Vol. XCIV   No. 1

Bible Expositor
and Illum

WINTER QUARTER   December

Looking Ahead 2
Editorial... 3

Triumph

UNIT I: Jesus' Triumphant Arrival

Dec. 5—Sorrow Before Triumph—Matt. 1:18-21; John 12:1-8 4
Dec. 12—A King Comes Forth—Isa. 9:6-7; John 12:12-16 18
Dec. 19—A Mission from Birth (Christmas)—Luke 2:25-35; John 12:23-26.......... 32
Dec. 26—A Humble Lord Is Born—Phil. 2:5-11; John 13:12-17 46

UNIT II: Teaching on Truth and Trials

Jan. 2—The Way, the Truth, and the Life—John 14:1-11 60
Jan. 9—Abide in the True Vine—John 15:1-8 74
Jan. 16—Peace and Trouble—John 16:19-33 88
Jan. 23—Jesus' Prayer for His Disciples—John 17:6-19 102

UNIT III: Triumph over Trials

Jan. 30—Jesus' Arrest—John 18:1-13 116
Feb. 6—Trials and Denials—John 18:15-27 130
Feb. 13—Pilate: What Is Truth?— John 18:28-40 144
Feb. 20—Crucifixion and Death—John 19:16-30 158
Feb. 27—Jesus by the Sea of Tiberias—John 21:1-14 172
     Topics for Next Quarter 188
     Paragraphs on Places and People 189
     Daily Bible Readings 190
     Review 191

Editor in Chief: Kenneth Sponsler

Union
Gospel
Press

Edited and published quarterly by
**THE INCORPORATED TRUSTEES OF THE
GOSPEL WORKER SOCIETY
UNION GOSPEL PRESS DIVISION**
Rev. W. B. Musselman, Founder
Price: $7.00 per quarter*
$28.00 per year*
*shipping and handling extra
ISBN 978-1-64495-189-7

LOOKING AHEAD

"Triumph" is a word that elicits many images: an army victorious in battle, a political candidate winning an election, or a sports team winning a championship. But the concept of "triumph" is also important in Scripture. In the New Testament, triumph is seen in a different light than it is ordinarily understood. To be sure, God will triumph over Satan, and good will triumph over evil, but the manner in which this will occur is quite different from the world's view of triumph and victory.

All of our lessons this quarter deal with texts from the Gospel of John—most of them exclusively so. The first unit of study is entitled "Jesus' Triumphant Arrival." It will be studied during the month of December. Since this is the month we celebrate the birth of Christ, each lesson will include a text from passages that in some way relate to that event. Selections from Matthew and Luke will consider what occurred immediately after Jesus' birth. A familiar prophecy from Isaiah about the Prince of Peace will be studied. Paul's great christological text from Philippians is also included in this unit.

The next unit of the quarter, "Teaching on Truth and Trials," will focus on four major discourses from Jesus' earthly ministry. The discourse on Jesus as the Way, the Truth, and the Life from John 14 will be studied first. Next we will examine the discourse on Jesus as the True Vine from John 15. Then we will study His discourse on peace and trials from chapter 16. The final lesson in this unit will deal with Jesus' High Priestly prayer from chapter 17. These lessons will examine the words of Jesus. His words are of supreme authority for understanding faith, life, and the world. He is the only object of our faith, the only source of eternal life, and the only Lord of heaven and earth.

The final unit is "Triumph Over Trials." We focus here on four texts from Jesus' Passion Week and a final lesson on events that took place after His resurrection. The first three lessons, all from John 18, deal with His arrest and trials before the Sanhedrin and Pontius Pilate. The fourth lesson focuses on the events surrounding Jesus' crucifixion and death. Our final lesson this quarter, from John 21, recounts the events of Jesus' third appearance to His disciples after He had risen triumphantly from the grave.

—John Alva Owston.

Born for a Purpose

ALAN ALLEGRA

Jesus' birth as told in the "Christmas story" of Luke 2 is nothing short of miraculous. It is a story we are all familiar with. We are also familiar with the depictions of His birth that pop up in homes, malls, shop windows, and greeting cards. Manger scenes depict a baby, two parents, lots of visitors and animals, and a star hovering overhead. While the typical crèche reveals little about the special circumstances of Christ's birth, other than that he was laid in a manger, Matthew 1:18-21 hints at the importance of Jesus' birth, a reality that ceramic or inflatable figures cannot convey.

We learn from this passage that Jesus' mother, Mary, was a virgin when He was conceived. That was certainly a miraculous and unique event! But beyond this, there is much more that makes this birth and the ensuing life of this Child even more unique. Matthew 1:21 tells us this child's gender, name, and His mission in life—all before He was even born!

From the time a woman learns that she is with child, both parents' curiosity is piqued: Is the baby a boy or girl? What shall we name the baby? What will he or she grow up to be? Sometimes, well-wishers may say, "He has a strong grip; he will become a ball player!" or "She has a lovely smile; she will be a heartbreaker!" or "What a loud voice! You have a future preacher!" Parents can hope and wish and pray, but they cannot know for certain who or what their child will become.

One of the unique features of Christ's birth is that His future destiny was plainly marked out for all the world to see. Matthew 1:23 tells us that Jesus would be born of a virgin and be known as "God with us." But that is not all.

Jesus did not have just one or two names—He had many names, all indicative of who and what He would become. Just like the prediction of His birth, these names were prophesied hundreds of years before (cf. Isa. 9:6-7). Even the time of Christ's death was prophesied (cf. Dan. 9:26) and the method of execution (cf. Ps. 22). These prophecies and many more indicate a life that triumphed over a lowly and controversial birth.

All of this makes the birth, life, and death of Jesus extraordinarily unique; after all, who else has had his life recorded in the Scriptures before His birth?

Believe it or not, though the details of your life are not explicitly recorded in Scripture, your path has also been planned from start to finish! God numbered all your days before you were born. Psalm 139:16 says, "Thine eyes did see my substance, yet being unperfect; and in thy book all my members were written, which in continuance were fashioned, when as yet there was none of them." Centuries before, Job exclaimed, "Seeing his days are determined, the number of his months are with thee, thou hast appointed his bounds that he cannot pass" (14:5). Before even the heavens and earth were created, we were "created in Christ Jesus unto good works, which God hath before ordained that we should walk in them" (Eph. 2:10). We, too, can triumph in Christ by seeking and obeying God's will. Your life's journey and purpose may not be spelled out publicly, but God has a plan, path, and purpose for

(Editorials continued on page 186)

SCRIPTURE LESSON TEXT

MATT. 1:18 Now the birth of Jesus Christ was on this wise: When as his mother Mary was espoused to Joseph, before they came together, she was found with child of the Holy Ghost.

19 Then Joseph her husband, being a just *man,* **and not willing to make her a publick example, was minded to put her away privily.**

20 But while he thought on these things, behold, the angel of the Lord appeared unto him in a dream, saying, Joseph, thou son of David, fear not to take unto thee Mary thy wife: for that which is conceived in her is of the Holy Ghost.

21 And she shall bring forth a son, and thou shalt call his name JESUS: for he shall save his people from their sins.

JOHN 12:1 Then Jesus six days before the passover came to Bethany, where Lazarus was which had been dead, whom he raised from the dead.

2 There they made him a supper; and Martha served: but **Lazarus was one of them that sat at the table with him.**

3 Then took Mary a pound of ointment of spikenard, very costly, and anointed the feet of Jesus, and wiped his feet with her hair: and the house was filled with the odour of the ointment.

4 Then saith one of his disciples, Judas Iscariot, Simon's *son,* **which should betray him,**

5 Why was not this ointment sold for three hundred pence, and given to the poor?

6 This he said, not that he cared for the poor; but because he was a thief, and had the bag, and bare what was put therein.

7 Then said Jesus, Let her alone: against the day of my burying hath she kept this.

8 For the poor always ye have with you; but me ye have not always.

NOTES

4

Sorrow Before Triumph

Lesson Text: Matthew 1:18-21; John 12:1-8

Related Scriptures: Matthew 26:6-13; Mark 14:3-9; Luke 7:37-39

TIMES: 6 or 5 B.C.; A.D. 30   PLACES: Nazareth; Bethany

GOLDEN TEXT—"Verily I say unto you, Wheresoever this gospel shall be preached in the whole world, there shall also this, that this woman hath done, be told for a memorial of her" (Matthew 26:13).

Introduction

Once we get to December, it seems that Christmas has already arrived, at least from the standpoint of the commercial world.

In many congregations, December's arrival heralds the beginning of the Advent season, a time for focusing on the events related to Christ's birth. Special programs begin to take shape.

Not all congregations are so inclined, however. As was true among the Puritans in early America, some churches feel that such celebrations are unscriptural and have no place in the regular worship of believers. But this is a minority view today, with most congregations seizing the opportunity to place special emphasis on Jesus' birth.

Since both Matthew and Luke provide significant information concerning the Messiah's arrival, it is appropriate that we likewise emphasize this world-changing event.

LESSON OUTLINE

I. A MOMENTOUS ANNOUNCE-MENT—Matt. 1:18-21

II. EXTRAORDINARY DEVOTION—John 12:1-3

III. A DUPLICITOUS OBJECTION—John 12:4-8

Exposition: Verse by Verse

A MOMENTOUS ANNOUNCEMENT

MATT. 1:18 Now the birth of Jesus Christ was on this wise: When as his mother Mary was espoused to Joseph, before they came together, she was found with child of the Holy Ghost.

19 Then Joseph her husband, being a just man, and not willing to make her a publick example, was minded to put her away privily.

20 But while he thought on these things, behold, the angel of the Lord appeared unto him in a dream, saying, Joseph, thou son of David, fear not to take unto thee Mary thy wife:

for that which is conceived in her is of the Holy Ghost.

21 And she shall bring forth a son, and thou shalt call his name JESUS: for he shall save his people from their sins.

Mary's condition (Matt. 1:18). Since Matthew's Gospel was addressed to a Jewish audience, the author is careful to trace the lineage of Jesus, as He was "the son of David, the son of Abraham" (1:1). Matthew therefore begins with Abraham, the father of the Hebrew people, and traces Jesus' lineage down to Joseph, His legal father. Of course, Christ was actually the Son of God (3:16-17), miraculously conceived by the Holy Spirit.

The narrative begins by telling us that Joseph and Mary were promised in marriage to each other. {While today we might use the words "betrothed" or "engaged" for their status, neither term accurately describes their relationship. Betrothal in New Testament Jewish culture was a legal arrangement made about one year before the actual marriage ceremony and consummation. To remove oneself from such a betrothal required a legal divorce.}**Q1**

{At some point it was discovered that Mary was with child. The conception had come about by the power of the Holy Spirit.}**Q2** In both Matthew's and Luke's account of the birth of Christ, there is no doubt that Mary was a virgin at both the time of the conception and the time of Jesus' birth (Matt. 1:25). While some have promoted the concept of the perpetual virginity of Mary, scriptural evidence suggests that after Jesus' birth, Joseph and Mary had a normal marital relationship and produced children (13:55-56).

Joseph's dilemma (Matt. 1:19-21). Since Joseph was a godly man, he did not wish to be married to a woman who had presumably been unfaithful to him with another man during their betrothal. Nor did he wish to disgrace Mary publicly or have her punished for her assumed unfaithfulness. Rather, {he was "minded to put her away privily"; that is, he intended to divorce her secretly.}**Q3** Note that Joseph is referred to here as Mary's husband, reflecting what was stated earlier concerning the binding nature of espousal.

Rather than making a hasty decision about his future with Mary, Joseph "thought on these things," mulling them over in his mind (vs. 20). No doubt he experienced many emotions, everything from anger, to sorrow, to confusion, to despair. Exactly how Joseph had discovered Mary's pregnancy is not stated, though it is likely that Mary herself told him, perhaps sharing the details of how the angel Gabriel had appeared to her (Luke 1:26-38). But Mary's story would almost certainly have been impossible for Joseph to believe—until the divine messenger himself revealed otherwise to him.

It was while Joseph was considering the dilemma in which he found himself that an angel of the Lord appeared to him. Encouraging him not to be afraid to wed Mary, the angel revealed that the child in Mary's womb actually was conceived by the Holy Spirit (Matt. 1:20). Joseph was further instructed that the child was to be given the name Jesus, which is the Greek equivalent of the Hebrew name Joshua, which means "the Lord saves"—an apt name indeed for the One who would "save his people from their sins" (vs. 21).

As we are told in the succeeding verse, this was in fulfillment of a prophecy concerning the birth of Messiah (cf. Isa. 7:14). Joseph then immediately took Mary as his wife (Matt. 1:24), and it was soon after this that they both departed for Bethlehem, where Jesus was actually born (cf. Luke 2:1-7), thus fulfilling another prophecy (cf. Matt. 2:4-6).

EXTRAORDINARY DEVOTION

JOHN 12:1 Then Jesus six days before the passover came to Bethany, where Lazarus was which had been dead, whom he raised from the dead.

2 There they made him a supper; and Martha served: but Lazarus was one of them that sat at the table with him.

3 Then took Mary a pound of ointment of spikenard, very costly, and anointed the feet of Jesus, and wiped his feet with her hair: and the house was filled with the odour of the ointment.

The setting (John 12:1). With a few exceptions, the bulk of our lesson material this quarter comes from the latter part of the Gospel of John, focusing mostly on events that occurred during the final week of the Saviour's earthly life. In fact, all the Gospels devote anywhere from one-third to one-half of their accounts of Jesus' life on earth to Passion Week. Obviously, the four evangelists saw these events as extremely significant.

As John 12 opens, it was six days before the Passover, the annual spring festival commemorating Israel's deliverance from Egyptian bondage. Since three Passovers are mentioned in John (cf. 2:13-25; 6:4; 11:55), this is one reason scholars have concluded that Jesus' earthly ministry lasted about three years.

Bethany was a village just outside Jerusalem and the home to {a family who were Jesus' good friends: Mary, her sister Martha, and their brother Lazarus.}Q4 Lazarus, of course, had just been raised from the dead (cf. 11:38-44). Were it not for John's Gospel, we would know nothing about Lazarus, since he is not mentioned in the Synoptic Gospels; nor should he be confused with a beggar by the same name mentioned in Luke 16:19-31. "Lazarus" was a rather common name in the culture of that time, be-ing the Greek equivalent of the Hebrew "Eleazar," a fairly common name in the Old Testament meaning "My God has helped me."

Extravagant devotion (John 12:2-3). Matthew 26:6-13 and Mark 14:3-9 also mention an anointing of Jesus at Bethany, although in those accounts the ointment is administered to Jesus by an unnamed woman who is mentioned only as anointing His head. There are so many similarities between these accounts that it is generally accepted that they describe the same event. The differences in their details are easily reconciled by reasonably supposing a difference in emphasis and perspective by the various narrators. But the accounts of this particular anointing should not be confused with a separate anointing by a sinful woman recorded in Luke 7:36-50.

From the parallel passages in Matthew and Mark, we learn that the dinner John describes took place in the home of a man called Simon the leper. It may be that Mary, Martha, Lazarus, and Simon all lived in the same dwelling. Most identify Simon as a disciple who had been healed of leprosy by Jesus, although some equate him with Lazarus himself. Whether there was some special occasion for this visit we are not told. They may have been honoring Christ for bringing Lazarus back from the dead (cf. vs. 9).

Since there are several women with the name Mary in the New Testament, it is always important to make sure that we do not confuse them. "Mary" was a very popular name given to girls, as it was derived from the name of Moses' sister, Miriam.

According to John 12:3, Mary took a pound of spikenard and anointed Jesus' feet with it. The parallel passages in Matthew and Mark mention that she also anointed His head. {Spikenard is a perfume derived from a plant that grows only in the

Himalayan mountains of India, Nepal, and China, and it is still very expensive today in its pure, organic form.}^{Q5} Even if Mary belonged to a wealthy family, this would have represented a very extravagant gesture of devotion.

{Showing her profound devotion and love for Jesus, Mary further honored Him by wiping His feet with her hair.}^{Q6} For a woman to let down her hair and behave in such a manner would have been considered unbecoming. Following Mary's example, our devotion to Christ should be extravagantly costly for us as well as unrestrained by human traditions.

As an eyewitness to these events, John mentions the aroma of the ointment filling the room where they were dining. The memory of fragrance is very powerful and persistent; if all those present ever got a whiff of spikenard in the future, they would surely be reminded of Mary's demonstration of devotion. As Jesus foretold, three of the Gospels also preserve the event for us today.

A DUPLICITOUS OBJECTION

4 Then saith one of his disciples, Judas Iscariot, Simon's son, which should betray him,

5 Why was not this ointment sold for three hundred pence, and given to the poor?

6 This he said, not that he cared for the poor; but because he was a thief, and had the bag, and bare what was put therein.

7 Then said Jesus, Let her alone: against the day of my burying hath she kept this.

8 For the poor always ye have with you; but me ye have not always.

Complaint (John 12:4-6). In the other accounts of this incident, Jesus' disciples collectively protested the extravagance of Mary's act of devotion. John's Gospel, however, makes it clear that it was Judas who complained most conspicuously about it.

When we hear the name Judas, we nearly always think of the disciple who betrayed Christ. Matthew and Mark both juxtapose this incident with Judas's act of making himself available to the chief priests to betray Jesus (Matt. 26:14-15; Mark 14:10-11). In the KJV New Testament, the name Judas appears some 33 times. The Greek name *Judas* is variously rendered "Jude," "Judah," "Juda," and of course, "Judas." Like many other Greek names that are equivalents of a Hebrew name, it was quite common, although today it is doubtful anyone would name their son Judas because of its odious connotations.

{As to the meaning of "Iscariot" (John 12:4), there is some debate. Most scholars hold that it merely means "man of Kerioth," which was a village in southern Judea. This is supported by the Greek text of 6:71, where Judas's father is actually named as "Simon Iscariot." Other suggested definitions tend to be rather dubious, including "false one," "dagger man," or "hanged one."}^{Q7}

{Judas protested that the costly ointment lavished upon Jesus could have been sold instead, and the money given to help the poor.}^{Q8} Under most circumstances, this might have been a valid objection, since such extravagance would hardly be justified among those who desire to be good stewards of the resources God entrusts to them.

"Three hundred pence" (vs. 5) represents the yearly earnings of a laborer, a significant sum even for the well-to-do. "Pence" translates the Greek "denarii" and is also used in the Parable of the Laborers in the Vineyard, where the workers agreed to work for a denarius a day (Matt. 20:2). This sounds like a negligible amount today, but it did in fact correspond to the current minimum wage for that time.

The apostle John tells us that Judas had no real concern for the poor. He was a thief and was only concerned about the amount of money he could steal from the disciples' treasury bag with which he was entrusted.

In most organizations, one person is usually given responsibility for the money. In many organizations, measures are instituted to prevent stealing from the treasury. But even when such preventative measures are in place, a dedicated thief can often find a way around them to take what does not belong to him.

People entrusted with finances invariably have reputations as trustworthy individuals, and most of them are. In some cases, people do not start out as thieves but become dishonest because of the temptation.

Defense (John 12:7-8). {Defending Mary, Jesus told Judas and those with him that they should cease their reproaches. He enlightened them to the fact that what she had done was a sign that He needed to be prepared for burial.}[Q9]

Jesus directed His disciples' attention to adjust their priorities in this special instance. While it is always commendable to give aid to those in need, the opportunity will always be readily available to all generations throughout history. But Jesus' time on earth would soon be over, and there would never be another chance to make such an offering concerning His impending death and burial. Mary therefore was honored for expressing her adoration. "For Christ also hath once suffered for sins, the just for the unjust, that he might bring us to God, being put to death in the flesh, but quickened by the Spirit" (I Pet. 3:18).

{Jesus' statement about the poor is an allusion to Deuteronomy 15:11, "For the poor shall never cease out of the land: therefore I command thee, saying, Thou shalt open thine hand wide unto thy brother, to thy poor, to thy needy, in thy land." Far from commending complacency, Jesus was bringing to bear the admonition of the Torah to encourage diligence in aiding the poor, since there will never be an end to the work that needs to be done in that matter.}[Q10]

—John Alva Owston.

QUESTIONS

1. What was the difference between a New Testament Jewish espousal and a modern engagement?
2. How did Mary come to be with child?
3. What was Joseph considering regarding Mary?
4. Who were Mary, Martha, and Lazarus?
5. What is spikenard?
6. After she anointed Jesus' feet with the spikenard, what further act of devotion and honor did Mary perform toward Him?
7. What are some possible meanings of the name Iscariot?
8. What reason did Judas offer for objecting to Mary's extravagant offering?
9. What significance did Jesus ascribe to Mary's act of devotion?
10. How should we understand Jesus' statement concerning the poor?

—John Alva Owston.

Preparing to Teach the Lesson

As we approach the Christmas season, our minds begin to think about the many holiday events that will be taking place as the month progresses. Christmas parties, programs at church, and of course, Christmas shopping. It is easy to forget what we are really celebrating with all of the hustle and bustle going on all around us. The reason for all of the good cheer in the air should be the birth of Jesus Christ, the most important person in all of history.

Jesus did not come simply to live a good life and leave a few good teachings behind. He came to take away the sins of the world (cf. John 1:29) and to reconcile man back to God (cf. II Cor. 5:18-19). The news of His impending birth came as quite a shock to His earthly father, Joseph, and He had a very humble beginning—being born in a stable in Bethlehem. However, He would later ride into Jerusalem triumphantly on a donkey as the King of the Jews and the Saviour of the world.

TODAY'S AIM

Facts: to discover that Jesus was born into this world to save us from our sins and that this salvation requires His death and burial.

Principle: to understand that as our conquering Hero, Jesus has defeated the sin in our lives and gives victory over sin.

Application: to turn away from the sin that Jesus' death and resurrection has freed us from and turn to God in Christ.

INTRODUCING THE LESSON

Our lesson begins with the most surprising birth announcement any father has ever received. Joseph, an otherwise anonymous carpenter from Nazareth in Israel, learned that his fi-ancée, Mary, was going to have a son. The news came as quite a shock since he and Mary had not been intimate. Joseph was assured by an angelic visitor, however, that the child had been conceived by the Holy Spirit and would save God's people from their sins.

DEVELOPING THE LESSON

1. A message only God could deliver (Matt. 1:18-21). Joseph was stunned when he heard that Mary was going to have a child. Since they had not yet been married, he knew the child was not his.

Joseph was a good man who found himself between a rock and a hard place. On the one hand, the law gave him the right to have Mary shamed and stoned for being unfaithful. On the other hand, it seems he could not stand to see her humiliated, much less killed. But how could he possibly stay with her if she was carrying someone else's child?

After contemplating this, Joseph decided to divorce her quietly. His plans changed, though, when he received an unexpected visit from an angel. The angel told him not to be afraid to take Mary as his wife. She had not been unfaithful to him! Rather, her child was conceived by the Holy Spirit.

The angel went on to tell Joseph that he was to name the child "Jesus," which means "Yahweh is salvation" or "the Lord saves." This particular name was chosen because the Child would save God's people—His people—from their sins. The baby that Mary was carrying was no accident nor the result of a sinful union. He was conceived by the Holy Spirit and sent by God to redeem people from the curse of sin (cf. Gal. 3:13).

2. Dinner with Jesus (John 12:1-3). We now fast-forward about thirty years to a time when Jesus had grown to adulthood and was nearing His death. Six days before Passover, Jesus arrived in Bethany, where Lazarus lived. Jesus had recently raised Lazarus from the dead, but this did nothing to dissuade His enemies from seeking to kill Him. In fact, it only made them seek His life more zealously (cf. 11:53).

One particular evening, a dinner was held for Jesus in the house of a man named Simon (cf. Mark 14:3-9). Martha, one of Lazarus's sisters, served at the dinner while Lazarus reclined at the table with Jesus. Mary, the other sister of Lazarus, came to Him carrying a container of pure nard. It amounted to around half a liter and was very expensive, but Mary did not think anything too expensive to give to Jesus.

Mary poured the ointment on Jesus' feet and also anointed His head (Matt. 26:7; Mark 14:3). She also wiped His feet with her hair, and the house was filled with the aroma of perfume. This was the sweet fragrance of worship.

3. Worship will not be denied (John 12:4-8). Not everyone was happy about what Mary was doing. Judas Iscariot, one of the Twelve and the one who would soon betray Jesus, objected to Mary's selfless act of worship by complaining that the ointment could have been sold for three hundred denarii and the money given to the poor. One denarius was equal to one day's wages, so three hundred denarii would amount to a sizeable sum.

Judas had no concern for the poor, however; his interests ended with himself. John points out that he had charge of the disciples' money and would help himself to it. He was the treasurer of the group, but he proved to be a crook. Jesus rebuked Judas by telling him to leave Mary alone. She had saved this gift for the time of His burial and had given what she had to worship Him. There would be plenty of opportunities to help the poor, but Jesus would not be with them for much longer. He was born to save His people from their sins, and to do that, He must die.

ILLUSTRATING THE LESSON

Sometimes it is easy to keep living in sin, but if we are Christ's, we should turn to Him.

TURN FROM SIN TO GOD

GOD

SIN

CONCLUDING THE LESSON

Our lesson began with a just man receiving news only God could deliver. The woman he was to marry was carrying someone else's child, and God was the Father! It is safe to say that this has happened to no one else. Mary's child would save His people. As we saw in the latter part of the lesson, Jesus would fulfill His purpose by dying.

ANTICIPATING THE NEXT LESSON

In next week's lesson, we will study a prophecy that looked forward to Jesus' birth and John's account of His triumphal entry into Jerusalem.

—*Robert Ferguson, Jr.*

PRACTICAL POINTS

1. The Lord may alter our plans so that He gets the glory (Matt. 1:18).
2. When faced with tough decisions, we should prayerfully consider what to do (vss. 19-21).
3. There are times when it is appropriate to serve the Lord and times when we simply enjoy His presence (John 12:1-2).
4. Our offering to the Lord should cost us something (vs. 3).
5. Though others may not understand our motives, the Lord knows our hearts (vss. 4-6).
6. We should keep our priorities straight and focus on what really matters (vss. 7-8).

—*Charity G. Carter.*

RESEARCH AND DISCUSSION

1. Joseph was described as a just man (Matt. 1:19). What does it mean to be a "just" person?
2. Why is it important to seek the Lord before making decisions (vs. 20)?
3. How would you feel if you learned that a gift you received had come at no cost to the giver (John 12:3)?
4. Why is it significant that Judas Iscariot was the one who took issue with the cost of the ointment (vss. 4-6)?
5. What did Jesus mean by saying, "The poor always ye have with you; but me ye have not always" (vs. 8)?

—*Charity G. Carter.*

ILLUSTRATED HIGH POINTS

Not willing to make her a public example (Matt. 1:19)

In Nathaniel Hawthorne's classic book, *The Scarlet Letter*, Hester Prynne is accused of adultery and forced to display a scarlet "A" on her clothing. The intent is to humiliate her before the entire community. It works: Prynne feels depressed on account of this letter. Although she may find ways to obscure it, "The pang of it will be always in her heart."

Hester's was certainly a bad situation, but Mary's involved undeserved shame. There would be no scarlet letter, but the gossip would be relentless. The Mosaic Law specified the death penalty for such an offense (Deut. 22:23-24). Though we do not know how often this was carried out, it does indicate the social stigma Mary would have experienced—almost like having a scarlet letter on her chest.

Ointment sold (John 12:5)

Judas offered a logical alternative to Mary's sacrificial act of loving devotion to Jesus, but he merely wanted this expensive perfume for himself and did not understand Mary's sacrifice.

We might recall the life of Jim Elliot. He gave his life to missionary service in Ecuador because he believed this would please God. He would ultimately be killed by the very tribe he was intending to reach. Some may consider that a tragic loss, but Elliot would surely not agree. He once wrote: "He is no fool who gives what he cannot keep to gain that which he cannot lose" (private journal entry, October 28, 1949). Though he was killed, the tribe who killed him later came to faith, and he no doubt has received eternal rewards that he will never lose.

—*David A. Hamburg.*

Golden Text Illuminated

"Verily I say unto you, Wheresoever this gospel shall be preached in the whole world, there shall also this, that this woman hath done, be told for a memorial of her" (Matthew 26:13).

The story of a woman anointing Jesus with costly ointment occurs in all four Gospels, each one offering a slightly different focus. Matthew contains fewer details than Mark, but both predict the worldwide tribute to be paid this woman, which Luke and John omit. All four Gospels, however, include one thing: criticism of Jesus and of this generous woman.

In the sexually charged atmosphere of the United States, we might expect Jesus and His female convert to be accused of an illicit affair, but no Gospel account even hints at such a criticism. Instead, the primary accusation is about wasting money that could have helped the poor. The charge seems to be partially leveled against Jesus for accepting such a luxurious gift.

His reply, however, is shocking: "Ye have the poor always with you; but me ye have not always" (Matt. 26:11). Jesus then justifies the woman's lavish present: it is a funeral expense worthy of Him; she was preparing His body for burial. Thus, Jesus predicts His imminent death.

Next week we will ponder Jesus' triumphal entry into Jerusalem, but this week we are reflecting on how sorrow often precedes joy. When Lazarus died, Mary, Martha, and their friends were sorrowful, but Jesus raised him from the dead. When this woman anoints Jesus' feet, everyone jumps on her, but Jesus defends her and says that her story will be told approvingly in all the world.

Although John notes that the allegation of wastefulness came from Judas (12:4-5), the accounts of Mark and Matthew disclose that other disciples were also saying the same thing. We could excuse their ignorance concerning the nearness of Jesus' death, but we cannot excuse their lack of faith. Many of them had followed Jesus for years. In that time, He had turned water into wine, healed the sick, cast out demons, calmed the storm, fed the multitudes, and raised the dead. Peter had recently called Jesus "the Christ, the Son of the living God" (Matt. 16:16).

But now some of His own disciples, witnesses to all these things, become petty over a vial of ointment. Jesus could have easily created barrels of pricy lotion or multiplied loaves and fish to feed all the poor in Israel. By criticizing Him for waste, they expose doubt in His ability to provide for His people and in His discernment in the use of resources.

Judas had a selfish reason for his irreverent words, while the others were likely just guilty of phony piety. They should not have doubted Jesus.

We do not know the sorrow that Jesus felt from their mistrust that day, but we do know His later plea in Gethsemane: "What, could ye not watch with me one hour?" (Matt. 26:40). Again, sorrow precedes joy.

Constructive criticism is sometimes necessary, but most criticism causes sorrow. Christians must not "bite and devour one another," or they will be "consumed" by one another (Gal. 5:15). We are not called to cause each other sorrow, but to love one another.

—David Samuel Gifford.

Heart of the Lesson

One Christmas many years ago, my mother received a bottle of designer-brand perfume from one of her third-grade students. She found out it cost $80. Mom felt that the perfume was too expensive to keep, so she returned it to the store and took me shopping with the refund money.

In this week's lesson, Jesus is the honored guest at a supper. Controversy erupts when a woman anoints Jesus' feet with a perfume far more costly than what my mother received.

1. Divine destiny (Matt. 1:18-21). Before Jesus' birth, His mother, Mary, was engaged to a man of Davidic descent. Because a Jewish engagement was legally binding, only divorce could end it. During the betrothal, Joseph learned Mary was pregnant.

No doubt, Joseph was devastated; any man would be who had reason to think his fiancée was unfaithful. And the Mosaic Law actually required stoning a betrothed woman caught in an affair. But Joseph loved Mary. A just and righteous man, he did not want her to face public humiliation. So he decided to divorce her privately.

One night, an angel appeared to Joseph in a dream and told him to proceed with the marriage without fear because the Holy Spirit had conceived Mary's baby, a son. Joseph was to name him Jesus, an alternative form of the name Joshua. This name, which means "Yahweh is salvation," foretold the Baby's destiny: He would save His people from their sins.

2. Honored guest (John 12:1-3). Years later, Jesus, now a grown man, was days away from His crucifixion and resurrection, the fulfillment of His life's purpose that His name explains. He had come to Jerusalem with His disciples to celebrate Passover. Before entering Jerusalem, they stopped in nearby Bethany to visit Jesus' dear friends Mary, Martha, and Lazarus.

A special dinner in His honor awaited Him. As usual, Martha showed her love by serving; she brought the food and waited on the guests. Lazarus showed his love by spending time with Jesus at the table. Mary showed her love by opening a jar of spikenard, an ointment worth a year's salary, and pouring it on Jesus' feet.

Kneeling, she wiped her long hair across Jesus' feet. She humbled herself by acting as a servant and using her own hair as a washcloth. She was unafraid to show her devotion to Jesus in front of her family and friends. She was not cheap, either. She poured out all the ointment, saving none for herself.

3. Hypocritical criticism (John 12:4-6). Judas, who later betrayed Jesus, considered Mary's actions a waste and questioned why she had not sold the ointment and given the money to the poor. The apostle John notes that Judas was a thief who regularly helped himself to the contents of the money bag. Judas did not care about the poor or Jesus; he wanted the money for himself.

4. Loving defense (John 12:7-8). Jesus told Judas to leave Mary alone. Jesus appreciated her loving and extravagant actions. They were in preparation for His upcoming burial. Perhaps Mary sensed the shortness of time she had left with Him. Regardless, Jesus pointed out the poor always would be present with them; He would be physically present only for "a little while" (14:19).

Which character in this lesson describes you most closely?

—*Ann Staatz.*

World Missions

In 1912, Dr. William Leslie went to minister to the tribal peoples of the Democratic Republic of Congo as a medical missionary. After seventeen years on the mission field, he returned home in seeming defeat. The seeds of the gospel he had faithfully scattered had never borne fruit; he had witnessed no conversions. Nine years later, he died, still filled with sorrow over his apparent failure to reach the tribal people.

Yet in 2010, about eighty years after he left Congo, a flourishing group of Christian churches was discovered nestled in the jungles near where Dr. Leslie had preached (Ellis, "Missionary Died Thinking He was a Failure," Godreports.com).

Although Dr. Leslie never knew while still on this earth, God had kept His promise. "So shall my word be that goeth forth out of my mouth: it shall not return unto me void, but it shall accomplish that which I please" (Isa. 55:11).

Dr. Leslie's efforts had led to the triumph of the gospel over sin. God had used "the foolish things of the world" (I Cor. 1:27) to bring people to salvation.

As humans, we have the tendency to believe that we need to have some great skill or talent in order to serve the Lord. We also tend to forget that God will use our sorrow to accomplish His ends. Dr. Leslie's story should show us that we can trust in God's faithfulness, as should the stories of the women in this week's lesson.

God spoke to a simple Jewish girl and told her that she would "bring forth a son" (Luke 1:31). Mary replied, "Be it unto me according to thy word" (vs. 38).

Mary would have known that she would face the ostracism and judgment of those around her. People—including Joseph (cf. Matt. 1:19)—might shame her for being an unwed mother. Further, she would endure the pain of childbirth. Still, she acquiesced to the will of God with complete surrender. And she brought forth the Saviour. God used her to give birth to His Son, who would triumph over death.

The woman with the costly ointment also experienced the judgment of her neighbors. But Jesus came to her defence, showing great love and compassion for her as He explained why He approved of what she had done. He also promised, "Verily I say unto you, Wheresoever this gospel shall be preached in the whole world, there shall also this, that this woman hath done, be told for a memorial of her" (Matt. 26:13).

Neither woman seemed important by the world's standards, but God used them and their sorrow. We still remember their lives many centuries later. He could use us too, though (maybe because) we feel inadequate!

The Lord might open the door for you to share Christ with the stranger sitting next to you on a plane or subway. You might have an opportunity to impart the gospel to the mailman. Sometimes, when years of prayers and sharing only result in the hardening of hearts, we grow discouraged. The world seems to embody the words of Paul, "Who knowing the judgment of God, that they which commit such things are worthy of death, not only do the same, but have pleasure in them that do them" (Rom. 1:32).

The seeds we sow might seem only to fall on the rocky, thorny, or shallow ground. But God is faithful. He also has prepared good soil (cf. Matt. 13:3-9, 18-23). Dr. Leslie never saw the seeds he scattered bear fruit, but God did.

—Jody Stinson

The Jewish Aspect

Jewish people have observed Passover since the time of the Exodus from Egypt, the "birth-night of the nation" (Edersheim, *Life and Times of Jesus,* Eerdmans). Passover is referred to in the Bible seventy-seven times, and various customs have developed around its observance.

Joseph and Mary attended Passover every year. When Jesus was twelve, they took Him with them, which was the custom at that time (Luke 2:41-51).

Jewish pilgrims greatly enlarged the population of Jerusalem, as they came to the city from all over Israel and from foreign nations. The Roman historian Tacitus says that at the time of Jerusalem's destruction by Rome (A.D. 70), its population "was six hundred thousand" (*Histories* 5.13). The apostle John writes that "the Jews' Passover was nigh at hand: and many went out of the country up to Jerusalem before the Passover, to purify themselves" (John 11:55).

How many are the "many"? Josephus gives more specific information. He writes that during the tenure of Cestius Gallus, governor of Syria from A.D. 63–65, a total of 256,500 lambs were slain at Passover in Jerusalem (*Wars of the Jews,* 6.9.3). Scholars assert that one lamb was sacrificed for approximately every ten people. Assuming that rate and that Josephus did not exaggerate, this places 2,565,000 worshippers at Jerusalem during Passover's observance, more than four times its normal population.

Pilgrims doubtless filled Jerusalem and all its surrounding area, extending miles outward. One can imagine how tents and shelters occupied every piece of open land, how the city streets bustled with people, how each flat roof had someone camped out on it, and how people prepared their homes for the influx of pilgrims (cf. Mark 14:15).

In addition to pilgrims who came to worship, beggars also came and stationed themselves around the city. Moreover, "merchants arrived early to sell or barter their wares" (Wilson, "Passover," *International Standard Bible Encyclopedia*, Eerdmans). Merchants sold clothing, ointments, jewelry, various food products, and most important, lambs for sacrifice. Greed and filthy gain infiltrated even the temple precincts. That is what prompted Jesus to drive out those who had turned the temple into "a den of thieves" (Matt. 21:13).

Edersheim observes that numerous preparations were made around Jerusalem before each Passover (*The Temple*, Kregel). Roads and bridges were restored, all burying places outside of cemeteries were whitewashed (cf. Matt. 23:27), sacrificial animals were chosen from the flocks and herds, and the temple treasure chests were emptied to prepare them to receive the financial gifts of pilgrims (cf. Mark 12:41-42). In addition, the *Babylonian Talmud* devotes an entire tractate with instructions on how a Jewish family should prepare for Passover, with great emphasis on eliminating all leaven in the home ("Pesachim," www.sacred-texts.com/jud/talmud.htm).

In the midst of all this religious activity, Jesus and His disciples also celebrated Passover. At the close of the meal, Jews took the third cup. This was the "cup of redemption" in remembrance of the original Exodus from Egypt (cf. Ex. 6:6). When Jesus took that cup, He declared, "This cup is the new testament in my blood, which is shed for you" (Luke 22:20). In Christ, Passover, along with the redemption it symbolized, found its total fulfillment.

—R. Larry Overstreet

Guiding the Superintendent

"Triumph" is the theme of this quarter's lessons. Unlike any other person, Jesus' triumph was in His death since His life's purpose was to pay the price for our sins. His future death was the point of His birth.

DEVOTIONAL OUTLINE

1. His death far away (Matthew 1:18-21). Confused and troubled by the pregnancy of his fiancée, Mary, Joseph contemplated what would be the right course of action for him (vss. 18-19). But while he was considering this, an angel of the Lord brought him a message. The infant in the womb of Mary was conceived by the Holy Ghost (vs. 20); she was still a virgin. Joseph was told to take Mary as his wife and to name the baby "Jesus," which means "Yahweh saves." This baby was born to die so that He could save His people from their sin (vs. 21). Before He was even born, the death of Jesus was being foreshadowed.

2. His death soon to come (John 12:1-8). Just six days before the cross, Jesus attended a dinner. Lazarus, who had been recently raised from the dead, was in attendance, and so were the disciples. But the guest of honor was Jesus Christ, who would soon go to the cross and rise from the dead.

Without announcement, Mary took a pound of ointment called spikenard and anointed Jesus' feet, wiping them with her hair. Her expression of extravagant love and devotion was shocking. The ointment was worth three hundred denarii—more than a year's wages for an average worker. The aroma of that powerful perfume filled the house. Mary had always been attentive to the teaching of Jesus (Luke 10:39). Perhaps she chose this time coincidentally, or perhaps she knew His death was near

(cf. John 12:7).

Judas objected to Mary's act of love. He said that the perfume could have been sold to meet the needs of the poor (vss. 4-5). However, his real motive was his own greed. He was treasurer for the disciples, and it was his custom to help himself to the money. At this point, the plan for betrayal had already entered Judas's mind, and perhaps he was seeking to grab all the money he could before he left Him.

Jesus did not hesitate to defend the actions and motives of Mary. She was anointing His body for burial (vs. 7). This was not a time for meeting the needs of the poor; it was a time to demonstrate love to Jesus. The poor would always be present, but the time of Jesus' departure by death was near (vs. 8).

Help your teachers see that Jesus was not insensitive to the needs of the poor. Throughout His ministry, He met the needs of the poor and downtrodden. But at this moment specifically, the most important action was to prepare Him for burial.

When we recognize the price Jesus paid for our salvation, we should respond like Mary. We should spare no expense, but offer Him lavish love.

CHILDREN'S CORNER

Your teachers will need to delicately discuss death in this lesson. They may explain this to the children by analogy to an animal's death or by the idea of not returning permanently.

Further, children likely will not have a concept of a year's salary. Prepare your teacher to ask the children what they consider to be most valuable in life and then relate the perfume to those answers.

—Robert Winter.

SCRIPTURE LESSON TEXT

ISA. 9:6 For unto us a child is born, unto us a son is given: and the government shall be upon his shoulder: and his name shall be called Wonderful, Counsellor, The mighty God, The everlasting Father, The Prince of Peace.

7 Of the increase of *his* government and peace *there shall be* no end, upon the throne of David, and upon his kingdom, to order it, and to establish it with judgment and with justice from henceforth even for ever. The zeal of the Lord of hosts will perform this.

JOHN 12:12 On the next day much people that were come to the feast, when they heard that Jesus was coming to Jerusalem,

13 Took branches of palm trees, and went forth to meet him, and cried, Hosanna: Blessed *is* the King of Israel that cometh in the name of the Lord.

14 And Jesus, when he had found a young ass, sat thereon; as it is written,

15 Fear not, daughter of Sion: behold, thy King cometh, sitting on an ass's colt.

16 These things understood not his disciples at the first: but when Jesus was glorified, then remembered they that these things were written of him, and *that* they had done these things unto him.

NOTES

18

A King Comes Forth

Lesson Text: Isaiah 9:6-7; John 12:12-16

Related Scriptures: Micah 5:2; Psalm 118:22-29; Zechariah 9:9;
Matthew 21:4-9; Mark 11:7-10; Luke 19:35-38

TIMES: about 733 B.C.; A.D. 30   PLACE: Jerusalem

GOLDEN TEXT—"[They] took branches of palm trees, and went forth to meet him, and cried, Hosanna: Blessed is the King of Israel that cometh in the name of the Lord" (John 12:13).

Introduction

While there are still kings in today's world, they do not usually wield the kind of power that was common throughout history. But when we think of kings, ideas such as thrones, crowns and absolute authority commonly come to mind.

Clearly, the Old Testament prophesied that Messiah would be a king (Gen. 49:10; II Sam. 7:16). Those anticipating His appearance seem to have focused on this aspect of His person almost to the exclusion of His other prophesied attributes, especially His role as Suffering Servant (cf. Isa. 53).

To be sure, Messiah is a king. He is in fact King of kings and Lord of lords (Rev. 19:16)! But the nature of His kingship varies, depending upon whether we are considering His first advent or His second coming. Standing before Pilate prior to His death, Christ declared, "My kingdom is not of this world" (John 18:36).

LESSON OUTLINE

I. PROPHECY OF THE KING—
   Isa. 9:6-7

II. WELCOMING THE KING—
   John 12:12-15

III. MISUNDERSTANDING THE
   KING—John 12:16

Exposition: Verse by Verse

PROPHECY OF THE KING

ISA. 9:6 For unto us a child is born, unto us a son is given: and the government shall be upon his shoulder: and his name shall be called Wonderful, Counsellor, The mighty God, The everlasting Father, The Prince of Peace.

7 Of the increase of his government and peace there shall be no end, upon the throne of David, and upon his kingdom, to order it, and to establish it with judgment and with justice from henceforth even for

ever. **The zeal of the Lord of hosts will perform this.**

Titles of honor (Isa. 9:6). While Jewish rabbis had many theories about when and how the Messiah would arrive, Scripture taught that He would be born of a virgin (7:14) in the town of Bethlehem (Mic. 5:2).

Jesus, of course, would be no ordinary child, since He was the very Son of God in the flesh (John 1:14). Unlike the rest of us, He was in no way tainted by sin (Heb. 4:15)—neither in His human nature nor in any thought, word, or deed during His earthly life. He could therefore offer Himself as a sinless sacrifice for sinners (cf. II Cor. 5:21).

Isaiah is often called the "gospel prophet" because he said more about the coming Messiah than any other prophet. The character of Messiah's reign is revealed in the titles given to Him by Isaiah's prophecies. "The government shall be upon his shoulder" (9:6) indeed indicates that Messiah would govern as king. Even the best of Israel's kings had many shortcomings, but Messiah would be a perfect king.

{What follows are some titles rightfully given to Messiah. The first is "Wonderful," or as many prefer, "Wonderful Counsellor."}[Q1]

In Hebrew, "Wonderful" is used in connection with the Angel of the Lord in Judges 13:18. Although the word is rendered as "secret" in that verse, it is usually translated as "wonder" or "miracle" throughout the Scriptures. Since many believe that the Angel of the Lord here was actually the preincarnate Christ, this could be seen as a confirmation that Messiah's name is "Wonderful."

As we think of Jesus' life and ministry, there are indeed many ways it could be described as wonderful. He spoke amazing words and performed miraculous deeds, confirming that He is both Saviour and Lord.

Christ is also "Counsellor." This Hebrew word denotes one who is the source of wise counsel, one who provides wisdom, meaning, determination, and purpose. During His ministry, Jesus never sought counsel from anyone other than His Heavenly Father (John 5:30; 6:38). As Creator (1:1-3), He never needs to seek counsel from any of His creatures.

Whether counseling a Pharisee like Nicodemus (John 3:1-19), a sinful Samaritan woman (4:4-26), or the grieving Mary and Martha (11:23-26), Jesus always had the wise, timely, comforting words they most needed to hear.

The title "The Mighty God" (Isa. 9:6) is the designation "God Almighty." While some in Isaiah's day might have been puzzled about how this could be true, New Testament believers can readily understand how Jesus deserves this prophetic title. As God incarnate, Christ was both "with God" and also "was God" (John 1:1). As the title "Immanuel" (Isa. 7:14) indicates, Jesus is "God with us" (Matt. 1:23).

When Jesus claimed to have existed before Abraham as the great I AM (cf. John 8:58), He was declaring Himself equal with God (cf. 5:18). He Himself asserted, "I am the Son of God" (10:36; Matt. 27:43). This is also affirmed elsewhere in Scripture (Phil. 2:5-6; Col. 1:15; Heb. 1:1-3).

Closely related to the preceding title is "everlasting Father" (Isa. 9:6). Some think this might be better rendered "Eternal Father." Christ Himself affirmed the truth of this title when He declared, "I and my Father are one" (John 10:30). In answering Philip's request to see the Father, Jesus replied, "He that hath seen me hath seen the Father" (14:9).

{Perhaps the best-remembered of the titles given to the Messiah, especially at this time of year, is "Prince of Peace" (Isa. 9:6).}[Q2] While many think of peace as only the cessation of earthly hostility, Christ offers so much more. At His birth, the angels announced,

"Peace, good will toward men" (Luke 2:14). This peace is only possible when we receive Christ as our Lord. Neither individuals nor nations can enjoy lasting peace if they reject the Prince of Peace. The apostle Paul writes, "Therefore being justified by faith, we have peace with God through our Lord Jesus Christ" (Rom. 5:1). This is the peace that matters most.

Just and righteous rule (Isa. 9:7). Concerning the Messiah's kingdom and the peace He brings, the prophet describes it as without end. All the earth will be subject to His divine authority.

When Gabriel appeared to Mary, he told her that "the Lord God shall give unto [Jesus] the throne of his father David: and he shall reign over the house of Jacob for ever; and of his kingdom there shall be no end" (Luke 1:32-33). {Unlike earthly kingdoms—often governed by unjust men—the Messiah will rule with "judgment and justice" (Isa. 9:7).}[Q3] Taking Christ as our example, Christians should live righteous lives and encourage justice in every possible way.

While we may wonder how Isaiah's original audience interpreted this message—which was given during a desperate time for their nation—we do know how it is to be accomplished: "The zeal of the Lord of hosts will perform this." Indeed, the Lord is zealous to establish Messiah's kingdom, and whatever He ordains will occur.

WELCOMING THE KING

JOHN 12:12 On the next day much people that were come to the feast, when they heard that Jesus was coming to Jerusalem,

13 Took branches of palm trees, and went forth to meet him, and cried, Hosanna: Blessed is the King of Israel that cometh in the name of the Lord.

14 And Jesus, when he had found a young ass, sat thereon; as it is written,

15 Fear not, daughter of Sion: behold, thy King cometh, sitting on an ass's colt.

Palm Sunday (John 12:12-13). Our second text begins shortly after the events of last week's lesson text, when Mary anointed the Lord with expensive perfume. Apparently, the chief priests wanted to kill not only Jesus, but Lazarus too (vs. 9). Raised from the dead, Lazarus was a living, breathing testimony to the messianic power of Jesus. Those who reject Jesus Christ will often go to great lengths to eliminate uncomfortable evidence about Him.

{While the chronology of some of the events of the final week of Jesus' earthly life may seem somewhat complex, we can be reasonably sure that "the next day" (vs. 12) was Sunday. Since Jews would abstain from travel on the Sabbath (Saturday), not even venturing very far from home on that day, we can assume that the Passover pilgrims would be making their way to Jerusalem on the first day of the week.}[Q4]

{Passover was a required feast for Jewish men (Ex. 23:14-17); multitudes, therefore, would be on their way to the city at this time.}[Q5] As was true with Pentecost, even Jews from distant lands commonly journeyed to Jerusalem for important gatherings such as this (cf. Acts 2:5-12).

John records many visits by Jesus to Jerusalem during His ministry. Although the other Gospels focus largely on His Galilean ministry, residents of Jerusalem as well as those from Galilee and other outlying regions would have heard that Jesus was coming to the city. Since people often traveled in large groups to these feasts, word would have spread very quickly concerning His imminent arrival.

Since Jesus' triumphal entry into Jerusalem is mentioned in all four Gospels (cf. Matt. 21:1-11; Mark 11:1-11; Luke 19:29-44), it was obviously considered a very significant event in Jesus' life. While the other Gospels all mention people casting their garments on the road as a carpet for the arrival of Jesus, only John specifically mentions the use of palm branches for this purpose. Thus, it is because of the account in John's Gospel that we now refer to the day honoring this event as Palm Sunday.

While nothing specific is mentioned in the Old Testament concerning palm branches at Passover, their use was common during the Feast of Tabernacles (Lev. 23:40). During the Maccabean revolt, almost two hundred years previous to Palm Sunday, palm branches were used to celebrate the rededication of the temple. The apocryphal book called II Maccabees says, "Therefore they now, carried boughs, and green branches, and palms for Him that had given them good success in cleansing his place" (10:7, *Douay-Rheims American Edition,* 1899).

{Consequently, the palm branch became something of a symbol of liberation for Israel.}[Q6] "On this occasion, then, the palm-branches may have signified the people's expectation of imminent national liberation, and this is supported by the words with which they greeted our Lord" (Bruce, *The Gospel of John,* Eerdmans). It was therefore significant that they welcomed Christ in this manner.

{The exclamation "Hosanna" (John 12:13) means "give salvation now" or "give victory now" (Bruce).}[Q7] Since God had liberated ancient Israel from Egyptian oppression at the first Passover, there was perhaps at this time an expectation that He might do the same thing by freeing His people from the oppression of the Romans.

We are all products of our times, especially with regard to our perceived needs. So it was with the Jews of Jesus' day; they thought their greatest need was freedom from Roman oppression. {Thus, their view of Messiah was one of a political deliverer and a military leader.}[Q8] Since He was to be the heir to David's throne, they assumed that He would be a great warrior, as was David.

What the crowd shouted came directly from the Psalms: "Save now. . . . Blessed be he that cometh in the name of the Lord" (118:25-26). In quoting this psalm, instead of using "he," the people inserted the phrase "the King of Israel" (John 12:13). The idea that they wanted Jesus to be their king was nothing new. A year previous, the people had actually wanted to "take him by force, to make him a king" (6:15). Had Jesus wanted to be the kind of king they sought, He could have submitted to their desires at that time. Recall also that Satan had once offered Him all the earthly kingdoms, but He refused (Matt. 4:8-9).

Prophecy fulfilled (John 12:14-15). While the other Gospels give details concerning how the donkey Jesus rode was procured, John merely informs us of the fact that He rode such an animal.

{Although donkeys were sometimes ridden by kings (II Sam. 16:1-2; I Kgs. 1:32-34), they were often seen as a poor man's beast and symbolic of peace and humility.}[Q9] Roman generals usually rode white horses. If Jesus had wanted to make a statement about His royal objectives, He would have secured such a large and impressive animal. At His second coming, Christ indeed is depicted as riding just such an impressive white war horse (Rev. 19:11-16). "Jesus riding into Jerusalem on a donkey was an acted parable, designed to correct the misguided expectations of the pilgrim crowds and to show the city its true way of peace" (Bruce).

Mentioned also in Matthew 21:5, John quotes Zechariah 9:9; "Rejoice greatly, O daughter of Zion; shout, O daughter of Jerusalem: behold, thy King cometh unto thee: he is just, and having salvation;

lowly, and riding upon an ass, and upon a colt the foal of an ass."

Of course, Christ *is* a king; He simply was not the kind of king Israel was expecting. To some degree, this is still true today. People say they believe in Christ, but what they believe about Him is often very different from what we find in Scripture. Just as Paul declared some so-called apostles of Christ to be false apostles and ministers of Satan (II Cor. 11:13-15), so we today can likewise be easily deceived by those who preach an unbiblical Jesus.

Clearly, what Christ came to offer at His first advent differs from what will occur at His second coming. At His first advent, it was necessary for Him to be "wounded for our transgressions" and "bruised for our iniquities" because "all we like sheep have gone astray" and "the Lord hath laid on him the iniquity of us all" (Isa. 53:5-6). As Hebrews 9:28 says, "So Christ was once offered to bear the sins of many; and unto them that look for him shall he appear the second time without sin unto salvation."

MISUNDERSTANDING THE KING

16 These things understood not his disciples at the first: but when Jesus was glorified, then remembered they that these things were written of him, and that they had done these things unto him.

That the disciples of Jesus did not comprehend many things should not surprise us. All of the Gospels seem to indicate that they were confused about many of His teachings, especially about certain aspects of His mission of salvation. {This may be partly due to the fact that He so often spoke in parables. Nor had they as yet received the fullness of the Holy Spirit, who would later greatly illuminate their understanding of His words (Luke 24:45; John 14:26; 16:13).}[Q10]

After Christ's death, resurrection, and ascension, His disciples would receive divine illumination through God's Spirit. What once had been unclear, the Spirit would make perfectly clear.

Today, the Holy Spirit likewise aids us in our comprehension of the Scriptures and our application of its teachings. For the unbelieving, it is not so: "But the natural man receiveth not the things of the Spirit of God: for they are foolishness unto him: neither can he know them, because they are spiritually discerned" (I Cor. 2:14).

After Jesus' ascension, the disciples "remembered" all these things (John 12:16). In other words, they were able to connect the dots regarding the promises of the Hebrew prophets with the prophetic words of Christ.

—John Alva Owston.

QUESTIONS

1. What is the first title given to Messiah in Isaiah 9:6?
2. Which of the titles in Isaiah 9:6 is the most commonly remembered at Christmas?
3. What are two qualities mentioned in Isaiah 9:7 that will characterize Messiah's reign?
4. On what day of the week did Christ triumphantly enter Jerusalem?
5. Why were there so many people in Jerusalem at this time?
6. How were palm branches significant in Jewish history?
7. What does "Hosanna" mean?
8. What kind of king were the Jews seeking at this time?
9. What did Jesus' riding on a donkey likely symbolize?
10. Why did Christ's disciples so often misunderstand Him?

—John Alva Owston.

Preparing to Teach the Lesson

Everyone loves to hear good news. It feels great when someone comes to us with a message that will change our lives for the better—even more so if it is for all eternity. That is precisely what our lesson this week discusses: a message of hope given to people in a dark time. The message let them know that God was with them and would one day save them from despair. The good news for us today is that God still hears us and that the gospel proclaimed in the Bible is just as relevant now as it was when it was originally given.

Jesus has come to us and fulfilled many Old Testament prophecies, one of which will be examined this week. He did not come on His own initiative with His own agenda but came to do the will of His Father, who sent Him. He has conquered sin for us so that we would not have to live as slaves to sin any longer. Because of Jesus, we have hope today.

TODAY'S AIM

Facts: to know that Isaiah prophesied the birth of a King centuries before Jesus entered Jerusalem as that King.

Principle: to recognize Jesus as the King who brings peace with God and eternal life by conquering sin.

Application: to accept His gift of peace and to follow His example and live peacefully with those who oppose and persecute us.

INTRODUCING THE LESSON

Isaiah made an astounding prophecy over seven centuries before Jesus was born that gave hope for God's people. God would send a Messiah, His Anointed One, who would overthrow all the oppressive governments of the world and establish His never-ending kingdom. The fulfillment of this prophecy was inaugurated when Jesus Christ entered Jerusalem over seven hundred years later as not only the King of the Jews, but as the King of kings!

DEVELOPING THE LESSON

1. The Messiah to come (Isa. 9:6-7). God's mission has been to save and redeem the world from the curse of sin that has afflicted it ever since Adam and Eve sinned in the Garden of Eden (cf. Gen. 3:15). In order to do this, however, something drastic had to be done.

God could not just wink at our sin and pretend it really is not a big deal. He must punish sin. The problem is that if God were to punish us for our sins as we deserve, we would spend eternity apart from Him because our own physical death would be insufficient as punishment.

To remedy our sin problem, God did for us what we could not do for ourselves. We could not get to God, so God in Christ came to us. Isaiah foretold this by the Spirit over seven centuries before Jesus was born.

His words "unto us a child is born, unto us a son is given" (vs. 6) are glorious because they show that God has not abandoned His people although we have all sinned. Through the Holy Spirit, Isaiah stated that salvation has been offered to everyone through the One whom God would send. The phrase "a child is born" speaks to the humanity of the Messiah.

The governments of the world are often known for corruption, deceit, and oppression. Even good governments are faulty because they are made up of faulty human beings. In the end, however, the government will rest on the shoulders of the Messiah, who will rule and reign in righteousness and truth. This prophecy will be fulfilled in the millennial reign of Christ after His second coming.

Isaiah described the Messiah with the terms "Wonderful" and "Counsellor." The birth of Jesus to a virgin was certainly a wonder, or miracle, and Christ counsels us with truth that leads to eternal life (cf. John 6:68). Notice the usage of the definite article in verse 6, stating that the Messiah is *the* Mighty God, *the* Everlasting Father, and *the* Prince of Peace. There can only be salvation through a Messiah that is both fully God and fully man. This meant that no mere human being could serve as the Messiah. He must be divine—God's Son.

There is no limit to the scope, power, and time of the Messiah's government. Justice will prevail in His reign, and no one will be mistreated or abused any longer.

2. The Messiah has arrived (John 12:12-16). We now look ahead in our reading to the Sunday before Jesus' crucifixion, which is often known today as Palm Sunday. Many people in Israel correctly believed Jesus to be the Messiah Isaiah prophesied about, and as He rode into Jerusalem, they went out to meet Him with palm branches and cries of "Hosanna" (vs. 13), which means "save us."

Palm branches were a Jewish symbol of victory. The people saw Jesus as a political or military king and expected Him to deliver them from the Romans. Jesus did not meet their expectations, as He had a greater enemy to defeat than Rome. He came to conquer sin.

Riding on a donkey as opposed to a horse was significant because kings rode donkeys during peacetime and horses during war. But more important, He rode on a donkey because of the prophecy of Zechariah 9:9. Jesus rode into Jerusalem two thousand years ago as the Prince of Peace, just as Isaiah prophesied.

We have peace with God today because of the faith we have in what Christ has already accomplished for us (cf. Rom. 5:1). The disciples did not understand this at first, but they did after Jesus was resurrected. Likewise, we do not always understand what God is doing, but by faith, we can trust that He is working for our good.

ILLUSTRATING THE LESSON

Jesus came to bring peace and salvation to all who believe in Him.

GIFTS OF THE KING

PEACE   SALVATION

CONCLUDING THE LESSON

Isaiah prophesied that God would send His Anointed One to set His people free. Our part is to trust in God's Messiah as the salvation from our sin. Note that this prophecy was fulfilled in Jesus Christ, but not in a way that people of His time expected. Have you felt disappointed because God has not answered your prayers as you expected? If so, be encouraged that He is working for your benefit and will not fail you.

ANTICIPATING THE NEXT LESSON

Next week, we will study an example of the blessing of waiting on the Lord.

—Robert Ferguson, Jr.

PRACTICAL POINTS

1. Jesus is the King who meets all needs (Isa. 9:6).
2. Though the world may be in a state of turmoil and confusion, God brings peace to those who believe in His Son (vs. 7).
3. When God has been faithful, we cannot help telling others about Jesus and what He has done (John 12:12-13).
4. Jesus' example shows us the humility we are to demonstrate when we live out and proclaim the gospel (vss. 14-15).
5. We will fully understand the ways of God when the time is right (vs. 16).

—*Charity G. Carter.*

RESEARCH AND DISCUSSION

1. Explain the meaning of each name that is ascribed to Jesus: "Wonderful, Counsellor," "The mighty God," "The everlasting Father," "The Prince of Peace" (Isa. 9:6).
2. The terms "government" and "peace" seem somewhat contradictory today. How does relating both terms to the promised Messiah make perfect sense (vs. 7)?
3. Why do you think Jesus allowed people to publicly celebrate His arrival (John 12:13)?
4. Why did the prophecy about Jesus' arrival include instructions about not being afraid (vss. 14-15; cf. Zech. 9:9)

—*Charity G. Carter.*

ILLUSTRATED HIGH POINTS

In Wonderful, Counsellor (Isa. 9:6)

Our Lord is indeed a "Wonderful Counsellor," but He is also amazingly Wonderful in His person and in His work of redemption. A songwriter put it this way:

> Wonderful, Wonderful Jesus Is to Me
> Counselor, Prince of Peace, Mighty
>   God is he.
> Saving me, keeping me
> From all sin and shame,
> Wonderful is my Redeemer
> Praise His Name!
> (Lillenas,
>   "Wonderful, Wonderful, Jesus
>   Is to Me.")

The Everlasting Father (Isa. 9:6)

More than once, my primary care physician has said, "You will probably not live another twenty years." He is probably right since at this moment, I am fourscore and one.

There is, however, life beyond this life provided by my Saviour who is "The everlasting Father." Someday, He will call me home where there is no pain, sorrow, or need of medicine.

The King of Israel (John 12:13)

It is possible that some Roman soldiers saw the crowd of people surging toward Jerusalem proclaiming Jesus as the King of Israel. It is also possible that they scoffed as they compared this event with one of Rome's victory parades of a conquering king or general riding in a chariot pulled by four horses, followed by defeated captives from the war.

This man was riding on a donkey. There were no captives. How could He be a king? But today, the entries of victorious Roman emperors are mostly forgotten while much of the world celebrates the royal entry of Jesus on each Psalm Sunday year after year.

—*David A. Hamburg.*

Golden Text Illuminated

"[They] took branches of palm trees, and went forth to meet him, and cried, Hosanna: Blessed is the King of Israel that cometh in the name of the Lord" (John 12:13).

The prophets had predicted a Messiah, and the time had finally arrived. The streets of Jerusalem filled when it was publicized that Jesus was coming. We should not deceive ourselves, however, and suppose that everyone in the crowd hailed Him as their Messiah. But some of Jesus' friends may have started the hosanna chant, and there is no doubt the masses were glad to see Him as well.

Jesus was well known for His healings and exorcisms, and the poor liked Him because He put the scribes and Pharisees in their place. We do not know the motivation of everyone that day, but we do know one thing: less than a week later, a crowd was shouting, "Crucify Him!"

Jesus had warned His disciples that His entrance into Jerusalem would result in His death, but they, too, may have been caught up in the euphoria. The crowds were paving Jesus' path with the leaves of palm trees, calling Him the King of Israel and quoting Scripture (Ps. 118:25-26). The word "hosanna" is a prayer for salvation: "Oh, save!"

Most of those present, however, were probably not asking to be born again. They were praying for deliverance from Rome, whom God was using to punish them for their sins. The people were not enacting typical customs of repentance: beating their breasts, wearing sackcloth, or throwing dust on their heads.

Jesus, by riding on a donkey's colt, was obviously encouraging this event (cf. Zech. 9:9), but He was under no illusion as to where this parade would end. Since the age of twelve, Jesus had been a Bible scholar. Surely, He had read, "But he was wounded for our transgressions, he was bruised for our iniquities" (Is. 53:5). Surely, He had calculated the 483 years "from the going forth of the commandment to restore and to build Jerusalem" (Dan. 9:25). Surely, He knew the meaning of His own cry, "O Jerusalem, Jerusalem, which killest the prophets, and stonest them that are sent unto thee" (Luke 13:34). Yet He rode on.

People like to watch parades, but it is also interesting to watch the end of a parade. When the marchers reach the end of the crowds, they suddenly realize no one is watching, and some faces fall. They quickly break rank and ramble off in every direction: some to find a restroom or drink, others to meet their ride home, and still others to hang out on the sidelines to savor the camaraderie of those who also stop to ponder, "Is that all there is?"

Jesus' triumphal entry into old Jerusalem was a necessary part of His messianic mission. But the week would close out with Him tried, crucified, killed, buried, and raised from the dead. The final stage of His earthly ministry, namely, atonement and forgiveness of sin, would be complete (cf. Heb. 1:3).

The next stage was still millennia away. After His bride, the church, would make herself ready, Jesus would return to rule the earth with her. What Adam and Eve had failed to do, Jesus would accomplish, along with His bride (Rev. 19:7; 20:4-6).

—David Samuel Gifford.

Heart of the Lesson

When employees at Seattle's Medical Dental Building heard that the queen of England was walking past their building, they headed for the windows. My dad, a resident carpenter, joined a denture maker in his fourth-floor lab.

Below, hundreds of people lined Fifth Avenue as Queen Elizabeth and her entourage arrived. A little girl presented the queen with flowers. Onlookers clapped. This was the closest Dad had ever been to royalty, and he said that he felt a shiver of awe as he watched.

In this week's lesson, pilgrims flooding Jerusalem for Passover give Jesus a royal welcome far beyond what Seattle offered Queen Elizabeth.

1. The gift (Isa. 9:6a). The prophet Isaiah predicted Jesus' advent more than seven hundred years before His birth. He wrote that "a child" will be born "unto us," indicating One who is born for all people, not just His parents. This Child will be "a son." God the Father Himself will give this Child, who is Himself God the Son.

2. The Messiah's reign (Isa. 9:6b-7). Next, Isaiah jumps to the time when Jesus assumes David's throne and establishes His kingdom. His titles will include descriptive names: "Wonderful, Counsellor, The mighty God, The everlasting Father, and The Prince of Peace" (vs. 6). Justice, righteousness, and peace will characterize Jesus' rule. Isaiah assures us of this event's certainty by saying, "The zeal of the Lord of hosts will perform this" (vs. 7).

3. The welcome (John 12:12-13). At the time of Jesus, Israel longed for the Messiah about whom prophets such as Isaiah had foretold. The people suffered under Roman rule. They wanted their nation restored to its former glory. As Jesus taught and healed, many wondered if He was the Promised One to come—their Messiah.

Five days before Passover, Jesus left the home of Mary, Martha, and Lazarus in Bethany to walk the two miles to Jerusalem. Jerusalem had been abuzz with people marveling about the raising of Lazarus from the dead. Now the word was out that Jesus Himself was on His way to the city.

Excited pilgrims cut palm tree branches and rushed from Jerusalem to meet Jesus. Waving the branches, they cried "Hosanna," which means "Oh save" or "Save now." The populace was saying, "Please save us now!" Most were probably looking for deliverance from Roman rule. They quoted Psalm 118:26: "Blessed be he that cometh in the name of the Lord," replacing the word "he" with the phrase, "the King of Israel."

4. The grand entrance (John 12:14-16). Instead of walking, Jesus rode into Jerusalem on a donkey's colt. He was deliberately fulfilling Zechariah 9:9, which foretold Israel's Messiah would come riding on a donkey. He was offering Himself to the Jewish nation as its Messiah.

In Jesus' day, kings rode horses in wartime and donkeys in peacetime. Jesus' choice not only fulfilled Scripture but also signaled that He was different from the Messiah they were expecting. He had come to die for their sins rather than to provide political deliverance.

The crowds joyfully celebrated the arrival of God's great gift. Through His Son Jesus, God has given us the gifts of eternal life and peace with God. In appreciation, have you given Jesus the gift of your heart and life? Can you cry, "Blessed be he that cometh in the name of the Lord"?

—Ann Staatz.

World Missions

Transportation in the middle of the Brazilian jungle is not easy. The roads are made of red clay that is slick in the rainy season and thick with dust in the dry season.

Jungle roads filled with ruts, craters, and puddles often left our vehicles broken and us stranded. With no cell phones, we never knew how long we would have to wait for rescue.

One night, my parents and I were headed home in our pickup truck when the vehicle shuddered to a stop on a jungle road—far from home or help.

Hours passed in the cramped, hot cab, with mosquitos coming through the windows to bite us. We were exhausted and longed for home.

At last, we saw the lights of a truck in the distance that soon grew closer. We grew hopeful, and that hope was rewarded, for our friends had shown up searching for us.

The anticipated rescue brought relief. How much greater joy must the Jews have felt to see their long-awaited Saviour arriving! Overcome by excitement, they cast palm fronds—and even their own garments—into the road (Matt. 21:8; John 12:13).

They welcomed their King, though it was probably not the king most of them were expecting. Jesus chose to arrive not on the back of an impressive horse or a golden chariot. He chose to arrive on a donkey's colt. Even in His birth, He chose to arrive in a humble manger—not a palace.

Nevertheless, He was their anticipated King, even though His kingdom was not of this world. As He would later say, "My kingdom is not of this world: . . . Thou sayest that I am a king. To this end was I born, and for this cause came I into the world, that I should bear witness unto the truth" (John 18:36-37).

When the Jews tried to kill Him in Luke 4, the Bible says that "he passing through the midst of them went his way" (vs. 30). They could not kill Him because he had all power, and His hour had not yet come (cf. John 7:30; 8:20).

As such, His eventual death was by His choice: "No man taketh it [my life] from me, but I lay it down of myself. I have power to lay it down, and I have power to take it again" (10:18).

Jesus' arrival had been anticipated for thousands of years (cf. Ps. 118:25-26; Isa. 9:6-7; Zech. 9:9). Yet even with the expectation of His arrival, no one, including His disciples, fully understood His life at the time. "These things understood not his disciples at the first: but when Jesus was glorified, then remembered they that these things were written of him, and that they had done these things unto him" (John 12:16).

Jesus fulfilled every Old Testament prophecy concerning His first advent—although not in the way some people expected. He is King, but of a kingdom that is not of this world.

One day, all will recognize this. Paul tells us, "That at the name of Jesus every knee should bow, of things in heaven, and things in earth, and things under the earth; and that every tongue should confess that Jesus Christ is Lord, to the glory of God the Father" (Phil. 2:10-11).

I have attended churches around the globe. Although the governments, cultures, and languages vary, we all bow to the same glorious King. Let us share the news of that King, who has come and is coming again!

—Jody Stinson

The Jewish Aspect

A frequently used word in Jesus' day is also heard in our time. While it was understood by ancient Jews, it may not be fully grasped today. It is the word that the Jews cried out at Jesus' triumphal entry: "Hosanna." This word occurs six times in the New Testament, always on the lips of the Jews.

At the triumphal entry, the Jewish crowd exclaimed, "Hosanna to the Son of David: Blessed is he that cometh in the name of the Lord; Hosanna in the highest" (Matt. 21:9). A short while later, children in the temple said, "Hosanna to the Son of David" (vs. 15). These words displeased the chief priests and scribes. Mark records the word twice at the triumphal entry: "And they that went before, and they that followed, cried, saying, Hosanna; Blessed is he that cometh in the name of the Lord: Blessed be the kingdom of our father David, that cometh in the name of the Lord: Hosanna in the highest" (11:9-10).

Jews spoke the word "hosanna" much more often, however, than merely at Jesus' triumphal entry. The word expressed specific desires of people's hearts. It was part of their ritual at the Feast of Tabernacles, at the Feast of Dedication (Hanukkah), and at the time of Passover. At each of these times, the Jews recited the Hallel (Pss. 113—118), wherein the term "hosanna" occurs.

The English word "hosanna" is transliterated from the Greek word *hosanna*, which is a transliteration of two Hebrew words: *hoshi'a na* ("save now"). As a priest chanted the psalms at one of the feasts in Jesus' day, the Jewish listeners responded occasionally with the word "hallelujah" and with the words of Psalm 118:25: "Save now (*hoshi'a na*), I beseech thee, O Lord: O Lord, I beseech thee, send now prosperity." On the seventh day of the Feast of Tabernacles, for example, the Jews "marched seven times round the altar, shouting . . . the great Hosanna to the sound of the trumpets of the Levites" (Smith, "Hosanna." *Cyclopedia of Biblical, Theological, and Ecclesiastical Literature,* Harper).

At Jesus' triumphal entry, the Jewish crowd identified Him as the promised Messiah. They proclaimed Jesus as the "Son of David" (Matt. 21:9) and directly connected Him with "the kingdom of our father David, that cometh in the name of the Lord" (Mark 11:10).They also identified Him as "the King of Israel that cometh in the name of the Lord" (John 12:13). They wanted Jesus, their Messiah, to "save now" as they cried out, "hosanna." The Jewish crowd said "hosanna" to Jesus, and in this way, He was "implored as Messiah to bring salvation" (Morris, *Gospel According to John*, Eerdmans).

For the vast majority of them though, that salvation was not a desire to be forgiven of their sins. The Jews were under Rome's dominion. Rome's legions were throughout Israel. Taxes to Rome were exorbitant. The Jews looked for a political Messiah, one who would militarily overthrow Rome and expel its soldiers from their borders. They looked for a physical "salvation" with a restoration of a kingdom similar to that of David. When Jesus did not fulfill that earthly expectation, the crowd's euphoric praise at His triumphal entry became a cry to "crucify him" (John 19:15).

The reality is that Jesus did accomplish salvation: spiritual and eternal and eventually physical. It is finished in His death and resurrection. It is available today for all Jews, and for Gentiles too.

—*R. Larry Overstreet*

Guiding the Superintendent

One of the greatest evidences of the inspiration of Scripture is the fulfillment of numerous prophecies concerning the Messiah. In our lesson today, we will study a prophecy which predicted the coming of the King.

DEVOTIONAL OUTLINE

1. A king will come (Isaiah 9:6-7). In this familiar prophecy, Isaiah reveals much of the character of the Messiah. He was to be a child, which points to His humanity, but also a Son, which may indicate His deity. The phrase "the government shall be upon his shoulder" points to His kingly authority (vs. 6). The title "Prince" and the reference to the throne of David also make this impression.

The nature of the Messiah is shown in four titles. As the Wonderful Counselor (cf. 28:29), He will possess the wisdom of God and give men wise advice. The title Mighty God stresses that by nature He is God and able to overcome all enemies. As the Everlasting Father, the Messiah will always show fatherly care and love for us. As the Prince of Peace, He brings the peace that our world craves.

Verse 7 points to the Second Coming when Jesus will return and make fully manifest His kingdom.

2. This King is coming (John 12:12-16). At His triumphal entry, Jesus entered Jerusalem and publicly presented Himself as the king that Isaiah had prophesied. There was no outward sign of a royal coronation, but only a symbolic act. A close study of Daniel 9:24-27 reveals that this entrance took place in the exact year Daniel had predicted.

It has been estimated that over 2.5 million people gathered in Jerusalem to celebrate Passover. Patriotic and religious fervor was great, and it exploded when the crowd heard that Jesus would be coming.

The crowds grabbed palm branches, which was the customary way to welcome and show submission to a king.

These pilgrims cried out the words of a messianic psalm: Psalm 118:25-26. "Hosanna: Blessed is the King of Israel that cometh in the name of the Lord" (John 12:13). "Hosanna" derives from Hebrew words that mean "save now." As already mentioned, it is probable that the crowds were looking for a deliverer who would overthrow Rome and reestablish the kingdom of Israel. But at His first coming, Jesus came to conquer sin and death, not the current political power.

John quoted a prophecy from Zechariah 9:9 which predicted that Israel would hail the Messiah when He rode into Jerusalem on the colt of a donkey. His entrance in this manner symbolized His humility. It was done to picture His meekness as well as His poverty. It is a graphic picture of the mission of the Messiah. The One who would bear our sin rode a beast of burden.

CHILDREN'S CORNER

You should equip your teachers to help younger children think about a King and a kingdom that would never go away. Before that they may have to explain the concept of kingship itself.

Your teachers should stress that the King in Isaiah 9 is Jesus, so your children do not wonder if every newborn baby is the King!

Your teachers will also need to be prepared to explain the metaphorical usage of "Daughter" in John 12:15 and likely replace the word "donkey" for "ass" in verses 14 and 15.

—*Robert Winter.*

SCRIPTURE LESSON TEXT

LUKE 2:25 And, behold, there was a man in Jerusalem, whose name *was* Simeon; and the same man *was* just and devout, waiting for the consolation of Israel: and the Holy Ghost was upon him.

26 And it was revealed unto him by the Holy Ghost, that he should not see death, before he had seen the Lord's Christ.

27 And he came by the Spirit into the temple: and when the parents brought in the child Jesus, to do for him after the custom of the law,

28 Then took he him up in his arms, and blessed God, and said,

29 Lord, now lettest thou thy servant depart in peace, according to thy word:

30 For mine eyes have seen thy salvation,

31 Which thou hast prepared before the face of all people;

32 A light to lighten the Gentiles, and the glory of thy people Israel.

33 And Joseph and his mother marvelled at those things which were spoken of him.

34 And Simeon blessed them, and said unto Mary his mother, Behold, this *child* is set for the fall and rising again of many in Israel; and for a sign which shall be spoken against;

35 (Yea, a sword shall pierce through thy own soul also,) that the thoughts of many hearts may be revealed.

JOHN 12:23 And Jesus answered them, saying, The hour is come, that the Son of man should be glorified.

24 Verily, verily, I say unto you, Except a corn of wheat fall into the ground and die, it abideth alone: but if it die, it bringeth forth much fruit.

25 He that loveth his life shall lose it; and he that hateth his life in this world shall keep it unto life eternal.

26 If any man serve me, let him follow me; and where I am, there shall also my servant be: if any man serve me, him will *my* Father honour.

NOTES

A Mission from Birth
(Christmas)

Lesson Text: Luke 2:25-35; John 12:23-26

Related Scriptures: Luke 2:21-24, 36-40; Matthew 26:18-45;
Mark 14:32-42

TIMES: 6 or 5 B.C.; A.D. 30   PLACE: Jerusalem

GOLDEN TEXT—"A light to lighten the Gentiles, and the glory of thy people Israel"
(Luke 2:32).

Introduction

Many passages of Scripture allude to the birth of Christ, both prophetically and historically. But two texts are used most frequently at this time of the year. One is from Matthew and the other is from Luke, the only Gospels that explicitly deal with Jesus' birth.

These accounts record the coming of the wise men (Matt. 2:1-12) and the angelic announcement of Christ's birth to the shepherds (Luke 2:1-20). Consequently, both are often used in sermons, children's programs, and Christmas pageants.

Besides the above passages, there are other texts that deal with the Messiah's advent. One of those was already covered in lesson 1, regarding Joseph's dilemma concerning his future bride. Our first lesson portion for this week concerns Simeon, a devout, aged man who was granted the privilege of living to see the advent of Messiah before he died.

LESSON OUTLINE

I. A BLESSED ENCOUNTER—
   Luke 2:25-28

II. BLESSING AND SORROW—
   Luke 2:29-35

III. HOUR OF GLORY—
   John 12:23-26

Exposition: Verse by Verse

A BLESSED ENCOUNTER

LUKE 2:25 And, behold, there was a man in Jerusalem, whose name was Simeon; and the same man was just and devout, waiting for the consolation of Israel: and the Holy Ghost was upon him.

26 And it was revealed unto him by the Holy Ghost, that he should not see death, before he had seen the Lord's Christ.

27 And he came by the Spirit into

the temple: and when the parents brought in the child Jesus, to do for him after the custom of the law,

28 Then took he him up in his arms, and blessed God, and said,

A promise to Simeon (Luke 2:25-26). Eight days after His birth, the infant Jesus was circumcised (cf. vs. 21), as commanded in the Mosaic Law (Gen. 17:12; Lev. 12:1-4). It was on the eighth day that a child was formally named. Both Joseph and Mary had been informed that the child's name would be Jesus (Matt. 1:21; Luke 1:31).

Forty days after His birth, Jesus was brought to Jerusalem and the temple for the customary dedication. Bethlehem was just a short distance away, so this would not have been a hardship. Since Joseph and Mary fled Bethlehem quickly after being informed of Herod's plot to murder the infant Messiah (Matt. 2:13-15), we have to conclude that the wise men did not arrive at the family dwelling until after His temple dedication. Hence, manger scenes that include the Magi are historically inaccurate.

It was at this time of dedication that Luke introduces us to Simeon. {Described as "just and devout" (2:25), Simeon was "waiting for the consolation of Israel."}^Q1 The word translated "consolation" is often translated "comfort" (II Cor. 1:3) and could be rendered "encouragement." Simeon was therefore anticipating the arrival of the Messiah, the One who would bring true and lasting consolation. {The Lord's imminent advent had in fact been revealed to Simeon by the Holy Spirit.}^Q2 Exactly how this happened is not stated, but it must have been so clear that Simeon had no doubts that it would occur soon.

The fact that Simeon would not see death until he saw the Messiah likely meant that he was quite aged. That the Holy Spirit was resting upon him tells us that he was filled with God's prophetic Spirit specifically for this occasion. By contrast, under the new covenant, the Spirit permanently indwells every believer.

A Spirit-arranged meeting (Luke 2:27-28). {Simeon, guided by the Holy Spirit, came into the temple seeking Messiah at the very time Joseph, Mary, and the infant Jesus were there for His dedication.}^Q3 Simeon was brought into the temple at just the right place and time to witness the fulfillment of the promise God had made to him.

While today we may not receive specific promises as Simeon did, there are nevertheless occasions when we likewise find ourselves at just the right place and time. Rather than attribute this to mere coincidence or some other impersonal force, we should recognize and acknowledge that it is actually God's guiding providence at work.

It is unlikely that Joseph and Mary knew Simeon previous to this occasion. It may have come as a surprise to them when he took their infant son in his arms. He seems to have simply walked up to them and taken Jesus from them as he began praising the Lord.

It is no secret that God blesses us, but we do not usually think of ourselves as blessing God. The Greek word translated "blessed" in verse 28 is *eulogeo,* from which comes our English word "eulogy," literally meaning "good word." While we usually think of a eulogy as a message delivered during a funeral, the biblical term has a much broader application. {In this case, Simeon's blessing meant that he was praising the Lord for fulfilling His promise to send the Messiah, as well as for allowing Simeon, before departing this world, to bear witness to Messiah's arrival.}^Q4

BLESSING AND SORROW

29 Lord, now lettest thou thy servant depart in peace, according to thy word:

30 For mine eyes have seen thy salvation,

31 Which thou hast prepared before the face of all people;

32 A light to lighten the Gentiles, and the glory of thy people Israel.

33 And Joseph and his mother marvelled at those things which were spoken of him.

34 And Simeon blessed them, and said unto Mary his mother, Behold, this child is set for the fall and rising again of many in Israel; and for a sign which shall be spoken against;

35 (Yea, a sword shall pierce through thy own soul also,) that the thoughts of many hearts may be revealed.

The light of salvation (Luke 2:29-32). Having seen and also taken into his arms the very Saviour of mankind, Simeon acknowledged that he could now die in peace, having experienced the greatest privilege of his life.

This was "according to thy word," that is, according to the promise made to Simeon. It is not clear whether this promise had been made many years previously or had been received recently. We might reasonably infer, however, that Simeon had been waiting a long time for the promise to come to pass.

With the infant Jesus still in his arms, Simeon declared, "Mine eyes have seen thy salvation" (vs. 30). {Simeon knew that he had now been privileged to behold the very embodiment of God's promised salvation to humankind. He knew that at that moment, the tiny infant in his arms was salvation personified.}Q5 We must never forget that salvation is found only in one specific Person, the Lord Jesus Christ. No other person or thing under heaven offers salvation (cf. Acts 4:12), for no one can come to God except through Him (cf. John 14:6).

Throughout the Old Testament, God had been working to bring about the realization of Christ's salvation. Jesus would be that seed of the woman who would crush the head of the serpent (Gen. 3:15). He would be the seed of Abraham who would bless the entire world (12:3). He would be born of a virgin (Isa. 7:14) in Bethlehem (Mic. 5:2). He would come from the tribe of Judah (Gen. 49:10) and be a Prophet like Moses (Deut. 18:15). He was destined to sit on David's throne (II Sam. 7:16). And His kingdom would never end (Dan. 2:44; 7:13-14).

{While Israel indeed had a unique role in bringing the Saviour into the world, the blessings of redemption had been promised to all peoples. Including Gentiles had always been God's plan.}Q6 Consequently, the message of salvation is to be taken to all the world, and disciples are to be made from all nations (Matt. 28:19). To be sure, not everyone who hears will be converted, but those who do receive Jesus as Lord and Saviour will become the very children of God (John 1:12). Like Paul, believers must do whatever they can to save souls (I Cor. 9:22). Indeed, God does not want anyone to be lost (I Tim. 2:4; II Pet. 3:9), but people must respond in repentance and faith to His gospel to be saved (Rom. 10:9).

That the Lord Jesus is "a light to lighten the Gentiles" (Luke 2:32) echoes what is found in Isaiah (9:2; 42:6; 49:6; 62:2). While Jesus' earthly ministry was primarily among His own people, the Jews (Matt. 15:24; John 1:11), the gospel was to be preached to Jews first, but then to all other peoples (Acts 1:8; Rom. 1:16). As those first Samaritan believers acknowledged, Jesus is indeed "the Saviour of the world" (John 4:42).

Perplexity (Luke 2:33). {Surprised by what Simeon proclaimed about their tiny infant, Joseph and Mary "marvelled at those things which were spoken of him."}[Q7] Considering what they already knew and had experienced relating to the birth of this Child, it is significant that this dramatic demonstration by the devout stranger took them by surprise, but it would not be the last turn of events in Jesus' life that would leave them astonished or bewildered.

Coming conflict (Luke 2:34-35). Next, Simeon's attention turned to address Joseph and Mary. He blessed them, but his message also contains an ominous element. Simeon prophesied that Jesus would become a polarizing figure in Israel. Those who rejected Him would fall, but those who received Him would rise. Although many would denounce Him, He would become the ultimate watershed between those who remained under God's righteous wrath, and those who would be delivered from that wrath to inherit the kingdom of God (cf. John 3:36). Even Joseph and Mary themselves would be pierced to their very souls by this conflict (cf. Heb. 4:12).

During His earthly ministry, Jesus' opponents leveled all sorts of charges against Him, everything from being a glutton and a drunkard (cf. Matt. 11:19) to being possessed by a demonic spirit (John 7:20; 8:48). As the early pages of Acts reveal, those who confessed Christ were frequently persecuted. As time went on, this persecution intensified. Many prominent Christians who attended the first ecumenical council at Nicaea in A.D. 325 were physically marked by the persecutions they had endured up to that time, including massive scarrings, missing limbs, and other cruel mutilations. Even today in many places, to acknowledge Jesus Christ as Saviour and Lord is to invite persecution, and in some cases even a martyr's death.

Mary's experience as Jesus' mother would not always be a pleasant one. There would be many painful moments, especially as she watched Him be rejected, tortured, and crucified. {Witnessing her son suffer on the cross must have been a most cruel sword that pierced Mary's soul.}[Q8]

HOUR OF GLORY

JOHN 12:23 And Jesus answered them, saying, The hour is come, that the Son of man should be glorified.

24 Verily, verily, I say unto you, Except a corn of wheat fall into the ground and die, it abideth alone: but if it die, it bringeth forth much fruit.

25 He that loveth his life shall lose it; and he that hateth his life in this world shall keep it unto life eternal.

26 If any man serve me, let him follow me; and where I am, there shall also my servant be: if any man serve me, him will my Father honour.

Christ's hour (John 12:23-24). Even when Jesus rode triumphantly into Jerusalem on Palm Sunday, a multitude of people lined the road as He made His way into the city. This included pilgrims who had journeyed far to attend the Passover (11:55), Pharisees and other religious leaders who opposed Jesus (12:19), and those who had witnessed the resurrection of Lazarus (vs. 17). Moreover, there were also curiosity seekers who had merely heard about Jesus' miracles (vs. 18).

It was at this time that some Greeks wanted to see Jesus (vss. 20-22). These were probably either converts to Judaism (proselytes) or Jews of the dispersion, that is, ethnic Jews who now resided outside Israel. Some have suggested that these Greeks were Gentiles like Cornelius (cf. Acts 10:1-2). Such individuals had attached themselves to Judaism but had not become full converts. Part of the reason for the ambiguity is that the term "Greek" is used to mean various things in the New Testament. These men approached Philip first. Philip then told Andrew, and both of them informed Jesus of the request. Whether these Greeks ever got their interview with Jesus is not recorded.

{The hour of Christ's glorification had arrived. While references to the Messiah's glory in Scripture can refer to a number of things, His atoning death and His resurrection seem to be in view in this instance.}[Q9] The fact that people other than native-born Jews were seeking Jesus indicates that the time had come for Christ's sacrifice for the sins of the world and for the spreading of the gospel to the farthest corners of the earth.

Throughout the Gospel of John, the idea of Christ's "hour" is prominent (cf. 2:4; 7:30; 8:20). With His arrival in Jerusalem for the final Passover, the hour had come for Him to be sacrificed and raised from the dead. Although Jesus struggled mightily with this prospect at Gethsemane, He would nevertheless persevere and submit to God's plan for Him (cf. 12:27; 18:11).

Just as a seed must die before it can produce new life, so it was with Christ. Jesus was about to die on the cross, but that would not be the end of the story. Rising from the grave not only affirmed that He was the Son of God but also made the promise of eternal life a reality for all who trust in Him.

Life and service (John 12:25-26). As Jesus was willing to sacrifice Himself for those who trust in Him, those who receive Him as Lord and Saviour must be willing to dedicate their lives to following Him. For the true disciple, loving his own life and loving this world must be replaced with a willingness to reject selfish interests and worldly concerns in exchange for eternal life, which is offered to us through God's grace.

"To love one's life here means to give it priority over the interests of God's kingdom; . . . The kingdom of God and 'eternal life' are in practice interchangeable terms, since eternal life is the life of the age to come, when God's kingdom is established on earth, but in this Gospel especially eternal life is something that can be received and enjoyed here and now through faith-union with Christ" (Bruce, *The Gospel of John,* Eerdmans).

In order to serve Christ, we must obey Him; we must not merely call Him "Lord, Lord" (Matt. 7:21-23). If we truly trust the Lord and follow Him in obedience, God the Father will honor our service. Christ died so that we could be with Him forever (John 14:1-6).

{Serving the Lord and following Him are two aspects of trusting Him as Lord and Saviour, and they are inseparable in the life of the true believer.}[Q10]

—*John Alva Owston.*

QUESTIONS

1. How is Simeon described?
2. What had been revealed to Simeon?
3. What event brought Joseph, Mary, Jesus, and Simeon together in the temple at the same time?
4. What does it mean that Simeon blessed God?
5. How did Simeon see God's salvation?
6. What promise had God made concerning salvation and the Gentiles?
7. How did Joseph and Mary respond to these events?
8. How would a sword pierce Mary's soul?
9. What hour had come for Christ? How would He be glorified?
10. How are serving and following Christ related?

—*John Alva Owston.*

Preparing to Teach the Lesson

Have you ever waited a long time for a prayer to be answered, only to think that God will never hear you? Sometimes God requires us to wait on Him patiently, but this does not mean that He has ignored you or refused you. It simply means that He is working to strengthen your faith and love for Him. He wants us to seek Him for Himself in love, not just treat Him like a genie in a bottle who appears to give us whatever we wish.

We can rest assured that God does what He has promised. He does not lie, nor does He fail (Num. 23:19; Titus 1:2; Heb. 6:18). We will find our prayer lives much more fulfilling if we seek to align ourselves with God's will rather than try to talk Him into lining up with our will. God works in His own time, but when the answer comes, we realize that He goes beyond our wildest imagination and exceeds our expectations (cf. Eph. 3:20).

TODAY'S AIM

Facts: to learn of the patient trust of Simeon and how Christ's followers must die to self as He died on the cross.

Principle: to grow closer to the Lord as we learn to patiently wait on Him.

Application: to learn to desire to know God as our sufficiency rather than just get our prayers answered.

INTRODUCING THE LESSON

In this week's lesson, we meet a man who learned how to wait patiently on God. This man was named Simeon, and he was known as a righteous and devout man who believed that God was going to send His Anointed One to Israel. He was so close to the Lord that God made a tremendous promise to him that may have seemed too good to be true. However, Simeon believed God, and his faith was rewarded in the end.

DEVELOPING THE LESSON

1. Simeon sees Jesus (Luke 2:25-27). Forty days after Jesus' birth, Mary and Joseph brought Him to Jerusalem "to present him to the Lord" (vs. 22). In accordance with the law's provision for those unable to afford a lamb, they brought two turtledoves for sacrifice (cf. Lev. 12).

In Jerusalem at the time of Jesus' birth was a man named Simeon, who was a just, righteous, and devout follower of the Lord. This is the only mention of this man by name in the Bible, and nothing else is known of him. Luke does not tell us his age or vocation; those were unimportant details. What mattered was that this man was faithfully devoted to God.

Simeon was waiting for "the consolation of Israel" (vs. 25), which meant that he was waiting for God to rescue and deliver His people. He greatly anticipated the coming of the Messiah because he believed that God would send His Anointed One to save Israel.

The Holy Spirit was upon Simeon and had revealed to him that he would not die until he saw "the Lord's Christ" (vs. 26), or Messiah. He walked so closely with the Lord that God promised him that he would not die until he laid his eyes on the One through whom consolation to Israel would come.

Simeon was led by the Spirit into the temple and saw Mary and Joseph there with the baby Jesus. They had brought Him into the temple to offer the sacrifices mentioned above. When Simeon saw the Child, he recognized Him and knew that his prayers had been answered.

2. Simeon prays and prophesies over Jesus (Luke 2:28-35). Simeon took Jesus in his arms and thanked God for answering him. He declared that he could depart, or die, in peace now that he had seen Israel's Messiah. We do not know how long Simeon had been waiting after hearing God's promise, but God kept His word to His faithful servant and allowed him to see the very One who would save Israel.

Simeon proclaimed that Jesus was not only sent for the Jews, but also for Gentiles. Jesus became a light to the Gentiles and glory to the Jews. There is a universal dimension to the mission of Christ. This does not mean that everyone will be saved in the end (universalism). Salvation comes only through Jesus Christ, but all can be saved through faith in Him. Hearing all this, Mary and Joseph marveled.

Simeon further told Mary that many in Israel would fall and rise because of Jesus. Some would reject Him, and others would follow Him. Those who humbly accept Him will be raised, and those who proudly reject Him will fall. As for Mary, her heart would be pierced when she saw her son die.

3. The cost of following Christ (John 12:23-26). As we celebrate the birth of Christ, let us remember that there is a cost associated with following Him. We must be willing to come and die to our own selves and agenda (vs. 25). Such daily sacrifice is a small reflection of the cross that Jesus Himself bore. For Him, death was His path to glorification, and unless He died, He would never have been able to bear fruit (vss. 23-24). But as it is, He is able to save all those who put their trust in Him.

Perhaps you are the recipient of gifts from various people right now. Enjoy those gifts as reminders of God's grace, but remember that the greatest gift is knowing Christ and being known by Him. Those who serve Christ must follow Him, which means we must always put Him first in our lives. Jesus is our greatest gift, and nothing compares to Him.

ILLUSTRATING THE LESSON

The real gift of Christmas is Christ Himself.

THE REAL GIFT OF CHRISTMAS

JESUS

CONCLUDING THE LESSON

Simeon was a man who knew what it meant to wait on the Lord. God had revealed to him that he would live to see the Messiah, and he rejoiced when that day came. He followed and served God, and God honored his obedience and devotion.

What are you waiting on? Are you being patient, or do you find yourself fidgeting in impatience? Rest assured that God will do what He has promised and will not let you down. Learn to be content with knowing Christ and accept Him as your greatest gift.

ANTICIPATING THE NEXT LESSON

In next week's lesson, we will study how Jesus, though God, humbly served as a man.

—*Robert Ferguson, Jr.*

PRACTICAL POINTS

1. Receiving a word from God calls for faith on our part (Luke 2:25-26).
2. Encountering Jesus is the most important thing in life for anyone (vss. 27-29).
3. The salvation God has brought in Jesus is something we should all marvel at (vss. 30-33).
4. Jesus brings salvation and hope, but many violently oppose Him, to their ruin (vss. 34-35).
5. When God has called you to a great work, do it with confidence (John 12:23-24).
6. True faith is marked by sacrificial service to the Lord (vss. 25-26).
—Charity G. Carter.

RESEARCH AND DISCUSSION

1. Define "consolation." Using that definition, describe what the "consolation of Israel" could be (Luke 2:25).
2. What did Simeon mean when he said, "Mine eyes have seen thy salvation" (vs. 30)?
3. How can Jesus be both "a light to lighten the Gentiles" and "the glory of thy people Israel" (vs. 32)?
4. What did Jesus mean when He said, "The hour has come" (John 12:23)?
5. What are some of the main differences between someone who loves his life and someone who hates his life (vs. 25)?
—Charity G. Carter.

ILLUSTRATED HIGH POINTS

He came by the Spirit (Luke 2:27)

When you leave an airplane, you encounter a crowd of people waiting to greet those who are coming and direct them to where they need to go next. Generally, there are a few uniformed limousine drivers holding up signs to find business visitors who need rides to a hotel or corporation headquarters.

But Simeon was guided to Mary, Joseph, and the baby Jesus not by human means but by the Holy Spirit.

He that loveth his life (John 12:25)

A young pastor wrote out his philosophy of ministry. Under "family life" he said, "Always put family before ministry." Does that mean no one in the church can get sick, be in an accident, or die on their pastor's day off? Of course not!

As this young pastor would also likely tell you, one has to "die" to his own desires or conveniences in order to fulfill ministry. This is true for all God's people, not just pastors.

If any man serve me (John 12:26)

A doctor, age 68, was stricken with a mysterious illness. His condition was controllable, but he was advised to give up his medical practice. Not to do so would be a threat to his life.

He decided he would continue because he cared for his patients. Twenty years later he died, not from his condition, but from a heart attack. The rest of the story: the doctor was a veterinarian, his patients were cats, and his condition was a severe allergy to cats (Aurandt, Destiny: *From Paul Harvey's "The Rest of The Story"*, Bantam).

If we can value the commitment of this man to cats, how much more should we be committed to Christ?
—David A. Hamburg.

Golden Text Illuminated

"A light to lighten the Gentiles, and the glory of thy people Israel" (Luke 2:32).

When God's Son came to earth, He was a man on a mission. That mission, however, can be as misunderstood today as it was in the first century. How many times have we heard someone say, "I love Jesus so much; He died for my sins"? This is a wonderful testimony, but it overlooks one thing: God's agenda. Jesus' mission is bigger than just saving you or me.

One aspect of Jesus' agenda involves Israel. When God sought a man to father the nation through whom He would send the Saviour, He chose Abraham. This man, whom we now call the father of faith, faced many trials. He not only had to worry that the Egyptians would kill him, he also had family problems. For example, when Sarah, his barren wife, finally conceived, Hagar and Ishmael harassed her and her child. Also, Lot's shepherds hated Abraham's shepherds.

The biggest problem that Abraham's family had, however, was not exposed for many years. In the final analysis, they underestimated their own capacity for sin (cf. Ex. 19:8); God had to show the people of Israel this through the Law (cf. Rom. 7:7-8; Gal. 3:24). Moses had warned Israel that one day their rebellion would cause them to be enslaved by other nations, and this happened between the eighth and sixth centuries B.C.

Paul speaks about a man hopelessly caught in the cycle of sin (Rom. 7), and this was the situation of the entire Jewish nation. With some even questioning God's faithfulness to the covenant (Rom. 11), the possibility of getting everyone together for repentance became nil. When Jesus bore the sins of Israel on the cross, however, God offered full release from their sin. Those who believed and confessed, "Jesus is Lord," received God's pardon, God's Spirit, and God's now-but-not-yet kingdom.

Jesus not only offered glory to Israel, He also enlightened Gentiles. Part of God's covenant with Abraham was that through his Seed, the Messiah, "all the nations of the earth [would] be blessed" (Gen. 22:18). In other words, one of the greatest blessings to Abraham was that the Saviour of the whole world would come through Him. Those of us who are not Jews tend to take this for granted, but if God had not included us in His covenant with Abraham, we would still be pagans worshipping lifeless idols.

Fortunately, God included the nations in the Abrahamic covenant, so Jesus also bore the sins of Gentiles. John, a Jew, writes, "He is the propitiation for our sins: and not for ours only, but also for the sins of the whole world" (I John 2:2). This has been proved true by people from all nations coming to trust Jesus as their Lord.

God's people today are called Christians, but they are not closed off to any who will repent. Jesus also died for the sins of those who currently consider themselves to be Muslims, Hindus, and atheists. Whether drug dealer or police officer, porn star or stay-at-home mom, Jew or Gentile—all who call Jesus Lord will receive God's pardon, God's Spirit, and God's now-but-not-yet kingdom. His glory is for all who believe.

—*David Samuel Gifford.*

Heart of the Lesson

"This is my time to play," a retired man told my friend. A job with good pay had enabled the man to retire early. Then when his mother died, he received a sizeable inheritance. He said he had given enough to the church. Now he is squandering his time and money at theme parks and auto races around the country. Everyone can see what he believes is important in life.

In this week's lesson, as Jesus is about to go to the cross, He explains what should be important in our lives.

1. Expectant life (Luke 2:25-28). Mary and Joseph had traveled to Jerusalem to present Jesus to the Lord at the temple, in accordance with the Mosaic Law regarding the firstborn. While they were there, the Holy Spirit prompted Simeon, a devout, righteous man who lived in Jerusalem, to go to the temple.

Like many people of his time, Simeon longed for the Messiah, the consolation of Israel, to come. His hope was more than wishful thinking; God had personally revealed to Simeon that he would live to see the Messiah. Simeon had lived in expectancy, never knowing when God would fulfill this promise. At last, the time had come. When Simeon saw Mary and Joseph, he took baby Jesus in his arms and praised God.

2. Saviour of all (Luke 2:29-32). Now Simeon could die in peace. God had given him the thing He had promised him: he had seen God's salvation for all people. Although Simeon was Jewish, he recognized Jesus had come for the Gentiles as well as for the Jews.

3. Obedient life (Luke 2:33-35). Simeon blessed Mary and Joseph and predicted that Jesus' life would be a source of division. Those who rejected Him would fall. Those who placed their faith in Him would rise. He would expose the hidden thoughts in many people's hearts.

Simeon warned Mary that she someday would suffer pain—like a sword piercing her very soul. This happened when she watched her firstborn die on the cross.

4. Sacrificial life (John 12:23-26). About thirty years later, during Passover week, just days before His crucifixion, Jesus entered Jerusalem to cheering crowds. Later that day, He announced the hour had come for Him to be glorified. His words may have given His listeners hope that He finally was going to free Israel from Roman tyranny.

Instead, Jesus shocked them. His glorification was going to be through His death for the sins of the world. Jesus said that He was like a lone grain of wheat. Unplanted, it remains just one seed. But when buried in the ground to die, it eventually sprouts and produces many more seeds. His death would produce many children of God.

Jesus warned His followers that those who cling to their lives in this world will ultimately lose their lives. It is better to despise this world, devoting ourselves to Jesus and His kingdom, and gain eternal life.

The person devoted to Jesus desires to serve Him: to minister, to help others in Jesus' name, and to meet both spiritual and physical needs.

Jesus said that the one who wants to serve Him must follow Him, or in other words, strive to be like Him. A follower's life should reflect Jesus' character, values, love, and sacrifice. Jesus said the Father will honor the person who serves the Son. A life devoted to Jesus is the life that is most satisfying, worthwhile, and full.

—Ann Staatz.

World Missions

In college, my grandmother knew a man who had been called to be a missionary. God laid on his heart, along with four others, to take the gospel to a South American tribe that was known for being extremely violent and trapped in the darkness of sin.

Filled with hope, they began their mission by dropping gifts for the tribe. Feeling that they had created a friendly relationship with the tribesmen, the men landed on a strip of land and set up a base camp.

They must have been excited and filled with joy that at last they might reach the souls of the lost.

Two days later, all five men were killed by the hands of the very people to whom they had come to witness.

The man my grandmother knew was Roger Youderian. His friends included Nate Saint and Jim Elliot.

Two years later, Elisabeth Elliot and Rachel Saint brought the light of the gospel to the people Elisabeth's husband and Rachel's brother died trying to reach.

We are tempted to see what happened to these men as tragic, but as Christians, we must see the story as one of victory. Many of this tribe (the Huaorani) came to faith in Christ—including some of the very men who had committed the murders.

From a human standpoint, the story of Christ would also seem to be one of defeat. He was born in a stable to poor parents—even though by His descent He was of the kingly line (Matt. 1:1). He lived as a nomad with nowhere to lay His head (8:20). And most significant of all, His life and ministry resulted in His being crucified.

But to see this as a tragedy would be to forget that Jesus came to serve, to die, and to rise again. "From that time forth began Jesus to shew unto his disciples, how that he must go unto Jerusalem, and suffer many things of the elders and chief priests and scribes, and be killed, and be raised again the third day" (Matt. 16:21; cf. Isa. 53:3-7). Jesus's mission on earth was to die because "without shedding of blood is no remission" (Heb. 9:22).

While holding the baby Jesus, Simeon praised God, calling Jesus "a light to lighten the Gentiles, and the glory of thy people Israel" (Luke 2:32). He also warned Mary, "A sword shall pierce through thy own soul" (vs. 35)—almost certainly a reference to His crucifixion.

In spite of Jesus' desire to let the cup pass from Him, He still ended His prayer the night before His death with, "nevertheless not as I will, but as thou wilt" (Matt. 26:39).

Do we say the same of our own lives? Christ's mission on earth led Him to the cross. We are called to follow in the footsteps of Christ. We do not know where that may lead. "If any man will come after me, let him deny himself, and take up his cross, and follow me" (Matt. 16:24).

Indeed, in John 12:23-26, Jesus explains that His mission will only be successful when He dies, and for those who wish to follow Him, they must also be willing to hate their life in this world to keep it unto eternal life.

For the five men who risked their lives to take the gospel to the Huaorani, obedience to Jesus' call led to their own deaths. Similarly, we should follow Christ regardless of the consequences (vss. 25-26).

—*Jody Stinson*

The Jewish Aspect

When Jesus said, "The hour is come, that the Son of man should be glorified" (John 12:23), the phrase "Son of man" is a recognizable title. It occurs eighty-seven times in the New Testament, with eighty-three of them in the Gospels, all referring to Jesus. Indeed, it was His favorite self-designation. But what did He mean by it?

When the Jewish crowds heard Jesus use this title concerning Himself, they would first have connected it with Daniel 7:13: "I saw in the night visions, and, behold, one like the Son of man came with the clouds of heaven, and came to the Ancient of days, and they brought him near before him." The word "like," which precedes the phrase "Son of man," shows that as Daniel looked at this heavenly person, he observed a contrast. This person was not like the beasts, but was like a man, that is, completely human.

More than that, Daniel 7:13 states that He "came with the clouds of heaven." That phrase indicates that this person is also Deity. In Scripture, clouds commonly characterize the revealing of Deity (cf. Ex. 13:21-22; 19:9, 16; I Kgs. 8:10-11; Isa. 19:1; Jer. 4:13). In addition, Daniel 7:13 asserts that a worldwide, everlasting kingdom encompassing "all people, nations, and languages" would be given to Him. Clearly, someone far above the average man is being described in Daniel.

When Jesus used the title Son of Man for Himself, He indicated His understanding of the nature of His messiahship. In so doing, He reached back to the person depicted in Daniel 7 and, in fulfillment of the prophet's vision, used it to explain His person and redemptive ministry in terms of glorification through suffering (Longenecker, "'Son of Man' as a Self-Designation of Jesus," *JETS*).

That the Jews of Jesus' day would have understood the messianic implications of Daniel 7:13 is clear from extrabiblical writings. The Jewish Book of Enoch, dated between 300-100 B.C., specifically refers to Daniel 7 and the identity of the "Son of man" there (46.2). In Enoch, an angel testifies of this Son of Man in messianic language, stating that in Him "righteousness dwells" (46.3). Further, He "will rouse the kings and the powerful," "break the teeth of the sinners" (46.4), and "cast down the kings from their thrones" who "do not exalt him" (46.5). Finally, the book applies the title "Messiah" to the Son of Man (48.10) (http://mrhebrew1. com/m/wp-content/uploads/2017/10/ TheBookOfEnoch.pdf).

The Babylonian Talmud (dated from A.D. 200–500) confirms that Jews were still anticipating the coming Messiah. This was based in part on their understanding of Daniel 7. The Talmud interprets this passage as referring to the coming of the Messiah ("Tract Sanhedrin," www.sacred-texts.com). By the time of the Jewish commentator Rashi (A.D. 1040–1105), however, "the messianic interpretation faded and the one like a human being was seen as representing Israel" (*Jewish Study Bible*).

Jesus used the title Son of Man to show Jewish listeners that He was the promised Messiah in His mission of salvation (Luke 19:10), His death (Matt. 12:40), His resurrection (Luke 24:7), His exaltation (Luke 22:69), His second coming (Matt. 24:37-44), and His judgment (John 5:27). The majority of those in His Jewish audience did not accept Him, but that does not change who He was, is, and always will be.

—R. Larry Overstreet

Guiding the Superintendent

On this Sunday before Christmas, we are reminded again that the birth of Jesus and His death are inseparably linked. When Jesus was only forty days old, Mary and Joseph brought Him to the temple to fulfill the rites of purification (cf. Lev. 12:1-8). While there, they met Simeon, who praised the Lord for the privilege of meeting the Messiah, but at the same time also prophesied His death.

DEVOTIONAL OUTLINE

1. Simeon's prediction (Luke 2:25-35). Scripture does not record that Simeon held any position of leadership, so he may have been a layman. But it does tell us that he was "just and devout" (vs. 25). This combination describes his actions and his character. The desire of his heart was to see the "consolation of Israel"—the Messiah. Because he was sensitive to the ministry of the Holy Spirit, he knew that he would live until this Messiah came (vs. 26) and was led to the temple at the precise moment when Jesus arrived (vs. 27).

When Simeon met Jesus (vss. 28-30), he made a significant prophecy. To the Gentiles, Jesus would be the light that would lead them out of their darkness to salvation. To Israel, He would be their glory (vs. 32). The reader of the Old Testament might connect "glory" with the visible presence of God (cf. II Chr. 7:1). Jesus would bring the glory that was lost back to Israel.

But not all of Simeon's prophecy was good news. Those who believed in Jesus would "rise," or receive salvation, but those who did not believe in Him would not receive salvation. They would "fall" (vs. 34).

Simeon further told them that Mary would experience a crushing blow. This refers to Jesus' death, which would pierce her heart (vs. 35). This was fulfilled when she watched her Son be crucified on the cross.

2. Jesus' picture (John 12:23-26). After His triumphal entry (John 12:12-19), a group of Gentiles recognized that Jesus was the Light and sought to follow Him (John 12:20-22)—a partial fulfillment of Simeon's prophecy (Luke 2:32). Jesus recognized that their arrival was a preview of the vast number of Gentiles who would come to salvation.

But before that could happen, Jesus had to die on the cross. His death would be the hour of His glorification (vs. 23). In verse 24, He uses a picture from farming to illustrate what must soon transpire. Until a kernel of wheat dies, it cannot multiply itself. Until Jesus died on the cross, He could not provide salvation for others. He must give up His life so that a harvest of souls could take place. The death of the Seed was required to produce life.

In verses 25 and 26, Jesus applied this same picture to anyone who would follow Him. Jesus demands that we practice the same principle of self-sacrifice. Our love and devotion to Him must be so strong that in comparison we hate everything else.

CHILDREN'S CORNER

Both passages in this lesson are filled with metaphors (light, a piercing sword, a grain of wheat, etc.). Children tend to be literal thinkers. Prepare your teachers to spend appropriate time on explaining what these metaphors mean.

Further, the concepts of Gentiles and glory may be new to some children. Your teachers could connect glory to the conversation about kings last week. With the term Gentiles, the emphasis should be on how Israel and Gentiles together comprise all people.

—Robert Winter.

SCRIPTURE LESSON TEXT

PHIL. 2:5 Let this mind be in you, which was also in Christ Jesus:

6 Who, being in the form of God, thought it not robbery to be equal with God:

7 But made himself of no reputation, and took upon him the form of a servant, and was made in the likeness of men:

8 And being found in fashion as a man, he humbled himself, and became obedient unto death, even the death of the cross.

9 Wherefore God also hath highly exalted him, and given him a name which is above every name:

10 That at the name of Jesus every knee should bow, of *things* **in heaven, and** *things* **in earth, and** *things* **under the earth;**

11 And *that* every tongue should confess that Jesus Christ *is* Lord, to the glory of God the Father.

JOHN 13:12 So after he had washed their feet, and had taken his garments, and was set down again, he said unto them, Know ye what I have done to you?

13 Ye call me Master and Lord: and ye say well; for *so* I am.

14 If I then, *your* **Lord and Master, have washed your feet; ye also ought to wash one another's feet.**

15 For I have given you an example, that ye should do as I have done to you.

16 Verily, verily, I say unto you, The servant is not greater than his lord; neither he that is sent greater than he that sent him.

17 If ye know these things, happy are ye if ye do them.

NOTES

46

A Humble Lord Is Born

Lesson Text: Philippians 2:5-11; John 13:12-17

Related Scriptures: John 1:14; Matthew 20:20-28

TIMES: A.D. 60-61; A.D. 30   PLACES: from Rome; Jerusalem

GOLDEN TEXT—"But [he] made himself of no reputation, and took upon him the form of a servant, and was made in the likeness of men" (Philippians 2:7).

Introduction

While the New Testament gives us few details concerning the planting of the early Christian congregations mentioned in its epistles, the book of Acts does furnish us with information concerning some of them. One of those is the church at the city of Philippi in Macedonia.

Arriving in the city on his second missionary journey, Paul and his three coworkers discovered there was no synagogue—the usual place they would have begun their evangelistic work in a new city. But they learned that some Jewish women met regularly by a nearby river on the Sabbath. This led them to Lydia, a businesswoman who readily received Christ and was baptized (cf. Acts 16:11-15).

At some point during his stay at Philippi, Paul cast a fortune-telling demon out of a profitable slave girl, leading to his arrest along with his fellow evangelist, Silas (cf. Acts 16:16-24). But all was not lost: as the result of an earthquake, the jailer was converted to Christ (cf. vss. 25-34). Thus, a church was successfully planted in Philippi, and unlike some other churches in the region, it remained faithful and steadfast in its ministry.

LESSON OUTLINE

I. EMPTIED—Phil. 2:5-8

II. EXALTED—Phil. 2:9-11

III. HUMILITY IN ACTION— John 13:12-17

Exposition: Verse by Verse

EMPTIED

PHIL. 2:5 Let this mind be in you, which was also in Christ Jesus:

6 Who, being in the form of God, thought it not robbery to be equal with God:

7 But made himself of no reputation, and took upon him the form of a servant, and was made in the likeness of men:

8 And being found in fashion as a man, he humbled himself, and be-

came obedient unto death, even the death of the cross.

A humble mindset (Phil. 2:5-6). It has been suggested that the church at Philippi was a favorite of Paul's because it did not have the level of controversies that were relatively common in some of the other congregations he founded. Moreover, the Philippians assisted Paul by supporting him financially (cf. 4:10-20).

{Paul was imprisoned in Rome when he wrote this letter. Therefore, this and three other letters written at about the same time (Ephesians, Colossians, and Philemon) are often referred to as the Prison Epistles.}[Q1]

In spite of the fact that no major problems plagued the Philippian church, there were some disagreements. But wherever people come together, there is always the possibility of discord and selfishness. {Consequently, Paul encouraged them to be "of one accord, of one mind" (vs. 2). He admonished them that nothing they did should be done out of rivalry or personal pride. Instead of being focused on their own individual interests, the interests of others should be paramount among them.}[Q2] What better way to show this than by the example of Christ Himself?

The mindset or attitude of Christ should be our continual model. Since He was ever and always concerned about others, so it should be for us. Putting others ahead of our own needs and desires is not easy, since we are by nature fallen, selfish creatures.

Because of the structure of the words that follow, they are often seen as an ancient hymn, either authored by Paul himself or cited by him. Either way, the cadence is suggestive of a poem or a portion of one.

Throughout church history there have been debates concerning the nature of Christ. In A.D. 325, at the Council of Nicea, two church leaders, Athanasius and Arius, debated the issue of Jesus' deity. While Athanasius maintained Christ's full divinity, Arius claimed that He was merely a superior created being. This controversy has resurfaced at various times, with one major cult today still promoting a modern form of Arianism.

Obviously, the Apostle Paul believed and taught that Christ was not only the Son of God but "equal with God" (vs. 6). The word translated "robbery" means "to grasp" or "cling." {While scholars debate the precise meaning, it is clear that the Son of God was willing to divest Himself of certain privileges to become human. He did not cling to His equality with the Father but gave up some divine prerogatives for a time.}[Q3]

Supreme obedience (Phil. 2:7-8). That Christ "made himself of no reputation" literally means that He *emptied* Himself. Of course, there are discussions concerning precisely how and in what ways Christ emptied Himself by becoming human. As seen in the Gospels, both the deity and humanity of Christ are affirmed and manifested in various ways in various contexts.

"'Christ indeed,' says Calvin, 'could not divest himself of Godhead; but he kept it concealed for a time . . . he laid aside his glory in the view of men, not by lessening it, but by concealing it'" (Motyer, *The Message of Philippians,* IVP).

In spite of the fact that Christ was "in the form of God" and "equal with God" (vs. 6), He voluntarily took upon Himself "the form of a servant" (vs. 7). While there are several words that can be translated "servant" in the New Testament, this is the Greek word *doulos,* regularly used of a common slave, which Paul frequently applies to himself.

As the Son of God, Christ could have come to earth in a glorious form, revealing instantly that He was the

Lord of glory. Instead, He came "in the likeness of men." This was "a voluntary deprivation of the exercise of Lordship" (Motyer). Though conceived by the Holy Spirit, Jesus' birth itself was like any other human birth. Like all humans, He felt pain, became hungry and thirsty, felt disappointment and discouragement, and was tempted to sin—although He never actually was guilty of any sin (cf. Heb. 4:15).

{While many examples of Christ's humility could be cited, the greatest was His willingness to obey the Father's will and go to the cross.}Q4 "Though he were a Son, yet learned he obedience by the things which he suffered" and "became the author of eternal salvation unto all them that obey him" (Heb. 5:8-9).

When Paul added the words, "even the death of the cross" (Phil. 2:8), he was emphasizing the horrendous nature of the suffering experienced by those who were crucified. Intense pain experienced in several different ways was the lot of the crucified. Added to this in Jesus' case was the humiliation and burden of bearing the sins of the world (cf. I Pet. 2:21-25).

"'This most cruel and hideous form of punishment' is the way it is described by Cicero, who expresses his feelings about crucifixion as follows: 'Far be the very name of a cross, not only from the body, but even from the thought, the eyes, the ears of Roman citizens'" (Martin, *Philippians,* IVP). This would be particularly relevant in Philippi, as it was a Roman colony. One benefit of Roman citizenship was that a condemned citizen could not be executed by crucifixion.

EXALTED

9 Wherefore God also hath highly exalted him, and given him a name which is above every name:
10 That at the name of Jesus every knee should bow, of things
in heaven, and things in earth, and things under the earth;
11 And that every tongue should confess that Jesus Christ is Lord, to the glory of God the Father.

Name above all names (Phil. 2:9). Because the Lord Jesus was willing to obey His Father and go to the cross for the sins of fallen humanity, "God also hath highly exalted him." This exaltation included not only His resurrection but also His ascension and His installation at the Father's right hand in heaven. "This pattern of exaltation following humiliation is thoroughly biblical, and especially evident in the teaching of Jesus" (Martin).

Although He was humiliated at the cross, {Jesus has been exalted and given a name that is above every other name in the universe.}Q5 This in no way implies that the Son of God gained any additional status within the Godhead that He did not have previous to His incarnation. Rather, as the unique person of the God-Man, He was exalted to the highest position in authority because of His perfect obedience and sacrifice.

In the hierarchy of God's entire universe, there is no other name that is exalted above all other powers and authorities. Jesus alone has accomplished divine salvation, and He is salvation personified. To confess Jesus as Lord is integral to our personal redemption (cf. Rom. 10:9-10).

Every knee, every tongue (Phil. 2:10-11). It is the will of God that everyone should come to repentance and confess Jesus as Lord (cf. II Pet. 3:9), but not everyone will actually do so. Those who reject Jesus are actually despising God's free offer of eternal life (cf. Acts 13:46), as well as scorning His grace and Christ's sacrifice (cf. Rom. 3:22-24; 5:1-2).

A time is coming, however, when every human being will humbly bow before Christ and confess Him alone as Lord of all (cf. Isa. 45:23). This will occur at the final judgment. Those who refuse to confess Christ before His coming in judgment shall nevertheless be forced to confess Him at that time.

But that latter confession will by no means lead to their salvation. Rather, it will merely confirm their eternal damnation. This "will not be a saving confession, but a grudging acknowledgement wrested by overmastering divine power from lips still as unbelieving as they were through their whole earthly experience. All will submit, all will confess, but not all will be saved" (Motyer). Even those who did not believe in the existence of God or the divinity of Jesus will bow before Him on that final day. Then they will hear the words, "Depart from me, ye cursed, into everlasting fire, prepared for the devil and his angels" (Matt. 25:31).

{The ultimate goal of confessing Christ is to bring glory to God the Father.}[Q6] All that we do should bring glory to God. Keep in mind that this passage was to remind the Philippian believers that they were to be like Christ, humbly obeying the Father's will and making the welfare of others their priority.

HUMILITY IN ACTION

JOHN 13:12 So after he had washed their feet, and had taken his garments, and was set down again, he said unto them, Know ye what I have done to you?

13 Ye call me Master and Lord: and ye say well; for so I am.

14 If I then, your Lord and Master, have washed your feet; ye also ought to wash one another's feet.

15 For I have given you an example, that ye should do as I have done to you.

16 Verily, verily, I say unto you, The servant is not greater than his lord; neither he that is sent greater than he that sent him.

17 If ye know these things, happy are ye if ye do them.

The Master's example (John 13:12-13). As this chapter opens, Jesus knew that His hour had come, that is, the time for His sacrificial death had arrived. His last meal would be the Passover. As the other Gospels record, it was during this feast that He instituted the Lord's Supper. John omits that detail, but he does relate that Jesus arose, took a basin of water, and began to wash the disciples' feet. Peter resisted this humble service, since it was the lowly task of the lowliest of servants. But after Jesus explained the necessity of the action, Peter wholeheartedly submitted to it.

Once Jesus had completed this task, He asked His disciples, "Know ye what I have done unto you?" He wanted to know if they had understood the significance of what He had done for them. {He had set them an example of how a Christian should humbly serve all fellow believers. As he had taught them previously, the greatest Christian is the one who makes himself the servant of all his brethren (cf. Mark 10:42-45).}[Q7]

Humble service (John 13:14-17). The liturgical day set aside to commemorate Jesus' washing of His disciples' feet is known as "Maundy Thursday," that is, the Thursday before Easter Sunday. It gets its name from the Latin word *mandatum,* meaning "commandment." This was the initial word of the hymn sung at the beginning of the traditional ceremony, which was a setting of John 13:34: "A new commandment I give unto you, That ye love one another; as I have loved you, that ye also love one another."

"Verily, verily" (vs. 16) represents the Greek *Amen, amen* and was used by Jesus to emphasize a teaching that was very important and of surpassing value. He prefaced many statements of His throughout John's Gospel with this expression to alert His hearers that what was about to be said was of crucial spiritual importance (3:3; 5:25; 6:53; 10:7).

{Starting with a timeless principle, Jesus instructed His disciples in the significance of His washing of their feet. No servant is greater than his master, and no messenger is greater than the one who sent him.}Q8 Since Jesus, their Master, has set this example for them, humbling Himself in service to His disciples, Jesus' true disciples should never consider themselves above likewise humbling themselves to serve one another. Even the lowliest task is no excuse to decline serving fellow believers.

Since their Master and Teacher had been willing to thus humble Himself, doing the most demeaning task of washing the feet of His disciples, then they themselves should follow His lead. Jesus was demonstrating to them that there was no service too undignified to perform on behalf of one another. Whatever is needed in the service of believing brothers and sisters—no matter how debasing it may appear—should never be regarded as beneath even the most highly respected individuals among them.

{For the present, the disciples might understand these things only in terms of service to one another. Eventually they would understand that in Christ, both masters and servants were also alike in the area of personal suffering.}Q9 Once Jesus ascended and the disciples began preaching the gospel on their own, they would realize that they were likewise meant to suffer just as He Himself had suffered at the hands of the world. As He would tell them, "If the world hate you, ye know that it hated me before it hated you. . . . Remember the word that I said unto you, The servant is not greater than his lord. If they have persecuted me, they will also persecute you" (15:18-20).

Those who realized these truths and put them into regular practice would be happy and blessed in their service to the Lord. The word rendered "happy" is the same one translated "blessed" in the Beatitudes (cf. Matt. 5:3-11).

We should not be misled into thinking what most people today mean when they use the word "happy." {True happiness is found in following, serving, and obeying Christ. The one who is truly happy is so because he knows that the Lord is with him; his heart is in tune with the priorities of the Lord Himself. Thus he knows in his heart that no matter how much he suffers in this life, he will one day surely reap the rewards of a faithful servant of Jesus Christ.}Q10

—John Alva Owston.

QUESTIONS

1. To what group of epistles does Paul's letter to the Philippians belong?

2. What was Paul saying in encouraging them to be of one accord?

3. What is clear from the word "robbery" in Philippians 2:6?

4. What was the ultimate demonstration of Christ's obedience?

5. Whose name is above every other name in the universe?

6. What is the ultimate goal of confessing Christ?

7. Why did Jesus wash His disciples' feet?

8. What principle did Jesus draw from the foot washing?

9. In what area are Christian disciples and their teachers alike?

10. What is meant by true happiness in Christ?

—John Alva Owston.

Preparing to Teach the Lesson

One of the great truths of the Christian faith is the fact that Jesus Christ is both fully God and fully man at the same time. This dual nature of Jesus is mysterious; nonetheless, it is true. It is because He is both God and man that He can reconcile the two back together.

The uniqueness of Christ is that He is the only one who is both God and man. He is not half-and-half, but wholly both simultaneously. Some have disputed this, saying that He can only be one or the other. In this week's lesson, however, we will see that there is no way to compromise Jesus' humanity or His deity and be consistent with sound biblical doctrine. Jesus endured the suffering we feel and was tempted as we are, though He did not commit sin (cf. Heb. 4:15). Most important, since He is also God, He can forgive our sins (cf. Mark 2:5-12).

TODAY'S AIM

Facts: to know the humility of Christ in His birth, life, and death.

Principle: to recognize Jesus as the ultimate example of humility and service.

Application: to put others' interests above our own by humbly serving them as Jesus gives us example.

INTRODUCING THE LESSON

All religions have leaders and teachers that adherents respect and follow. The difference between all of these people and Jesus is that He is God in the flesh while these other teachers are mere human beings. They dispense wisdom; He reconciles all who trust in Him to Himself. An important truth in our lesson this week is that though He is God, Jesus humbled Himself to become man and serve in life and death.

Along the way, we will learn how it is that Jesus Christ can be both fully God and fully man.

DEVELOPING THE LESSON

1. The humiliation of Christ (Phil. 2:5-8). Paul tells us that we are to have the same mind as Christ and be willing to humbly serve others. He then goes into great detail as to how far Jesus lowered Himself in order to be a servant. It begins with the Son subjecting Himself to the frailties of a human nature.

It must be stated clearly that Jesus' existence did not begin when He was born as a baby in Bethlehem. He has always existed as the Son of God, the second Person of the Trinity. He added humanity to His deity and came into this world by being born of a woman, like everyone else. The difference is that Jesus was conceived by the Holy Spirit, so He has no biological father.

The Council of Chalcedon (A.D. 451) clarifies this unique, dual nature of Jesus by teaching that in His incarnation, His human and divine natures were united in the Person of the Divine Son while remaining distinct from each other. Chalcedon understands Jesus to be one Person with two natures, which is a summation of what Paul teaches in this passage.

But the addition of humanity is only the beginning of our Lord's humility. He further humbled Himself by being obedient to the will of the Father to die on the cross. Jesus' true service is not simply living among us as a human, but the sacrifice of His life on the cross—a sacrifice which secured our redemption. That sacrifice is the pinnacle of humility we are called to imitate.

2. The exaltation of Christ (Phil. 2:9-11). Although Jesus humbled Himself by being "made in the likeness of men" (vs. 7), He was exalted by God. In fact, it was because Jesus humbled Himself that He has been highly exalted.

Jesus never came to make a name for Himself. As a result, God has given Him a name above all names. His name is so great that at its proclamation, everything in heaven, on earth, and below the earth will bow down to Him and confess Him as Lord. All of this will be done to the glory of the Father.

3. The servanthood of Christ (John 13:12-17). We are told to imitate not just the humility seen in Jesus' death, but also that which we observe in His life. For instance, the night before His crucifixion, Jesus met with His disciples in an upper room where they ate their final Passover supper together. After supper, Jesus performed one of the most astonishing acts of service ever recorded: He washed His disciples' feet.

After washing their feet, Jesus asked them if they understood what He had done to them. The disciples were correct in calling Him Master and Lord, which meant that they were to follow His example and do for each other what He had done for them.

Foot washing was an undesirable task that was typically left for the lowest of slaves, or the person would wash his feet himself. Hosts were expected to provide for the washing of the the feet of guests, but not to perform it themselves. Indeed, it would have been taboo even for Jesus to ask His disciples to wash His feet. What makes this instance so stunning is that Jesus, their Master and Lord, stooped down and washed their feet. Afterward, He told them to wash one another's feet.

Servanthood is not glamorous, nor was it intended to be. If we are to be like Christ, then we must serve others in humility, never seeking anything in return. Jesus is our ultimate example in all matters of life, and servanthood is no exception. If our Lord and Master served others, then we must do the same.

ILLUSTRATING THE LESSON

Jesus had the mindset of a servant and calls us to serve as well.

CONCLUDING THE LESSON

Jesus said that a servant is not greater than his Lord (John 13:16; 15:20). Since Jesus is our Lord and Master, if a task is not too low for Him, it is not too low for us. Servanthood is the very heartbeat of Christ. Let us humble ourselves and take on the mind of Christ and seek to help and bless other people. Servants do not look for anything in return but simply seek to help people and glorify God in all that they do.

ANTICIPATING THE NEXT LESSON

In next week's lesson, Jesus makes an exclusive claim to be the only way to God. Apart from Christ, there is no way to reach God and enter heaven.

—Robert Ferguson, Jr.

PRACTICAL POINTS

1. Christ humbled Himself. We should do the same (Phil. 2:5-8).
2. Our greatest joy should be knowing that our Saviour will be elevated to the place of supreme authority (vss. 9-11).
3. It is important for us to realize that if we are truly serving the Lord, no task is beneath us (John 13:12).
4. Christians should follow Jesus' example in leading by serving (vss. 13-15).
5. We are not greater than our Lord, who willingly served (vs. 16).
6. Joy comes from doing the Lord's will for us (vs. 17).

—Charity G. Carter.

RESEARCH AND DISCUSSION

1. It seems that most people are determined to build a great reputation for themselves. How and why would people make themselves "of no reputation" (Phil. 2:7)?
2. Describe a time when you witnessed someone being "highly exalted" to a new level. What was their attitude and demeanor (vs. 9)?
3. Define "confess." What does it mean to "confess that Jesus Christ is Lord" (vs. 11)?
4. What are some ways you have symbolically washed other people's feet?
5. How can submitting to authority lead to happiness (vs. 17)?

—Charity G. Carter.

ILLUSTRATED HIGH POINTS

He humbled himself (Phil. 2:8)

Paul's epistle to the believers at Philippi is known for its emphasis on joy. The words "joy," "rejoice," "rejoiced," and "rejoicing" occur eighteen times in the book.

This joy comes through the Lord Jesus Christ and is more fully experienced when a Christian operates in the proper way. To cite a well-known acronym, JOY comes from putting *J*esus first, *O*thers next, and *Y*ourself last.

Jesus led the way. He, who was very God, willingly subjected Himself to the frailty of human nature and humbled Himself to die on a cross to satisfy God's justice. He did this that His enemies could have life.

Highly exalted (Phil. 2:9)

Jesus taught that the way to greatness is service (Matt. 20:25-28). He also demonstrated it as He voluntarily humbled Himself to become a man, served others, and then suffered the agony and shame of the cross in order to provide salvation for sinful men.

An unknown author wrote: "Wouldst thou be chief?—then lowly serve. / Wouldst thou go up?—go down; / But go as low as ere you will / The Highest has been lower still."

An example (John 13:15)

Jesus' example goes beyond simply washing the dust off someone's feet. There are many other ways we should serve others even when it is not easy or convenient.

For instance, one night, after midnight, our friend Sam called our home. Could we come and watch the boys while he took his wife to the ER? The answer was a no-brainer; of course we would be right over.

—David A. Hamburg.

Golden Text Illuminated

"But [he] made himself of no reputation, and took upon him the form of a servant, and was made in the likeness of men" (Phil. 2:7).

Hardly any nation's military would ever conduct a huge parade to hail the enlistment of a rookie soldier, but that is just about what we see in the staging of Jesus' birth. Magi were summoned, angels employed, shepherds distracted, rabbis consulted, and Bethlehem's infants slaughtered. A star was launched, a new tax instituted, a virgin discredited, and Herod bypassed. This was all arranged for what was from an earthly perspective, an unproven king's birth in a barn.

William Shakespeare, Walt Disney, and Steven Spielberg together could not have scripted this story. In fact, God Himself would not have let it happen if this humble child was not also Creation's "Word" and Revelation's "Lamb." That the eternal Son of God would accept such a role in the first place (and that He would also sweat blood in agony over the coming climax) seems like folly—except for one thing.

Love hurts. This is not because of what love is, but because of what it works to overcome: sin, the real cause of pain. To defeat sin, God's Son started at the bottom and stayed at the bottom until He died. Overcoming humanity's entrenched arrogance required absolute humility.

Did the Son of God have to feign humility? We know that "the Lord . . . is a jealous God" (Ex. 34:14), and the Messiah's role also suggests supremacy: "Thou shalt break [the heathen] with a rod of iron; thou shalt dash them in pieces like a potter's vessel" (Ps. 2:9). Because of His power, this question is valid, but the answer is that His humility was real. Jesus said, "I am meek and lowly in heart" (Matt. 11:29), and God's Son cannot lie.

Again, Jesus "was made in the likeness of men." This word, "likeness," comes from the Greek word *homoioma*. The Bible uses the same word in Genesis 1:26: "Let us make man in our image, after our likeness." We were made like God, and Jesus was made like us. Christ's likeness to the Father is seen in John 14:9: "He that hath seen me hath seen the Father."

God intended a big happy family, but sin, pain, and human arrogance came and stood in the way. Jesus is the Eternal Son of God, but for His mission to succeed, He had to lower Himself in at least three ways. First, He had to be subjected to human weakness and this sin-cursed world. Second, He had to sacrifice His reputation, both His reputation as the Son of God and the prospect of being a respected Jewish rabbi. Third, He had to become a servant unto death for two arrogant people groups: Jews and Gentiles.

God threw Jesus an impressive welcome, but the devil fought back. When God led Mary to Bethlehem, there was initially no room to stay. When the Magi told Herod of the new King's star, he tried to have Him murdered. When Jesus fasted before launching His public ministry, Satan tempted, "If thou . . . worship me, all shall be thine" (Luke 4:7). Our only hope for salvation is Jesus' sacrifice, which involved inconceivable humiliation. Thank God that He swallowed His pride!

—*David Samuel Gifford.*

Heart of the Lesson

Raking the leaves that drop from my maple tree in the front yard is a time-consuming task every year. But one fall day, I came home to find every leaf raked and not a bag of leaves in sight. A hand-scribbled note on my front door read, "Jesus loves you."

I began talking to my neighbors. Eventually, I learned my benefactor was the young adult Sunday school class from a nearby church. I have gratefully reflected many times on the Christlike service those believers provided to someone they did not even know. In this week's lesson, Jesus provides a stirring example of serving others.

1. Humble servant (Phil. 2:5-8). Jesus is God in His very nature and essence. He is and always has been fully Deity. Yet when He came to earth as a man in what theologians term the incarnation, Jesus willingly emptied Himself of the outward expression of His Deity. He did not cease being God; rather, His glory was veiled, hidden from human eyes. When people looked at Him, they saw a man in His very nature and essence. The God who made us became like us.

As a man, Jesus is a servant. He exchanged heaven's worship and glory for an earthly life of humility and of obedience to His Father. His greatest humiliation was the cross, where He paid for our sins and suffered the excruciating death Rome reserved for criminals.

2. Exalted Lord (Phil. 2:9-11). As a result of Jesus' obedience, God the Father has exalted Him to the highest position in heaven and on earth. The Father has given Him a name above all other names.

Our world today does not recognize Jesus' supremacy. But at the end of time, at the mention of Jesus' name, all human beings, dead or alive, will prostrate themselves before Him. As they behold Him in His power and glory, they will audibly confess He is Lord. No matter what their opinion has been about Jesus, they will acknowledge that He is the Sovereign, the Lord of all, and above all others. Through God the Son's exaltation, God the Father will also be glorified.

3. Perfect example (John 13:12-17). In the final hours before Jesus' trial and crucifixion as He and His disciples shared the Passover meal, He washed His disciples' dusty, sweaty feet, a job normally left to a lowly household servant. As Jesus rejoined them at the table, He asked if they understood what He had just done for them.

During their life together, the disciples had correctly addressed Him as their Master and Lord. Yet He, their superior and teacher, had just stooped to wash their grimy feet.

The lesson for them? They should follow His example and serve one another. In life, the servant is never greater than his master. If Jesus, their Lord and Maker, could serve by washing others' feet, so should they.

Many churches today practice foot washing, especially around the Easter season. A friend told me of washing his wife's feet at a couple's conference.

Foot washing was the symbol Jesus used to help His disciples remember His deeper message: His followers are to serve one another in love—no matter how menial the task. We are not given the option of limiting our service to tasks we enjoy.

Serving one another may mean washing someone's feet. But it can also mean doing someone's grocery shopping, emptying a bed pan, or even raking leaves for a neighbor.

—Ann Staatz.

World Missions

When you become a foreign missionary, you leave your home, culture, and language behind.

My family answered God's call to enter the mission field of Brazil. Before we left, our Portuguese lessons consisted of some tapes that taught basic phrases. After arriving in Brazil, we realized that the tapes had not prepared us. Simple tasks grew much harder through the barrier of a foreign language.

The experience was humbling. One of my family members wanted to order a soda pop, but instead asked the waiter if he had a cold (The words for pop and a sick cold are similar in Portuguese).

Even hosting a dinner was humbling when we put avocado on the salad platter (Brazilian salad consists of piles of individual vegetables served without dressing). The kind wife of a fellow missionary told us that avocado was a dessert in Brazil.

The list of mistakes we made could fill a book. We literally became as children, having to humbly submit to the guidance of those who knew better.

As humbling as that experience was, the humiliation of Jesus Christ was infinitely greater. He, Sovereign Ruler of all, humbled Himself "and took upon him the form of a servant, and was made in the likeness of men" (Phil. 2:7). And more than that, He died a shameful death on the cross (vs. 8)!

From His birth in a stable to His death on a cross, Jesus embodied a true example of humility. One such instance is found in John 13 when Jesus washed the feet of His disciples.

In the culture of His day, open-toed sandals were worn, and entering someone's house required a washing of feet. For wealthier hosts, the job of foot washing belonged to their slaves.

For people without slaves, guests washed their own feet upon arrival. It was unthinkable for a non-slave to wash someone else's feet. The act of the Master washing His disciples' feet would have been shocking indeed.

But Christ did not wash only the feet of those who would follow Him faithfully. He also washed the feet of Judas Iscariot, the man who was already planning to betray Him (John 13:2).

What an amazing act! He provided His disciples with an example to follow: they should humbly serve one another.

The disciples struggled to learn the humility taught by Christ. The mother of two of them sought for her sons the honor of sitting beside Christ in His kingdom (Matt. 20:20-28). All the disciples argued amongst themselves about who would be the greatest (Luke 9:46).

Jesus' teachings went counter to the culture of His day. The religious leaders did their works "to be seen by men," loved "the uppermost rooms . . . and chief seats," and desired "to be called of men, Rabbi, Rabbi" (Matt. 23:5-7). Jesus contrasted this with His own teaching of, "But he that is the greatest among you shall be your servant" (vs. 11).

For the disciples, learning the teachings of Christ must have been much like learning a new culture—the culture of a heavenly kingdom. In a world where sin is normal, right and wrong are twisted, and people speaking the truth are called haters, we too need to act counter to culture.

To think back to my experience in Brazil, the type of humility that was called for in that situation is what all Christians are called to. We need to follow our humble King with the humility of sinners saved by grace.

—Jody Stinson

The Jewish Aspect

Humility is "a freedom from arrogance that grows out of the recognition that all we have and are comes from God" (*Nelson's Illustrated Bible Dictionary*, Thomas Nelson). The Jews of Jesus' day knew that God required humility (cf. Deut. 8:2, 16; Isa. 57:15). For most of us, humility is difficult to maintain. As soon as we think we have it, we get proud of it. Even Jesus' disciples struggled with humility. To them, Jesus gave the classic example of humility: He washed their feet (John 13:12). What was so significant about this act?

Foot washing was an essential part of life in the long history of the Jews. It was practiced from the time of Abraham through the time of Jesus. In contrast to today's lifestyles, people in ancient days wore open sandals and walked on dirt roads. Because this practice dirtied feet, a host commonly provided water for his guests to wash their feet, as Abraham did (Gen. 18:4). Indeed, "Among the Israelites it was the first duty of the host to give his guest water for the washing of his feet (Gen. xviii. 4, xix. 2, xxiv. 32, xliii. 24; Judges xix. 21); to omit this was a sign of marked unfriendliness" ("Feet, Washing of," jewishencyclopedia.com).

Sandals were typically removed when entering a home (whether a tent or a house), and the feet were washed. It was also common to wash one's feet before going to bed at night (cf. S Sol. 5:3). Putting on sandals indicated that a person was leaving home, ready for action (cf. Ezek. 24:17). Failure to wash feet for an extended period was an indication of grief (cf. II Sam. 19:24).

Later, the task of washing someone's feet passed to a servant (cf. I Sam. 25:41). By New Testament times, many believed that no Jew, not even a slave, should be required to wash another person's feet. A rabbi's disciples were expected to serve their rabbi, but no disciple was ever expected to wash his rabbi's feet. That is what makes John the Baptist's statement in Mark 1:7 so remarkable. John knew that it was the servants' task to meet their masters' needs and to "remove their sandals and to wash their feet" (Barbieri, *Mark*, Moody). John knew that he was unworthy to do even this lowliest servant's task for his Lord.

Only the Gospel of John records that Jesus assumed this humble position in washing His disciples' feet. While the Synoptic Gospels do not record the event, Luke does provide potential background for it. The disciples had strife over who was the greatest among them (22:24). "It may be that they were quarreling about which of them should perform this service for the others (22:26)" ("Foot Washing," *International Standard Bible Encyclopedia*, Eerdmans). Jesus rebuked them and then said, "I am among you as he that serveth" (vs. 27).

In John's account, Jesus took the towel, girded Himself with it, and began to wash His disciples' feet—the notable task of a lowly servant. By washing their feet, Jesus set forth two particular lessons for them. The first lesson concerned His atoning death, which fully washed them from their sins (John 13:8). The second lesson was that of humility. While the apostles thought of personal greatness, Jesus demonstrated by His example that the primary way to achieve greatness before God is through humility. No follower of Jesus is greater than our Lord who humbled Himself, even to death on the cross (Phil. 2:8).

—*R. Larry Overstreet.*

Guiding the Superintendent

We celebrate Christmas by focusing on the birth of the Son of God on earth. It is also possible to look at Christmas from the heavenly point of view. In our lesson this week, we will look at how the descent of Jesus from heaven to the cross is the greatest demonstration of humility possible.

DEVOTIONAL OUTLINE

1. Humility in heaven (Phil 2:5-11). In Philippians 2, Paul teaches the importance of living in humility (vss. 3-5). To illustrate what genuine humility is, he uses the example of Jesus. This is the story of Christmas from the viewpoint of heaven. Jesus, who is the sovereign God, was willing to come down to earth and be subjected to suffering (vss. 6-7). The word "form" means Jesus possesses the exact nature of God. He was equal with the Father, yet He was willing to come to earth and make "himself of no reputation," meaning that He took on a human nature (vs. 7).

Of course, Jesus never stopped being God, but He was willing to veil His glory for a time. He showed ultimate humility by voluntarily going to the cross and dying for our sins (vs. 8).

Because Jesus was willing to submit Himself to the plan of salvation, the Father exalted Him (vs. 9). At the name of Jesus, all creation should bow down (vs. 10). All will one day recognize Him as the sovereign ruler of the universe (vs. 11).

2. Humility on earth (John 13:12-17). Compared to the steep step down from heaven to the cross, the example of Jesus' humility on earth may not seem quite as significant. However, in John 13, He gives us a visual demonstration of humility as He washes the feet of the disciples. The sovereign God of the universe not only became flesh; He also willingly washed dirty feet!

Just like each of us, these proud disciples needed to learn the importance of being humble servants. The issue was not deciding who was the greatest; what was crucial was living out genuine humility and love. So, in verse 12, after having washed their feet, Jesus asked them if they understood the meaning of what He had just done for them.

Jesus wanted them to follow His example. If the Son of God was willing to kneel down with a towel and wash the feet of others (vs. 13), then His servants should be willing to serve in the same way (vs. 14). The display of genuine humility is needed between believers. To the world, it demonstrates that we are different. They are able to see our humility in action.

Jesus reminded the disciples that they were not greater than He was, so they should follow the example He had provided for them (vs. 16).

The same principle is still true today. If we want to experience genuine joy and happiness, we should follow the model of Jesus: we need to be serving others. What specific way can you put this principle into practice this coming year?

CHILDREN'S CORNER

Explaining the Incarnation is difficult. Provide your teachers (including your adult teachers) a resource like the "Chalcedonian box" (you can find it online) to give them appropriate boundaries for orthodoxy in their explanation of the Incarnation.

Your children need to hear the gospel. In a lesson that correctly focuses on the Christian's responsibility for humble service, you will want to remind your teachers that the gospel is what the non-Christian (and Christian) children need first.

—Robert Winter.

SCRIPTURE LESSON TEXT

JOHN 14:1 Let not your heart be troubled: ye believe in God, believe also in me.

2 In my Father's house are many mansions: if *it were* **not** *so,* **I would have told you. I go to prepare a place for you.**

3 And if I go and prepare a place for you, I will come again, and receive you unto myself; that where I am, *there* ye may be also.

4 And whither I go ye know, and the way ye know.

5 Thomas saith unto him, Lord, we know not whither thou goest; and how can we know the way?

6 Jesus saith unto him, I am the way, the truth, and the life: no man cometh unto the Father, but by me.

7 If ye had known me, ye should have known my Father also: and from henceforth ye know him, and have seen him.

8 Philip saith unto him, Lord, shew us the Father, and it sufficeth us.

9 Jesus saith unto him, Have I been so long time with you, and yet hast thou not known me, Philip? he that hath seen me hath seen the Father; and how sayest thou *then,* Shew us the Father?

10 Believest thou not that I am in the Father, and the Father in me? the words that I speak unto you I speak not of myself: but the Father that dwelleth in me, he doeth the works.

11 Believe me that I *am* in the Father, and the Father in me: or else believe me for the very works' sake.

NOTES

The Way, the Truth, and the Life

Lesson Text: John 14:1-11

Related Scriptures: John 13:31-38; John 14:12-21;
Colossians 1:15-20; John 12:44-50; John 5:19-30

TIME: A.D. 30   PLACE: Jerusalem

GOLDEN TEXT—"Jesus saith unto him, I am the way, the truth, and the life: no man cometh unto the Father, but by me" (John 14:6).

Introduction

While some funerary practices have changed in recent years, one thing seems to have remained constant: the Scripture passages commonly read at funerals and memorial services. One of the most popular is the beginning of John chapter 14.

Jesus spoke these words not to comfort His disciples in the face of their own deaths but to prepare them for His. Since these words were spoken after He had instituted the Lord's Supper and washed the feet of His disciples, we can assume that it was late in the evening, but before they eventually made their way to the Garden of Gethsemane (cf. John 18:1). While we cannot ascertain the precise time of these events, we do know that Jesus' crucifixion was not more that twelve hours away.

LESSON OUTLINE

I. A PLACE PREPARED—
   John 14:1-3

II. THE WAY REVEALED—
   John 14:4-7

III. THE FATHER SHOWN—
   John 14:8-11

Exposition: Verse by Verse

A PLACE PREPARED

JOHN 14:1 Let not your heart be troubled: ye believe in God, believe also in me.

2 In my Father's house are many mansions: if it were not so, I would have told you. I go to prepare a place for you.

3 And if I go and prepare a place for you, I will come again, and receive you unto myself; that where I am, there ye may be also.

Believe in Me (John 14:1). Chapters 13 through 17 record what occurred in the upper room at Jesus' final Passover. To set the background for this week's lesson, we note that Jesus had washed the disciples' feet and also revealed that there was a traitor among them. John divulges the identity of the betrayer to us (13:26), but the disciples at this time did not know it (vss. 28-29). Once Satan had entered Judas, Jesus commanded him, "That thou doest, do quickly" (vs. 27).

With the betrayer now absent, Jesus began to reveal to those who remained the events that would soon befall them. He also gave some instructions meant not only for them but for all future believers as well. Jesus informed His disciples that He would only be with them a little while longer and that He would soon be going where they could not now follow Him.

When Peter asked Jesus where He was going, He answered by saying merely that he could not follow Him now but would follow later. But Peter again asked why this was so and added that he was willing to lay down his life for Jesus. The Lord's response appears to have ended Peter's persistent enquiry, prophesying that he would deny Him three times before morning dawned.

So when Jesus said to His disciples, "Let not your heart be troubled" (14:1), His intention was to reassure them. {After all, Christ had just spoken ominous words that had shocked and saddened them. He had been their Teacher and constant Companion for three years; now He spoke of His imminent departure.}[Q1] Actually, Jesus had previously warned them on numerous occasions that He would one day be rejected and killed at Jerusalem.

In verse 1, Jesus is not telling His disciples to merely put troubling thoughts out of their minds, but to see those troubling thoughts in the new light of their eternal hope in Him. The reasoning is that since they already believed in God the Father, they should likewise place the same trust in Him, for He had always faithfully revealed the Father to them as they had been following Him over the course of their discipleship. They themselves were witnesses to both the Father's love and faithfulness toward Him and His love and faithfulness toward the Father.

It is possible to vaguely believe in God but not believe in Christ, as is the case with various world religions. Many people believe in the existence of the God of the Bible but have never trusted Christ as Lord and Saviour. What such people believe about God is often rife with many unbiblical ideas about Him. But in reality, even holding correct beliefs about God does not save anyone (cf. Jas. 2:19). If we believe in the true God of Scripture according to the testimony of Scripture, we will also trust and believe in His Son, Jesus Christ, who has fully and faithfully revealed Him (cf. John 1:18).

My Father's house (John 14:2-3). {The Father's house is generally understood to be heaven.}[Q2] Jesus, of course, was not going to heaven directly from the upper room. Between this time and His actual ascension into heaven a number of events had to occur, most significantly His crucifixion and resurrection.

Our English word "mansion" comes from the Latin *mansio,* meaning "a place to stay." Hence, it generally could be understood as any house or home of any description. But for most of us today, a mansion conjures up the idea of a large, stately home, usually occupied by the wealthy.

The Greek word rendered "mansions" appears only twice in the New Testament, here and in verse 23 where it is translated "abode." It is the noun form of the verb translated "abide" in 15:4, 6, 7, and 10. {Therefore, we should not assume that Christ is saying here that each individual will have his own private, large, stately home in heaven. Jesus is saying that there are many places for believers to live in heaven, indicating nothing about their relative size but rather emphasizing the tremendous privilege of abiding eternally with Him and the Father.}[Q3]

While the words, "I go to prepare a place for you" (14:2) are usually seen as referring to heaven, we should not imagine that Jesus was returning there to engage in a construction project to accommodate His new followers. We should see it more along the broader lines of the invitation, "Come, ye blessed of my Father, inherit the kingdom prepared for you from the foundation of the world" (Matt. 25:34).

{Christ would soon die and rise from the dead. In this way, He was making the necessary preparations for His true disciples to be with Him forever.}[Q4] Apart from His redemptive work, we are all hopelessly lost, with no abiding place in God's presence. Heaven is indeed a place prepared for a people whom God has likewise prepared to inhabit it.

{The fact that Christ would "come again" (John 14:3) is usually understood as a reference to His Second Coming.}[Q5] Some think this is a reference to His resurrection, but His stated purpose was having His disciples be where He would be—surely the kingdom He would establish. In any event, the apostles had to trust in Christ to receive these promises. What was true of them is also true of us.

THE WAY REVEALED

4 And whither I go ye know, and the way ye know.

5 Thomas saith unto him, Lord, we know not whither thou goest; and how can we know the way?

6 Jesus saith unto him, I am the way, the truth, and the life: no man cometh unto the Father, but by me.

7 If ye had known me, ye should have known my Father also: and from henceforth ye know him, and have seen him.

Momentary confusion (John 14:4-5). Although Jesus said that the disciples knew the way to get where He was going, they apparently did not fully grasp His meaning. As we think about these men who were with Jesus day and night during His ministry, we may often wonder why they did not better comprehend the things He said and did. We probably think that somehow we would have been different.

Whether we would have understood Jesus any better in their place is doubtful. The crucial difference between them and us is that we have the advantage of looking back on things after the completion of Christ's redemptive work, whereas they were in the midst of experiences and events that preceded its fulfillment. We also have the advantage of the illumination of the indwelling Holy Spirit, who would not come upon them until Pentecost.

Thomas is mentioned in the other Gospels, but only in passing when listed among the other apostles. In John, however, he is mentioned several times, the most famous being when he doubted the testimony of the others concerning Jesus' resurrection (cf. 11:16; 20:24-28; 21:2).

{Whatever else might be said about Thomas, he does seem to have been inquisitive and willing to speak his mind. On this occasion, he openly stated that he and the other disciples did not know where Christ was going, nor did they know the way.}[Q6]

Eternal clarity (John 14:6-7). Verse 6 is one of the most famous and frequently quoted declarations of Jesus. It is also one of the most controversial, since it denies the possibility that faith in anything other than Jesus Christ can actually lead a person to the true God. {Jesus corrected Thomas's objections by revealing to him that, in fact, they did know the way because they knew Him, and He Himself is that way! The way is not a thing but a Person; to know that Person is to know the Way.}[Q7]

Christ is also the truth. Yes, He spoke the truth, but He is as well the very embodiment of the truth in human form. Jesus declared that God's Word is truth (cf. 17:17), and He Himself is God's Word made flesh (cf. 1:14). To look upon Jesus is to look upon Truth personified. More important, to know Jesus is to know the Truth, for He Himself is the truth that sets us free from sin and death to live abundantly (cf. 8:32; 10:10). Moreover, never did Christ deceive anyone about the truth, distort the truth, or deny the truth in any way whatsoever.

Christ is also the life. Life is a common theme in John's Gospel, and it usually refers specifically to eternal life (3:36; 5:21; 6:33; 8:12; 10:10), which actually begins when we receive Christ as Lord and Saviour by faith (5:24). Moreover, Christ is the Creator of all physical and spiritual life in the universe (1:3-4).

Commenting on the truth of John 14:6, the German monk Thomas à Kempis (1380-1471) famously wrote, "Without the way there is no going; without the truth there is no knowing; without the life there is no living."

{That no one can come to the Father except through Christ has some implications regarding the effectiveness of prayer, but the primary implication here has to do with salvation. Simply put, no one can be saved apart from Jesus Christ (Acts 4:12; I Tim. 2:5-6).}[Q8]

While many feel that the idea of Christ alone being the way to God is narrow-minded and judgmental, this truth is foundational to any understanding of who Christ really is. While it is true that similarities in spiritual teachings overlap in many religions, there are always, by definition, similarities between all counterfeits and the true original; otherwise, they could never hope to pass for the original!

To know Christ is to know the Father (John 14:7). The disciples not only knew the Father; they had actually seen Him in the Person of His Son. They had not really grasped that truth up to this point, but Jesus assured them that from then on they would know the Father intimately. This was possible only because they had seen Him in Christ, who would continue to make the Father known to them.

THE FATHER SHOWN

8 Philip saith unto him, Lord, shew us the Father, and it sufficeth us.

9 Jesus saith unto him, Have I been so long time with you, and yet hast thou not known me, Philip? he that hath seen me hath seen the Father; and how sayest thou then, Shew us the Father?

10 Believest thou not that I am in the Father, and the Father in me? the words that I speak unto you I speak not of myself: but the Father that dwelleth in me, he doeth the works.

11 Believe me that I am in the Father, and the Father in me: or else believe me for the very works' sake.

Seeing the Father (John 14:8-9). To know Christ is to also know the Father. It is a wonderful truth that the disciples had actually seen the Father—seen Him in the Person of Jesus. While this concept may seem difficult to grasp for us today, it may have actually been easier in the ancient world, since a son traditionally represented and spoke for his father in a way that is rarely acknowledged in our current culture.

Like Thomas, Philip is mentioned briefly in the apostolic lists in the Synoptics, but nothing is actually said about him. According to John, however, Philip was one of the first followers of Christ, and he brought Nathanael to Jesus (cf. 1:43-45). Philip is also noted in the feeding of the five thousand (cf. 6:5-7) and in bringing some Greeks to see Jesus

(12:20-22). In all of the above instances, Andrew is mentioned as well, likely meaning that they were close friends.

Still confused about what Jesus was saying concerning the Father, Philip asked Him to show the Father to them. If the disciples could just be granted an actual look at God Himself, Philip reasoned, that would be the fulfillment of all their needs forever.

In answer to what seemed such a bold request, reminiscent of Moses' request to behold the Lord's glory (cf. Ex. 33:18), Jesus redirected Philip's thinking with a gentle rebuke: "Have I been so long time with you, and yet hast thou not known me, Philip?" (vs. 9). In other words, Jesus was saying, "After all this time, Philip, haven't you seen enough of Me to be convinced that I am Myself the full revelation of the Father?"

{For us to know God, to see the Father, all we have to do is look at Jesus. He perfectly reveals God Himself. If we want to know how God behaves towards people, look at how Jesus treated people. If we want to know God's character and integrity, examine Christ's character and integrity in the Gospels. All the attributes of God the Father are revealed in God the Son.}[Q9]

Words and works (John 14:10-11). There should have been no doubt in the minds of the disciples that the Father was in the Son and the Son was in the Father. Moreover, the words of Christ are the words of God. Jesus did not come to do His own will but His Father's will. His words were not His own but the Father's words. His works likewise were the Father's works. What Jesus said here, He had already said in other places (cf. John 5:36; 10:37-38; 12:49-50), so this was not any new teaching, but merely a review, so to speak.

{The works in this case had to do with the miraculous signs Christ had performed, which are presented throughout John's Gospel as testifying to His divine identity and forming the foundation for saving faith (cf. 20:30-31).}
[Q10] While John is very selective concerning the miracles he records in his Gospel, relating only seven of them, he acknowledges that there were so many more that they were actually innumerable (cf. 21:25).

Both miraculous signs and other works would continue under the ministry of the apostles and their successors (cf. 14:12; Mark 16:17-20; I Cor. 12:4-11, 28-30; Heb. 2:1-4). Today, since we have the completed canon of the written Scriptures (II Tim. 3:16-17), it is generally unnecessary to verify God's truth by means of miracles, for faith comes by hearing God's Word (Rom. 10:17).

—John Alva Owston.

QUESTIONS

1. Why were the disciples troubled?
2. What is the "Father's house" (John 14:2)?
3. What was Jesus emphasizing in using the term "mansions?"
4. What preparation did Christ make for us to go to heaven?
5. What did Jesus mean when He said He would come again?
6. Which apostle insisted that he and the other disciples did not know where Jesus was going or how to get there?
7. What did Jesus declare about the way?
8. What primary implication follows from the fact that no one can come to the Father except through Jesus?
9. How can we see God the Father?
10. What were the works of the Father that Jesus did?

—John Alva Owston.

Preparing to Teach the Lesson

Many skeptics and critics of Christianity criticize what they believe is the arbitrary exclusivity of our faith. Many wonder how we can say that there is only one way to heaven. Who are we to say what the right way is? Jesus is often seen as nothing more than a good teacher who showed one way to get to heaven. But He is much more than just a good teacher, and He did not just show us a way to get to heaven. In His words, He *is* the Way—the only Way.

Christianity is exclusive in that Jesus is the only way to God. While the gospel is exclusive, its offer is inclusive in that anyone who turns from their sinful ways to follow Christ in faith and love can come to the Father through Him. All who want to come to God through Him will not be turned away, but all who seek another path will not find it. This claim of exclusivity does not originate with the church; it is the claim of Jesus Christ Himself.

TODAY'S AIM

Facts: to see that Jesus claims to be the way to the Father and the revelation of Him.

Principle: to understand that Jesus is the way to God and the way to understand Him.

Application: to not waver when people or our own inclinations try to propose other ways to God, such as religious practices or good works.

INTRODUCING THE LESSON

Jesus had just told His disciples that He was going to suffer and die. To make matters worse, one of them would betray Him and another would deny Him (John 13:21-38). At this, the disciples were dejected and troubled.

Jesus gave them good news, however: He would come again for them, and He is in fact the way to God. He is worthy of our trust even when we are upset or confused, and He will never leave us.

DEVELOPING THE LESSON

1. Our hope is found in Jesus (John 14:1-3). In the opening sentence of chapter 14, Jesus tells the disciples to not let their hearts be troubled. He informs them that they should trust Him even in their worst hour. This trust in Him is the reason they will be able to keep their hearts from being troubled, and it is grounded in their trust in the Father. God's Word is still true even in extreme heartbreak.

He then begins to describe His Father's house to them. In it are many mansions. The term Jesus used does not emphasize the luxury of the Father's house so much as the abundance of room for all God's people. In other words, by saying "many mansions," Jesus is guaranteeing them a place in His Father's house. God has a place for you as well to live in His house, and He sent His Son to pay your mortgage.

Jesus promises that He will come again for them. They will not have to find Him because He will return for them and receive them to Himself, so they can be with Him forever. Never think that God has forsaken you, no matter your circumstances. God knows where you are and has prepared a residence in His house for all who love and trust Him.

2. The way to God is Jesus (John 14:4-6). Jesus tells His disciples that they knew where He was going and the way there. Confused by this statement, Thomas asks Him how they could know the way when they did not even know where He was going. Jesus responded by saying that He is the Way, the Truth, and the Life. No one comes to the Father except through Him.

The reason the disciples knew the way to where Jesus was going is because Jesus is the Way, and they knew Him. He was not giving them a road map to follow. They were to follow Him.

Any attempts to find God apart from Christ are sure to end up in futility. Other religions and philosophies will never lead anyone to God, regardless of how devout and sincere its followers are. We know that Jesus is the only way to God directly from His own mouth. The church does not make this claim of its own ambition, contrary to what our opponents often claim. This is the direct claim of Jesus Himself. Christians simply believe it.

3. To see Jesus is to see God (John 14:7-11). After hearing this, Philip speaks up and says that if Jesus would just show them the Father, it would be enough for them. Wanting to see God is a noble desire; however, Philip has already seen God in His Son (cf. 1:18).

Jesus asks him how long they had been together and Philip still did not recognize who was right in front of him. Anyone who had seen Jesus had also seen the Father. Jesus is God's Son and is the "express image of his person" (Heb. 1:3).

Jesus said that He is in the Father and the Father is in Him. One cannot be separated from the other. To believe in Jesus is to believe in God because they are one. Jesus did not speak on His own authority, but the Father was doing His work through Jesus. We are to believe in the deity of the Son based on His words and His works, both of which originate in the Father. They are completely united, and there is no conflict between the two. Have you asked God to do His work through you and yielded yourself to total obedience to Him?

ILLUSTRATING THE LESSON

Many religions claim to have the way to God, but only Jesus can take you to the Father.

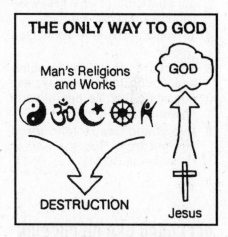

THE ONLY WAY TO GOD

Man's Religions and Works

GOD

DESTRUCTION

Jesus

CONCLUDING THE LESSON

Heartbreak can often cloud our thinking and rattle our faith. Jesus tells us, however, that we are to trust Him even in these times. He has not forgotten you, and even death cannot separate a believer from Christ. Christ has prepared a place in the Father's house for all who believe in Him and persevere by His grace to the end. Do not be fooled by other claims to get to God; Jesus is the only way.

ANTICIPATING THE NEXT LESSON

In the next lesson, we see that we are completely dependent upon Christ for everything, just as a branch is completely reliant on the vine for life and nourishment.

—*Robert Ferguson, Jr.*

PRACTICAL POINTS

1. The best way to maintain peace of mind is to trust in Jesus (John 14:1).
2. We can rest assured that we have a place in God's presence (vss. 2-3).
3. When we do not know where to go, what to do, or what to say, we can ask God (vss. 4-6).
4. To know Jesus is to know God (vs. 7).
5. The Lord does not become angry or frustrated when we ask questions that He has already answered (vss. 8-9).
6. Everything Jesus tells us is straight from God the Father Himself (vss. 10-11).

—*Charity G. Carter.*

RESEARCH AND DISCUSSION

1. What are some things you can do to keep your heart from being troubled (John 14:1)?
2. Was Jesus talking about literal mansions or using figurative language (vs. 2)?
3. What does it mean that Jesus will receive us to Himself (vs. 3)?
4. Philip asked a question that Jesus had just answered. What does Jesus' second response teach us about dealing with difficult people (vss. 7-9)?
5. Why do people have a hard time believing that Jesus and the Father are one (vs. 10)?

—*Charity G. Carter.*

ILLUSTRATED HIGH POINTS

Believe also in me (John 14:1)

Doubt generally has a negative meaning.

Some doubt, however, can be good. There is phishing on the Internet, and there are many who imitate their "father the devil" who "was a murderer from the beginning, and abode not in the truth, because there is no truth in him" (John 8:44). Thus, it is wise to be careful.

Thankfully, truth is available in Jesus Christ, who is the epitome of truth. He simply asks us to "believe in God, believe also in me" (14:1).

How can we know the way? (John 14:5)

Oxana, our Ukrainian interpreter, and Andrew, her husband, took us to Yalta in Crimea. Although Andrew had been there before, he often stopped and asked people for directions.

He commented with a smile that people in Ukraine were always anxious and willing to help show you the way even if they did not know it.

But by me (John 14:6)

In Wilmette, Illinois, stands a nine-sided temple of the Baha'i faith. It features nine entrances, but each enters the same room. The implication is that whatever religious leader or religion you follow (including diverse figures such as Jesus, Muhammad, Buddha, and Confucius), you come to the same truth. It does not matter that these religions are not in agreement; in Baha'i thinking, they all reveal the same "god" in different ways.

Our Lord Jesus is exclusive. He is the way—the only way. As He said before, "I am the door" (John 10:9)—again, the only door.

—*David A. Hamburg.*

Golden Text Illuminated

"Jesus saith unto him, I am the way, the truth, and the life: no man cometh unto the Father, but by me" (John 14:6).

The young John who followed Jesus around the Holy Land spent many years pondering Jesus' life before he wrote about it. The last half of John's Gospel (chaps. 11—21) covers Jesus' final days, and chapter 14 includes some of His last instructions to His disciples. To understand today's oft-quoted verse, we must pay close attention to Jesus' words.

When Jesus tells His disciples that He is getting ready to leave, He also tells them that they know where He's going and how to get there. However, Thomas, replying for the group, protests that they know neither His destination nor the route. Jesus is clear about the destination, the Father's house, but the disciples do not understand the travel route.

Jesus answers their query with the simple statement: "I am the way." As explained later in the verse, no one comes to the Father except through Jesus. If the disciples want to enter the place in the Father's house that He will prepare for them, they will need to have faith. Those who place their faith in Jesus will receive the Holy Spirit and obey His commandments.

The statement "I am the truth" means more than just "I tell he truth," or even "I am life's ultimate reality." Right from his prologue, John establishes that Christ is the Word of God, who perfectly reveals the Father (John 1:1, 14, 18; 5:19; 8:29; 14:7-11). John also connects Jesus' work as the Word to the fact that He is "full of grace and truth" (1:14) and that these come through Him (vs. 17). Thus, Jesus is the very embodiment of Truth because He is the complete self-revelation of God.

"I am the life" means more than "I am alive." John's Gospel is well known for its stress on "life." His prologue contains two of the most vital of the book's forty-four uses of the term: "In him was life, and the life was the light of men" (1:4). Indeed, God sent Jesus into the world so that those who believe in Him might experience abundant life (3:16-17; 10:10), and "this life is in his Son" (I John 5:11; cf. vs. 20). Thus, "I am the life" means that eternal life is found in Him.

As Jesus prepared to die for the sins of the world, He also began to prepare His disciples for their roles following His death. "I am the way, the truth, and the life" is more than Jesus' claim to fame. He calls His disciples to know that He is the way to life with the Father because He is the truth of the Father.

Jesus also said that no one can reach the Father except through Him. No one else can justify people before God; it is Jesus alone who brings us to God. It also implies that we will travel the route that Jesus Himself established: the way of obedience and sacrifice.

Yet regardless of the implications of John 14:6, Jesus' main message to His disciples is encouragement. This chapter begins with Jesus telling His disciples, "Let not your heart be troubled" (vs. 1) because it is Jesus who prepares a place with the Father for all His people (vss. 2-3). Further, it is He who is the Way to that place He prepares, not failing to bring any who place their faith in Him to it.

—*David Samuel Gifford.*

Heart of the Lesson

Remember MapQuest? The first time I used it for directions, it sent me to a farmer's backyard instead of the Clark County Quilters' annual rummage sale. I still don't remember how I found the actual sale location.

In this week's lesson, Jesus' disciples also struggle with directions as He tells them about heaven.

1. Comfort (John 14:1-4). Jesus had just told His disciples in the upper room that He would soon be leaving them. Just as He knows our troubled hearts, He noticed their despondency. Despite His own troubled heart (13:21), Jesus worked to encourage them. He started by asking them to believe in Him just as they believed in God the Father.

He assured them His Father's heavenly abode contains ample space for all. He would not have told them this if it were not true. He was going away for a purpose: to prepare a place for them in His Father's house. Their great hope, and ours as well, is His promise to return and receive His followers to Himself.

Jesus describes the abundant blessing of this place not in terms of its luxury, but in terms of fellowship—between Him and the Father and us. He then assured the disciples they knew where He was going—to the Father—and how to get there.

2. Direction (John 14:5-6). The disciple Thomas countered that he and the other disciples did not know where Jesus was going. How could they possibly know the way?

Jesus answered with the words many believers have memorized: "I am the way, the truth, and the life: no man cometh unto the Father, but by me." Only one way to God the Father exists, and that is Jesus. Through faith in Him and His work on the cross, we can have a relationship with the Father and hope of eternal life with Him. Yes, the way is narrow, but it is open to all.

Jesus is the truth. William Barclay points out that He perfectly embodied what He taught. Others may teach truth; only He can say He is *the* truth (*The Gospel of John, Vol. 2,* Westminster).

Jesus is life. He always has existed and always will. He gave life to creation and sustains it even today. To those who put their trust in Him, He gives abundant, meaningful life today and eternal life with Him in the future.

3. Oneness (John 14:7-11). If the disciples had known Jesus deeply, they would have known the Father. He assured them that from this time on, they both knew and had seen the Father.

Philip asked Jesus to show them the Father. Then they would be satisfied and ask no more. Even after their years together, they did not understand His relationship to the Father. He explained that whoever has seen Him has seen the Father.

All the teachings they had heard from Jesus were the Father's words and ideas. The Father lived in Jesus and did His work through the Son. When the disciples watched Him do miracles, they saw the Father work through Him. The Father was in the Son, and the Son was in the Father. They were and are one.

Many analogies try to explain God as three Persons yet one God, but none fully succeed. Like Jesus' disciples, we must believe His words, examine His works (which could not have been done by a mere man), and bring Him our doubts. He indeed is God.

—Ann Staatz

World Missions

The world is full of religions that claim to be a way to God—whatever they mean by the term. People either believe they can reach heaven going their own way, or they deny the very existence of God or a need for salvation.

My father once had a conversation with a man who said, "For you God exists; for me He doesn't."

My father picked up a glass of water and set it out of sight. He then said, "I believe there is a glass on the next table; you believe there isn't. Does my belief make the glass appear or does your unbelief make the glass disappear? No, the glass exists regardless of what we believe about it. So does God."

Yet even if a person believes in some form of deity, many followers can only hope that their actions will be enough to save them. While serving in Brazil, my father would walk around the villages and invite people to the service we held. People would refuse with the excuse that they were of some other religion, but many had no idea what their religion taught and merely had a vague hope that in the end their good works would be enough.

Jesus leaves no room for uncertainty about how we can obtain salvation. He says, "I am the way, the truth, and the life: no man cometh unto the Father, but by me" (John 14:6).

Jesus is not just a way—He is the only Way. He clearly states, "For wide is the gate . . . that leadeth to destruction, and many there be which go in thereat . . . and narrow is the way, which leadeth unto life, and few there be that find it" (Matt. 7:13-14). These are sobering words.

Like a child resisting the help of an adult, people want to believe that they can save themselves by their own skills or righteousness; this is the broad way. But "all our righteousnesses are as filthy rags" (Isa. 64:6).

No matter how many seemingly good works a person might perform, without salvation in Christ, they are lost. They need the Saviour; this is the narrow way.

The truth is that no man could do what Christ did. He lived a perfect life. And wholly guiltless, He still chose to sacrifice His life for those who were His enemies (Rom. 5:6).

What amazing love! He declared Himself to be the Way, knowing how much He would suffer to be the way of salvation for us. "For he hath made him to be sin for us, who knew no sin; that we might be made the righteousness of God in him" (II Cor. 5:21). Believers are clothed with the righteousness of Christ. What a great protection and privilege this is.

We can believe He is the Way since Jesus is also the Truth. In a world where many religions claim to be the means of knowing God, He alone can truly claim to be the perfect revelation of God. Further, He is the Life, for in Him alone can we receive life. Paul tells us that God, "even when we were dead in sins, hath quickened us together with Christ" (Eph. 2:5). John is even more explicit: "He that hath the Son hath life; and he that hath not the Son of God hath not life" (I John 5:12).

There is no other way to God, and yet the world is filled with people who believe they can reach God through their own strength. We need to share the Way, the Truth, and the Life with them.

—*Jody Stinson*

The Jewish Aspect

When we read Jesus' words, "In my Father's house are many mansions" (John 14:2), we may think of particular songs. Harriet E. Buell composed "A Child of the King" in 1877, writing, "A tent or a cottage, why should I care? They're building a palace for me over there." Ira Stanphill's "Mansion Over the Hilltop" (1949) echoes a similar thought. Many people think of heaven as some type of southern plantation with elaborate houses, tree-lined driveways, and large verandas with white pillars stretching across the front. No Jew in Jesus' day could have imagined any such thing.

The word "mansions" in John 14:2 is from the Greek word *morē*, which means "room" or "dwelling place." Jesus said there are many such abiding places in the Father's "house." In Scripture, God's "house" is sometimes the tabernacle (Matt. 12:4) or the Jerusalem temple (Matt. 21:12-13). The earthly temple, as God's "house," pictures God's eternal house. Significantly, the word "house" is singular in all references. Just as the earthly temple had various rooms in it, so God's heavenly house has many abiding places in it for His children.

The Jewish disciples listening to Jesus' words would have particular pictures in their minds. "The average home of the common people was a one-room dwelling" (Wight, *Manners and Customs of Bible Lands*, Moody). These homes may only be about nine-by-twelve feet (108 square feet) or twelve-by-fifteen (180 square feet) in size.

In contrast, a wealthy aristocrat would have a larger home. Archaeologists have found remains of such homes in Jerusalem. Many are about 650 square feet, but one was discovered that "covered almost 2000 square feet" (McRay, *Archaeology and the New Testament*, Baker). For Jesus' day, that was palatial. Common Jews knew of these homes and no doubt envied them.

This is the picture of the Father's house in John 14. Such a house was built with its rooms surrounding a large courtyard. A locked door was attended by a servant (cf. Acts 12:13). A well or fountain was often in it. All the surrounding rooms (the "mansions") opened into the courtyard. The owner of the home had a special room. Each family member was also assigned a particular room, a dwelling-place. As a family grew larger, rooms were built and prepared for each one.

A family's growth could occur through the birth of children. It could also occur through the marriage of sons, who brought their wives to live with them in the family estate. When additional rooms were needed, they were constructed along the sides of the courtyard. Regardless of how many rooms were added to the wealthy Jewish owner's home, it remained a single house. This is similar to a contemporary family adding on to their home.

The emphasis in ancient times was on the family unit. Each member had a dwelling place, but there was unity in the family. Such is the emphasis of Jesus' words in John 14. Jesus assured His Jewish disciples that He was going to heaven to prepare a place for them in the Father's house. The emphasis is on the unity of God's family and the intimate fellowship among its members. Jesus did not stress the magnificent beauty of a "gold mansion." Rather, He emphasized the harmonious, never-ending relationship of all believers in the family of God.

—R. Larry Overstreet.

Guiding the Superintendent

There are many things that could happen in this new year that would cause our hearts to be troubled. The possibility of the loss of a job or a divorce causes great stress and anxiety. The death of a spouse or child would cause us great emotional pain.

In this week's passage, the disciples were disturbed when they finally realized that Jesus' death was soon going to be a reality. Jesus guided His anxious followers with wise counsel that would provide them with future comfort.

DEVOTIONAL OUTLINE

1. Believe His promises (John 14:1-3). Jesus commanded His disciples to believe in Him just as they believed in God the Father. To overcome anxiety, the disciples needed to rely on Him completely (vs. 1).

Jesus told the disciples that they could find needed comfort in His promises. He told them that when He left, He would be preparing a place for them (vs. 2). They would have a home with the Father for eternity. He also promised that He would personally return and take them to be with Him (vs. 3). Though heaven is a real place, the emphasis concerning heaven in Scripture is on our intimate relationship with a Person, Jesus Christ. We will be with Him forever.

2. Know the way (John 14:4-7). Jesus told His disciples that they knew the way to heaven (vs. 4), but Thomas disagreed. So, he asked how they could know the way when they did not even know where He was going (vs. 5). This question prompted Jesus to answer with what would become one of the best-known verses in Scripture. Jesus declared that He was the Way, Truth, and Life (vs. 6). The only way to heaven is through faith in Jesus Christ. Jesus told them that their knowledge of Him was incomplete. If they really knew Him, they would also really know the Father (vs. 7). This is a clear claim by Jesus to be God.

3. Believe in His person (14:8-11). Philip did not understand Jesus' answer, so he asked Jesus to visibly show them God the Father (vs. 8). Jesus' answer reveals a hint of reproof. They had been with Him for so long and seen all the things He did, yet they still did not understand who He was. He told them that in seeing Him for three years they had been seeing the Father (vs. 9).

The problem was not a lack of empirical evidence, but a lack of faith (vs. 10). Philip wanted an experience, but Jesus taught that He was enough. His deity was confirmed by His words, which came from the Father (vs. 10). If His words were not clear proof, all the works Jesus performed had been done by the power of the Father through Him (vs. 11). There was sufficient reason for belief!

There are many important lessons that we will need to apply this year. One lesson is that fear can be overcome when we believe God's truth. Ignorance of God's Word and a weak understanding of the power of God will lead to a failure to fully experience the peace God offers to us.

CHILDREN'S CORNER

Your teachers will need to be sure to contextualize their examples of fear and anxiety to the appropriate age group.

You should prepare your teachers to communicate to the children that being troubled in heart is not sinful, but that our response should be faith. Further, your teachers should communicate that overcoming fear and anxiety is a matter of growth; the children should not expect its total absence.

—Robert Winter.

SCRIPTURE LESSON TEXT

JOHN 15:1 I am the true vine, and my Father is the husbandman.

2 Every branch in me that beareth not fruit he taketh away: and every *branch* **that beareth fruit, he purgeth it, that it may bring forth more fruit.**

3 Now ye are clean through the word which I have spoken unto you.

4 Abide in me, and I in you. As the branch cannot bear fruit of itself, except it abide in the vine; no more can ye, except ye abide in me.

5 I am the vine, ye *are* the branches: He that abideth in me, and I in him,

the same bringeth forth much fruit: for without me ye can do nothing.

6 If a man abide not in me, he is cast forth as a branch, and is withered; and men gather them, and cast *them* **into the fire, and they are burned.**

7 If ye abide in me, and my words abide in you, ye shall ask what ye will, and it shall be done unto you.

8 Herein is my Father glorified, that ye bear much fruit; so shall ye be my disciples.

NOTES

Abide in the True Vine

Lesson Text: John 15:1-8

Related Scriptures: John 15:9-17; Romans 11:11-21;
Matthew 7:15-20

TIME: A.D. 30   PLACE: Jerusalem

~~~

GOLDEN TEXT—"I am the vine, ye are the branches: He that abideth in me, and I in him, the same bringeth forth much fruit: for without me ye can do nothing" (John 15:5).

~~~

Introduction

People in the Northern Hemisphere are currently in the midst of winter. For many, this can mean brutally cold weather and the dangers of snow and ice. Looking outside can lead one to conclude that much of life has ceased to exist, at least for the time being.

While some love cold weather, many more long for spring. Those who plant flowers and vegetable gardens begin to think about the new life that will emerge within the next few months. Thoughts of green grass, blooming trees, beautiful flowers, and home-grown vegetables are not just flights of fancy; it will actually happen! While some plants will grow without human tending, others thrive only with careful planning and hard work.

Whether you are a farmer, gardener, or an interested onlooker, we all understand the necessity for plowing, planting, and harvesting. In Jesus' parables, these concepts are often used to teach important spiritual lessons.

LESSON OUTLINE

I. THE VINEDRESSER—
   John 15:1-3

II. ABIDING IN THE VINE—
   John 15:4-5

III. A WARNING AND A PROMISE—
   John 15:6-8

Exposition: Verse by Verse

THE VINEDRESSER

JOHN 15:1 I am the true vine, and my Father is the husbandman.

2 Every branch in me that beareth not fruit he taketh away: and every branch that beareth fruit, he purgeth it, that it may bring forth more fruit.

3 Now ye are clean through the word which I have spoken unto you.

The true vine (John 15:1). Over the last few lessons, Jesus has been relating His final instructions to the apostles in the upper room prior to His arrest. The news that He was about to leave them brought sadness to their hearts. Moreover, the fact that "the prince of this world," the devil, was on the move must have sounded an ominous note in the disciples' ears (14:30).

That Jesus begins this section with "I am" is noteworthy. This is the eighth and final time in John's Gospel that Christ has used this expression to identify Himself. Previously, He had said, "I am the bread of life," "I am the light of the world," "Before Abraham was, I am," "I am the door of the sheep," "I am the good shepherd," "I am the resurrection, and the life," and "I am the way, the truth, and the life" (6:35; 8:12, 58; 10:7, 11; 11:25; 14:6).

{By using these various "I am" statements, Christ was actually identifying Himself as Yahweh, the Lord—the very God of Abraham, Isaac, and Jacob (Ex. 3:6).}[Q1] "Thus shalt thou say unto the children of Israel, I AM hath sent me unto you" (vs. 14). When, in John 8:58, Jesus declares to the Jewish religious leaders, "Before Abraham was, I am," they pick up rocks to stone Him for blasphemy because they understand that Jesus is claiming that He Himself is equal to God.

{When Jesus speaks metaphorically of Himself as "the true vine," He is identifying Himself as the true Israel personified.}[Q2] One of the most famous Old Testament parables using the vine imagery is found in Isaiah 5:1-7. There, Israel is called "the vineyard of the Lord of hosts" (vs. 7). The Lord expended great effort and care upon His vineyard, but instead of a good crop, He got only wild, sour grapes. Where He looked for justice, He found only oppression; where He looked for righteousness, He heard only the outcry of the exploited. The vine metaphor is also used in a similar way in Psalm 80:8-19.

Interestingly, during the Maccabean period, two hundred years before the discourse in John 15, Jewish coinage itself depicted Israel as such a vine. "Assuming that the Lord's Supper had just been instituted by Jesus the metaphor of the vine is naturally suggested by 'the fruit of the vine' (Mark 14:25; Matt. 26:29)" (Robertson, *Word Pictures in the New Testament,* Broadman).

In John 15, Christ is "presented as the true Israel, the genuine vine, the man of God's right hand" (Bruce, *The Gospel of John,* Eerdmans). The Heavenly Father is identified with the "husbandman," the Vinedresser who cares for the vineyard. Unlike most seasonal crops that sprout quickly after planting, vineyards require many seasons to develop. God had taken centuries to prepare the nation of Israel for the Messiah's coming, but alas, "He came unto his own, and his own received him not" (John 1:11).

True disciples (John 15:2-3). {As those who work with trees and vines know, if a branch bears no fruit, it needs to be removed, since it uses resources that would otherwise be devoted to fruit-bearing branches.}[Q3] {If a branch *is* bearing fruit, then pruning—thinning some of it away—is necessary. This maximizes the productivity of the vine by channeling its resources toward producing increased fruit rather than majoring on leaves.}[Q4]

When we come to Christ, we do so as spiritual babes (cf. I Cor. 3:1-3). Some converts mature spiritually sooner than others. Sadly, some seem to remain stuck in spiritual babyhood, hardly moving beyond an elementary knowledge and application of the Christian faith (cf. Heb. 5:11—6:3).

For those who do mature, however, it is important to continue maturing. We should never be content to remain where we are. Continued progress invariably includes "pruning" in the form of trials, sacrifices, and tribulations.

While such experiences challenge and test our faith, they also deepen it. Warren Wiersbe writes, "Your Heavenly Father is never nearer to you than when He is pruning you. . . . Pruning does not simply mean spiritual surgery that removes what is bad. It can also mean cutting away the good and the better so that we might enjoy the best. Yes, pruning hurts, but it also helps. We may not enjoy it, but we need it" (*BE Transformed,* Cook).

The eleven remaining disciples in the upper room were clean (John 15:3) by the word of Christ. They had listened to Him, believed Him, and obeyed His teachings. But Judas Iscariot, now absent, was unclean (cf. 13:10-11), meaning that he was a false disciple.

There are those who profess faith in Christ who do not really possess genuine faith in Him. Faith indeed comes through hearing the Word of God (cf. Rom. 10:17), but genuine faith will always be manifested through good works (cf. Jas. 2:14-26). Maturing in our faith is vital to both spiritual growth and our personal assurance of salvation (cf. II Pet. 1:5-11). "The only way to continue 'clean' (pruned) and to bear fruit is to maintain vital spiritual [connection] with Christ (the vine)" (Robertson).

ABIDING IN THE VINE

4 Abide in me, and I in you. As the branch cannot bear fruit of itself, except it abide in the vine; no more can ye, except ye abide in me.

5 I am the vine, ye are the branches: He that abideth in me, and I in him, the same bringeth forth much fruit: for without me ye can do nothing.

The word translated "abide" appears over one hundred times in the New Testament, mostly in the Gospel of John and in I John. It is sometimes used in a physical sense, of remaining or staying in a certain place (cf. John 1:38). But it is also used in a spiritual sense, as it is here in John 15.

There is, of course, a sense in which Christ is holding on to us, as when He said concerning His sheep, "Neither shall any man pluck them out of my hand" (10:28). But at the same time, we must hold on to Him, that is, abide in Him. He also abides, or remains, in us.

In short, following Christ is a two-way street. True, both our decision to come to Christ and our ability to remain in Him depend on divine initiative and power. But this does not nullify our responsibility to persevere in the faith. We are not merely coasting to heaven. We are pressing on (cf. Phil. 3:14), running a race (cf. Heb. 12:1). As great a man of God as he was, Paul refused to presume upon God's saving grace (I Cor. 9:27).

A branch that is severed from its tree or vine is thereby cut off from the nutrients that produce fruit. {To abide in Christ means to remain spiritually connected to Christ.}Q5 Otherwise, no fruit can be produced. "The living sap from the stock flowing into it enables it to produce grapes; otherwise it is fruitless. So with Jesus' disciples" (Bruce).

This should also remind us that any fruit we produce in the Christian life or in evangelism is not the result of our own power or ability. As Paul points out, the virtuous qualities that reflect Christian conversion are, in fact, "the fruit of the Spirit" (Gal. 5:22). Peter likewise teaches that Christian virtues keep us from being barren and unfruitful (cf. II Pet. 1:8).

"This abiding relationship is natural to the branch and the vine, but it must be cultivated in the Christian life. It is not automatic. Abiding in Christ demands worship, meditation on God's Word, prayer, sacrifice, and service—but what a joyful experience it is! Once you have begun to cultivate this deeper communion with Christ, you have no desire to return to the shallow life of the careless Christian" (Wiersbe).

Although Jesus was speaking to His chosen apostles when He said, "Ye are the branches" (John 15:5), this applies to all followers of Christ, both ancient and modern.

Among other things, abiding in Christ makes it possible for the believer to bring forth "much fruit." This includes those qualities that make up the fruit of the Spirit, but it also certainly includes leading others to Christ. If the fruit of a grape vine is grapes, then the fruit of the Christian should be more Christians. Sadly, most believers never lead anyone to Christ. To be sure, there are people who are specially gifted in evangelism, but that does not mean those who are not so gifted can ignore the unsaved.

At some level, all of us need to be seeking to reach the lost. If nothing else, we must make sure that our lives and lips match our profession of faith. "The word results is often heard in conversations among Christian workers, but this is not actually a Bible concept. A machine can produce results, and so can a robot, but it takes a living organism to produce fruit. It takes time and cultivation to produce fruit; a good crop does not come overnight" (Wiersbe).

{When Jesus said, "Without me ye can do nothing," He was not talking about secular activities. Even people who do not believe in God can accomplish many things in the world. But from the standpoint of that which has eternal value and significance, only what we do for Christ truly matters, and for that we need Him.}[Q6] As missionary C. T. Studd famously said, "Only one life, 'twill soon be past; Only what's done for Christ will last."

A WARNING AND A PROMISE

6 If a man abide not in me, he is cast forth as a branch, and is withered; and men gather them, and cast them into the fire, and they are burned.

7 If ye abide in me, and my words abide in you, ye shall ask what ye will, and it shall be done unto you.

8 Herein is my Father glorified, that ye bear much fruit; so shall ye be my disciples.

Dead branches burned (John 15:6). Just as a branch that does not remain connected to a rooted tree will wither and die, so it is with those who are alienated from Christ. Such dead branches are good for nothing but to be gathered and burned. While fire is sometimes used as a symbol for purification from sin (cf. Isa. 6:5-7), it is most often used as a symbol of judgment and destruction, both in the Old Testament (cf. Ezek. 15:1-8) and in the New (cf. Matt. 13:36-43).

While polls indicate that more people believe in heaven than in hell, if we take the Bible seriously, especially the teachings of Jesus, we must conclude that a fiery judgment awaits unbelievers (Rev. 20:12-15; 21:8). {Many who profess faith are nevertheless among the lost. As Christ pointed out, even the ability to prophesy, exorcise demons, and perform miracles is no guarantee that a person is a true believer (Matt. 7:21-23). Jesus was not speaking of people losing their salvation either, since He said to them, "I *never* knew you" (vs. 23, emphasis added). The Lord chooses His words carefully, and He means what He says!}[Q7]

{The reality that we cannot be taken from the Lord's hand (John 10:28), that nothing can separate us from God's love (Rom. 8:38-39), and that God is able to keep us from falling (Jude 1:24), should not lead us to presumption concerning our salvation. New Testament exhortations to faithfulness and obedience are not superfluous. The prospects of spiritual ruin, a destroyed testimony, and uselessness for God's kingdom work are real and catastrophic. To make light of such things is to play into the devil's hands. "Wherefore let him that thinketh he standeth take heed lest he fall" (I Cor. 10:12).}[Q8]

God's glory magnified (John 15:7-8). {Jesus promised that the prayers of those who remained steadfastly in Him would always be answered.}[Q9] Although God answers all prayers with either yes, no, or wait, keep in mind that this promise was originally spoken to Jesus' apostles. How and when their prayers were answered may differ from how God answers ours. Other passages, however, assure us that God's people can expect to be heard by our Heavenly Father.

We should not take this to mean that everything we pray for will be automatically granted. It is common for even Christians to pray amiss and for the wrong things. Nevertheless, "Receiving an answer to the prayer of faith is one form of spiritual fruitbearing" (Bruce).

As it was with Jesus, our words and works should be for the purpose of glorifying God. {One way to bring glory to God is to "bear much fruit" (vs. 8). In this way, we show that we are true disciples of Christ.}[Q10] A fruitless disciple is an oxymoron, a self-contradiction. Our purpose in coming to Christ is not just to receive the salvation He offers, but to glorify Him by being fruit-bearing followers. In this regard, our actions speak louder than our words.

Bearing fruit is reflected in our willingness to keep His commandments (vs. 10) and to love one another (vs. 12). Whether dealing with the original apostles or modern-day disciples, this does not mean it will be easy to live the Christian life. As the world hated Christ, so it will always hate His followers (vs. 18). We therefore cannot expect any better treatment than was received by our Lord (vs. 20).

—*John Alva Owston.*

QUESTIONS

1. What was Jesus' point in the various "I am" statements found in John?

2. What did Jesus mean when He referred to Himself as "the true vine?"

3. What must be done to a branch on the vine that does not bear fruit?

4. What does pruning accomplish in branches that do bear fruit?

5. What does it mean to abide in Christ?

6. What did Jesus mean when He said, "Without me ye can do nothing?"

7. What is the significance of the burning of dead branches?

8. Why does the New Testament exhort us so strongly to faithfulness and obedience?

9. What promise did Jesus make about prayer?

10. What is a prime way we can bring glory to God?

—*John Alva Owston.*

Preparing to Teach the Lesson

In last week's lesson, we learned that Jesus is the only way to God. There are no other choices for those who want to have eternal life. Jesus did not come to show us a way; He is the Way. He did not come simply to give us a plan of truth to live by; He is the Truth. He did not give us a step-by-step plan to have a better life; He is the Life. No one else compares to Him, and no one else can take us to God.

This week, we will see the importance of staying connected to Jesus at all times. Just as He is the only way to God, He is the only way to fruitful life for God. It is vital that we stay connected to Him. Anything apart from Him will certainly result in death and separation.

TODAY'S AIM

Facts: to learn how Jesus claims to be the True Vine.

Principle: to know with certainty that without the Lord Jesus Christ, we can do nothing.

Application to stay connected to Jesus through faith, love, and obedience.

INTRODUCING THE LESSON

Jesus had been preparing His disciples for His suffering and death, which would come the very next day. He tells them, however, that without Him, they can do nothing. How could a man who is going to die the next day ensure success for them? He could do this because He would rise from the dead three days later. Even death cannot separate us from Him (cf. Rom. 8:38-39), and life is only found in Christ.

DEVELOPING THE LESSON

1. The vine and the vinedresser (John 15:1-3). Throughout the Old Testament, the vine was used as a metaphor for Israel (cf. Isa. 5:1-7). Israel, however, failed to become what God called her to be. God had planted a vineyard, but it failed to yield good grapes. Jesus now declares that He, not Israel, is the True Vine. God the Father is the Vinedresser, meaning that He has all authority and oversees the vineyard.

Two types of branches are contrasted in verse 2, but notice that both kinds are, in some sense, related to Christ. The first type of branch is one that does not bear fruit, which Jesus says is taken away.

Some interpret the Greek verb *aireo* as "to lift up." In this view, the fruitless branch is a backslidden Christian whom God will lift up, so that by gaining access to the light, it can be fruitful. Others argue that *aireo* does mean "to take away," indicating that the branch was never truly connected to Christ by faith (cf. 2:23; 6:64, 66, 70; 8:30-31, 37) and is eventually "cast forth" (15:6). Those who hold this view argue further that such fruitlessness is possible only if one is not abiding in the Vine (cf. vs. 5).

Branches that do bear fruit are pruned, so they can bear more fruit. These are Christians who are growing in the Lord. God's purpose is to produce fruit in us.

2. Abide in Christ (John 15:4-6). To abide means to stay put without struggle. We do not have to struggle in order to stay in Christ. We simply have to trust Him.

As branches, we are not called to produce fruit. This is something the branch cannot do. The production of fruit in our lives depends on the Vine, which is why we as branches must stay connected to Him.

Abiding is more than just us being in Christ. It is also Christ being in us. When we are in Christ, we will bear fruit because of our connection to Him. When we bear fruit, we are purged so that we can bear more fruit. Bearing fruit is a byproduct of abiding in Christ.

Refusing to abide will cause a believer to wither and dry up. He is then gathered and burned by men. Those who believe unfruitful branches are merely lifted up argue that the burning by men puts a serious dent in the belief that Jesus is referring here to eternal judgment: men do not pronounce eternal judgment on other men. In this view, people will ridicule the one who claims to be a Christian but is not bearing fruit. God lifts such unfruitful believers up and exposes them to the light while the world "burns" them with insults and ridicule, dismissing them as hypocrites.

Those who hold that the unfruitful branches are removed point out that ridicule by the world seems more the result of faithfulness in the Christian life than unfaithfulness (cf. John 16:1-3, 33; II Tim. 3:12). Further, the burning involves *gathering* branches away from the Vine and throwing them into a fire. That coheres more with imagery of judgment than with the idea of being lifted up for exposure to light. It is also possible that the men mentioned here are hired hands of the Husbandman, who Himself is the Judge.

3. The blessings of abiding in Christ (John 15:7-8). Those who abide in Christ and bear fruit have the tremendous privilege of communion with God. Jesus states that we can ask for anything in His name, and it will be done for us. This does not mean that we are to ask for selfish things but that when we seek God's will, He will answer our prayers. The key is to always stay connected to the Vine. Our desire should always be to bear much fruit for our Father in heaven.

ILLUSTRATING THE LESSON

A wise Christian will always stay connected to Jesus through the Word and prayer.

In this way, a Christian will be able to bear much fruit to the glory of God the Father and the Lord Jesus Christ.

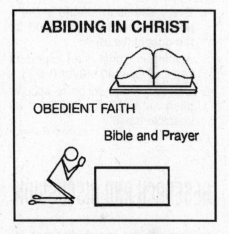

ABIDING IN CHRIST

OBEDIENT FAITH

Bible and Prayer

CONCLUDING THE LESSON

The only way for us to live productive lives is to stay connected to Christ. It is wrong to think that we can please the Lord while being separated from Him. The only way for a branch to bear fruit is to stay connected to the Vine. All life and nourishment come from the Vine, not the branches. Likewise, Christians are to stay connected to Jesus because we can do nothing without Him.

ANTICIPATING THE NEXT LESSON

Next week, we will see that the only way to have triumph in our lives is to experience hardships. No need to fear, though, because Jesus has already secured victory for us.

—*Robert Ferguson, Jr.*

PRACTICAL POINTS

1. True life is in Jesus, and it is given to us by the Father (John 15:1).
2. Those who belong to God have a responsibility to proclaim who He is (vss. 2-3).
3. We cannot bear fruit for God if we are living apart from Christ (vss. 4-5).
4. Every Christian should make a positive impact on the world for the gospel (vs. 6).
5. Abiding in Christ is an important key to answered prayer (vs. 7).
6. Our desire should be to accomplish as much for the Lord as possible (vs. 8).

—*Charity G. Carter.*

RESEARCH AND DISCUSSION

1. How can the knowledge that Jesus is the Vine give us confidence and security (John 15:1)?
2. Why are branches that do not bear fruit taken away while branches that do bear fruit are pruned (vs. 2)?
3. Abiding in Christ means to remain in Him (vs. 4). How can we abide in Christ?
4. Why are we unable to bear fruit if we do not abide in Christ (vs. 5)?
5. Abiding in Christ is a command rather than a suggestion. What are some consequences for not abiding in Christ (vs. 6)?
6. What does it mean to "bear much fruit" (vs. 8)?

—*Charity G. Carter.*

ILLUSTRATED HIGH POINTS

He purgeth it (John 15:2)

Just as a gardener will prune branches to help a plant flourish, our Heavenly Father will discipline His children to enable them to be more spiritually fruitful (cf. Heb. 12:5-11).

Abide in me (John 15:4)

A bouquet of flowers is almost always a welcome gift to a mother, wife, or girlfriend. Today a fellow does not even have to go to a florist since flowers are often available in a variety of grocery and convenience stores. Cut flowers are pretty, but they soon fade and shrivel up since they have been severed from their source of life. Some will choose a potted plant because the blooms will last longer.

Similarly, those who learn to abide in Christ will flourish and bear fruit for the glory of God, while those disconnected from Christ—the source of life—will fade and shrivel up.

Ye can do nothing (John 15:5)

Phillips Brooks (1835-1893), the Boston clergyman who wrote "O Little Town of Bethlehem," once wrote, "It is almost as presumptuous to think you can do nothing as to think you can do everything." To think we can do everything is a blatant pride in our abilities, but to think that we can do nothing—that we could occupy no role in God's kingdom—is to undervalue His creative and redemptive work in us.

On the one hand, Jesus said, "Without me ye can do nothing" (John 15:5), and by that, He meant doing anything of value that would glorify God. We must abide in Him and let Him work in and through us. By ourselves, in our flesh, we can do nothing. But in Him, we will bring forth much fruit.

—*David A. Hamburg.*

Golden Text Illuminated

"I am the vine, ye are the branches: He that abideth in me, and I in him, the same bringeth forth much fruit: for without me ye can do nothing" (John 15:5).

Jesus lifts a metaphor from the pages of Isaiah and calls Himself "the Vine." Israel, according to Isaiah, was God's vineyard, and Judah was His favorite plant, though both were failing to bear fruit (Isa. 5:7). In light of this, Jesus remarkably calls Himself the "true vine" (John 15:1).

That is only the beginning of Jesus' rhetorical boldness. He then calls His eleven disciples (Judas is excluded) "the branches." They, of course, represent all who put their faith in Him, Jews or Gentiles. All non-believing Jews and Gentiles are in trouble; they might soon be fuel for a fire (cf. vs. 6).

After Jesus' blaze of rhetoric is complete, He explains what a person must do to bear fruit and keep safe. The person must remain "in" Jesus, and herein lies the text's mystery: what does that mean?

Further down the page in John 15, we read that abiding in Jesus is associated with letting His words abide in us (vs. 7). We also read that He gives "commandments" that we must "keep" (vs. 10). At first, Jesus seems to echo Moses: to avoid being thrown in the fire, we must obey commandments and bear fruit. But that can hardly be, for Paul later declares such a works-based theology—please allow the pun—fruitless (cf. Gal. 3:10-11).

John 15:12, however, defines Jesus' commandments as primarily a single commandment: "Love one another, as I have loved you." Jesus said this, however, before He was crucified, and the Eleven may have thought that He was referring to teaching one another,

helping one another make ends meet, sticking up for one another in a dispute with the Jewish or Roman authorities, or helping one another escape tough situations.

In retrospect, however, we see that Jesus was asking them to help one another even if it resulted in death. Jesus would literally offer Himself for their freedom from bondage, and they should plan to do things like this for one another. Christians would later share their last meals with one another, go to jail refusing to tell where the others were hiding, and defend one another at the cost of their own lives.

Because of their selfless love, Jesus' group would bear fruit. He had told them, "By this shall all men know that ye are my disciples, if ye have love one to another" (John 13:35). Other people would see their love for one another and want to join God's vineyard. Jesus had eleven true disciples, and by loving them, He invited the whole world into God's community of love. This is what abiding in Christ signifies. When Jesus told His disciples to love one another as He had loved them, He was asking them to do *more* than Moses required.

But this naturally raises the question of our source of power to do this. If sinful man is unable to abide by the words of the law (cf. Deut. 29:4; Rom. 3:19-24), how can we handle the more challenging law of Jesus? The golden text makes it clear: "Without me ye can do nothing." It is only by abiding in the Vine that we are able to love in this way. In other words, this love is the consequence of faith, which truly allows us to abide in Him.

—*David Samuel Gifford.*

Heart of the Lesson

My grandfather, a farmer, showed me how to prune grapes after I planted grapevines in my backyard. When I followed his advice and heavily pruned the previous year's growth, I picked enough grapes in the fall to make pies and can juice.

When I did not prune, branches grew uncontrollably and produced no fruit. The lack of fruit was disappointing, but instructive. In this week's lesson, following the Passover meal, Jesus says that He is the True Vine; to bear fruit, we must abide, or remain, in Him and submit to the pruning of the Vinedresser.

1. Identities (John 15:1-3). Jesus said He is the Vine—the thick, rough, woody, and brown stalk that grows out of the soil. The Father is the Vinedresser. A vinedresser is a gardener who prunes the fruitful branches that emerge from the vine. Pruning removes unnecessary, diseased, or insect-ridden foliage. Pruning exposes the branches to sunlight, which promotes the growth and ripening of fruit. God's pruning shapes, disciplines, and chastens us. Though it may be unpleasant, it results in increased fruitfulness.

2. Connection (John 15:4-6). Because a vine carries nutrients to the branches, a branch cannot produce fruit without connection to a vine. Thus, Jesus urges His disciples, the branches, to remain in Him, the Vine. If they do so, He will remain in them.

Matthew Henry explains that Jesus abiding in us is equivalent to a vine's sap flowing through the branches (*Commentary on the Whole Bible*, Zondervan). The Vine is the source of all we need for an abundant, fruitful spiritual life. We can do nothing on our own.

To abide in Jesus is a choice we make daily. Practically, we abide in Him by such things as: praying throughout our day; reading, studying, meditating, memorizing, and obeying God's Word; fasting; confessing our sins to maintain fellowship with Him; and worshipping with other believers. These actions strengthen the faith that connects us to the Vine. This connection enables us to bear fruit—much fruit.

A severed branch quickly wilts and becomes limp. The leaves droop. Over time, a severed branch, once green and supple, turns brown and brittle, only good for a fire. Anyone who does not remain in Jesus is like that severed branch.

3. Results (John 15:7-8). Answered prayer results if we abide in Jesus and His words abide in us. Jesus told His disciples to ask whatever they will, and it would be done unto them, but only if they abide in Him and His words abide in them. For His words to abide in us, we must know, recall, and obey them. Devote time to God's Word.

Abiding in Jesus and producing much fruit glorifies the Father. Perhaps this is because others will see God's power and work in us (cf. Matt. 5:16). During Jesus' earthly ministry, He sought to bring the Father glory; this should be our aim, too.

In this passage Jesus does not define fruit; other New Testament passages, however, do. Fruit is a life characterized by qualities such as love, joy, peace, longsuffering, gentleness, goodness, faith, meekness, and self-control (Gal. 5:22-23). Fruit is righteousness—a holy life in conformity with God's moral character (Heb. 12:11). Fruit is making disciples—leading others to faith in Jesus and helping them become fruitful by abiding in Him (Rom. 1:13). Abiding is the key to a fruitful life.

—Ann Staatz.

World Missions

The deprivations of missionary life can include the physical and the emotional. Most missionaries rely on support from home churches, as my family did, or missionary societies. We need the support of our fellow believers as much as we would if we were in the American church.

For instance, in Brazil, my family worked with the very poor. Some of the recent converts were convicted that they were sinning because they were not legally married. Unfortunately, the cost of having a simple civil ceremony exceeded a month's salary. For these people who lived hand-to-mouth, their conviction tore at their consciences, but their financial limitations prevented them from marrying.

When we told supporting churches in the States, believers got together to supply the money so that ten couples could have legal marriages. Without the support of those home churches, we never would have been able to help these Christians in Brazil. While this support was monetary, the support of letters, packages, and prayers was just as important throughout our time in Brazil.

Such acts of Christian love exemplify Christ's teachings. In this week's passage, Jesus says, "I am the vine, ye are the branches: He that abideth in me, and I in him, the same bringeth forth much fruit: for without me ye can do nothing" (John 15:5). In dependence upon Him, believers can bear fruit. Jesus continues by describing our need to abide in His love (vs. 9), clarifying that we do this by keeping His commandments (vs. 10). These commandments are summed up in the command to "love one another" (vs. 12).

Perhaps this is why Jesus can both say, "Wherefore by their fruits ye shall know them" (Matt. 7:20) and, "By this shall all men know that ye are my disciples, if ye have love one to another" (John 13:35). The fruit we are called on to produce is love, particularly for our fellow Christians.

When we look at missionary work, we can see a picture of believers showing love to those who are laboring for a harvest of souls. It is a beautiful picture of bearing the fruit of love, but we must remember that the point of John 15 is that we cannot do this without Christ (vs. 5). Without Christ, we are nothing. Christ is the Vine. Without a root system drawing nutrients from the soil, a branch is lifeless and cannot bear fruit.

In another use of an agricultural analogy, Paul writes, "I have planted, Apollos watered; but God gave the increase" (I Cor. 3:6). Continuing in the same context, Paul begins to speak of the church as a house to which many ministers may contribute. But he is quick to point out, "For other foundation can no man lay than that is laid, which is Jesus Christ" (vs. 11). We know that a house without a firm foundation will collapse (cf. Matt. 7:24-27). Christ is that foundation for the church—and the chief cornerstone (Eph. 2:20-21).

Humans are incapable of producing life or fruit without God. From another of Paul's analogies: "But speaking the truth in love, may grow up into him in all things, which is the head, even Christ" (Eph. 4:15).

May we all "grow in grace, and in the knowledge of our Lord and Saviour Jesus Christ" (II Pet. 3:18), without whom we can do nothing, and support our fellow branches here and abroad.

—Jody Stinson.

The Jewish Aspect

When Jesus referred to the "vine" and each "branch," He used a figure of speech that His Jewish disciples knew well. Grapevines were common in biblical lands, and Jews were familiar with how their Scripture (the Old Testament) uses the analogy of the vine to refer to Israel. Asaph wrote of Israel's Exodus from Egypt and their movement into the Promised Land using the metaphor of Israel as God's vine: "Thou hast brought a vine out of Egypt: thou hast cast out the heathen, and planted it. Thou preparedst room before it, and didst cause it to take deep root, and it filled the land" (Ps. 80:8-9).

The first biblical reference to a vine is when Noah planted a vineyard (Gen. 9:20), and from there, it appears frequently in Scripture. When Jesus' disciples heard Him speak, they would have drawn upon both cultural and biblical knowledge.

Jews knew that vines required regular care to maintain their fruitfulness. They observed that some vines grew along the ground, and others grew on trellises and poles. The actual grapes, however, were always lifted off the ground so that they would not be damaged by contact with soil.

Jews also knew that "immediately following the harvest the grapes were pruned severely in the fall and all leaves were stripped from the plants to induce dormancy. Spring trimming of the vines was practiced before blooming as well as after" (Derickson, "Viticulture and John 15:1-6," *Bibliotheca Sacra*). Compare Leviticus 25:3 with Isaiah 5:6. They were further aware that vines must be guarded, since various creatures (Ps. 80:13; S Sol. 2:15) could damage them.

Jesus' audience would also remember their Scriptures, which testified that "every man under his vine" (I Kgs. 4:25) indicated Jewish peace and affluence (cf. Mic. 4:4; Zech. 3:10). Having a prosperous vineyard indicated that Israel had an established territory (cf. II Kgs. 19:29; Ps. 107:37). They would remember that when the spies entered Canaan, they found clusters of grapes so large that they carried them on a pole between two men (Num. 13:23). Even in contemporary times, "large clusters of grapes weighing about five kilograms (12 pounds) each" have been harvested in Israel ("Plants," *Nelson's Illustrated Bible Dictionary*, Thomas Nelson).

If Jesus' Jewish listeners gave careful thought, they would also remember that in judgment God destroyed Israel by leaving "no grapes on the vine" (Jer. 8:13; cf. Hab. 3:17). They knew that Israel was the unfaithful "vine" (Ps. 80:8; Hos. 10:1) and "vineyard" (cf. Isa. 5:7; Jer. 12:10). They also knew that God was the vinedresser in those texts and that He judged the nation (Isa. 5:1-7). Jesus' disciples should also have remembered that Jesus Himself used this metaphor of God as the judging vineyard owner (Mark 12:1-12).

Jesus' disciples heard Him use "vine" language in a totally new manner in John 15. In contrast to Israel, the failed and fruitless vine under judgment, Jesus said He is "the true vine" (vs. 1). Jesus is fully faithful in service to the Father. "The implication is that in contrast to Israel, which became unfaithful and incurred the judgment of God, Jesus remains faithful and thus fulfills Israel's calling to be the vine of God" (Tashjian, "The Symbolism of Vine in Scripture," www.crivoice.org). Jesus is the True Vine, and all believers in Christ who desire to bear fruit in God's service, whether they be Jewish or Gentile, must abide in Him.

—R. Larry Overstreet.

Guiding the Superintendent

Jesus Christ was clearly the greatest teacher who ever lived. In John 15, Jesus used the picture of a vine and branches to teach His disciples the importance of cultivating an intimate relationship with Him.

DEVOTIONAL OUTLINE

1. The symbolism of the vine (15:1-3). Jesus begins by identifying the key elements of the analogy. Verse 1 states that Jesus is the True Vine and the Father is the Husbandman. However, there is great debate over the identity of the branches. It is clear that the fruitful branches are believers, but the identity of the unfruitful branches is debated.

The fruit-bearing branches are pruned, so they can produce more fruit. In agriculture, pruning describes the process of eliminating the dead wood and cutting back the living wood. This allows for a greater production of fruit. Spiritually, when God prunes His children through trials, greater fruit is produced.

However, fruitless branches are removed (John 15:2). A likely understanding of the identity of the fruitless branches is that they represent professing believers who are removed from the Vine because they never had a genuine relationship with Christ (cf. Matt. 7:21-23). John has previously described professions of faith that were not genuine (cf. John 2:23-25).

Jesus said that the disciples did not have to worry about their faith. They were already clean (vs. 3). This verse connects to the metaphor since the pruning process is in many ways a cleaning process for overgrown branches.

2. The significance of the picture (15:4-6). The key to understanding the picture is the word "abide," which means "to stay or to remain" in either a physical place (Acts 27:31) or a certain state. In our context, the command to "abide" is synonymous with believing in Christ. It is a plea to have a genuine relationship with the Vine, Jesus Christ.

It is impossible to produce genuine fruit if you are not connected to the Vine (John 15:4). Conversely, if you have a genuine relationship with Christ, you will bear fruit. As Jesus said, "Even so every good tree bringeth forth good fruit" (Matt. 7:17). Christ is the One who supplies what is needed to bear genuine fruit. When He said, "Without me ye can do nothing" (John 15:5), He was saying that without Him it is impossible to produce any genuine fruit. The unfruitful branches cannot produce fruit, which proves that they do not have a relationship with Christ (vs. 6).

3. The benefits of abiding (15:7-8). Jesus told His disciples that if they remained in Him, and His word or teaching remained in them, they would have a fruitful prayer life (vs. 7). A lack of power in prayer is a sign that one of these two conditions is not being met. Second, when a believer has a genuine relationship with Jesus Christ, that life (with its dependence on Him) will bring glory to the Father by bearing even more fruit (vs. 8). This growth is the natural overflow of abiding.

CHILDREN'S CORNER

The children in your church may become more confused with the continued addition of metaphors. How can Jesus be both a road and a vine? Help your teachers to continue to explain what figurative language is and how it works, but also help them not to lose sight of teaching the need for dependence on Christ for salvation and the Christian life.

—*Robert Winter.*

Scripture Lesson Text

JOHN 16:19 Now Jesus knew that they were desirous to ask him, and said unto them, Do ye enquire among yourselves of that I said, A little while, and ye shall not see me: and again, a little while, and ye shall see me?

20 Verily, verily, I say unto you, That ye shall weep and lament, but the world shall rejoice: and ye shall be sorrowful, but your sorrow shall be turned into joy.

21 A woman when she is in travail hath sorrow, because her hour is come: but as soon as she is delivered of the child, she remembereth no more the anguish, for joy that a man is born into the world.

22 And ye now therefore have sorrow: but I will see you again, and your heart shall rejoice, and your joy no man taketh from you.

23 And in that day ye shall ask me nothing. Verily, verily, I say unto you, Whatsoever ye shall ask the Father in my name, he will give *it* you.

24 Hitherto have ye asked nothing in my name: ask, and ye shall receive, that your joy may be full.

25 These things have I spoken unto you in proverbs: but the time cometh, when I shall no more speak unto you in proverbs, but I shall shew you plainly of the Father.

26 At that day ye shall ask in my name: and I say not unto you, that I will pray the Father for you:

27 For the Father himself loveth you, because ye have loved me, and have believed that I came out from God.

28 I came forth from the Father, and am come into the world: again, I leave the world, and go to the Father.

29 His disciples said unto him, Lo, now speakest thou plainly, and speakest no proverb.

30 Now are we sure that thou knowest all things, and needest not that any man should ask thee: by this we believe that thou camest forth from God.

31 Jesus answered them, Do ye now believe?

32 Behold, the hour cometh, yea, is now come, that ye shall be scattered, every man to his own, and shall leave me alone: and yet I am not alone, because the Father is with me.

33 These things I have spoken unto you, that in me ye might have peace. In the world ye shall have tribulation: but be of good cheer; I have overcome the world.

NOTES

Peace and Trouble

Lesson Text: John 16:19-33

Related Scriptures: Romans 8:31-39; II Corinthians 4:7-12;
Ephesians 2:11-18; I Peter 1:3-9; I John 4:4-6

TIME: A.D. 30   PLACE: Jerusalem

GOLDEN TEXT—"These things I have spoken unto you, that in me ye might have peace.
In the world ye shall have tribulation: but be of good cheer; I have overcome the world"
(John 16:33).

Introduction

Jesus said, "In the world ye shall have tribulation" (John 16:33). Most of us know this to be all too true.

Trials can arise in almost any area: health, family, finances, career, and more. Sometimes trouble comes because of bad choices we have made, though we may be reluctant to admit it. At other times, trouble is brought by other people, by forces beyond our control, or by Satan. God permits these things to occur, and we naturally wonder why.

Rather than blame God—or even Satan—for our troubles, we should seek to profit from them. This does not mean evil is good, but merely that God even uses evil to bring about our ultimate good.

LESSON OUTLINE

I. SORROW AND JOY—
John 16:19-22

II. PRAYER IN JESUS' NAME—
John 16:23-28

III. COMFORT IN TRIBULATION—
John 16:29-33

Exposition: Verse by Verse

SORROW AND JOY

JOHN 16:19 Now Jesus knew that they were desirous to ask him, and said unto them, Do ye enquire among yourselves of that I said, A little while, and ye shall not see me: and again, a little while, and ye shall see me?

20 Verily, verily, I say unto you, That ye shall weep and lament, but the world shall rejoice: and ye shall be sorrowful, but your sorrow shall be turned into joy.

21 A woman when she is in travail hath sorrow, because her hour is come: but as soon as she is delivered of the child, she remembereth no more the anguish, for joy that a man is born into the world.

22 And ye now therefore have sorrow: but I will see you again, and your heart shall rejoice, and your joy no man taketh from you.

A burning question (John 16:19-20). {As Jesus continued the final teaching session with His disciples, He issued a puzzling statement: "A little while, and ye shall not see me: and again, a little while, and ye shall see me, because I go to the Father" (vs. 16). As our lesson text begins, the disciples are feverishly discussing among themselves what He meant by it. They were confounded and just dying to ask Him about it, but none of them wanted to be the first one to speak up.}^Q1

Knowing their dilemma, Jesus took the initiative and asked the question for them, offering at the same time to provide the answer. {He was, of course, speaking about His impending death by crucifixion and His subsequent resurrection on the third day.}^Q2

Numerous times in the Gospel of John, Jesus' "hour" has been alluded to (cf. 7:30; 8:20; 12:23; 13:1). Just before His first miracle, He had told His mother, "Mine hour is not yet come" (2:4). But shortly after the present discussion He would declare that His hour had arrived (cf. 16:32; 17:1). The time of fulfillment had arrived—Jesus' ministry on earth would soon come to an end.

Jesus was telling them that after He was crucified and entombed, He would be hidden from them for a short time. Then, on the third day after his crucifixion, He would rise from the dead and appear to them again in a glorified body. His intent in telling them this was to provide comfort to them in the midst of their impending grief and dismay over witnessing His torture and death on the cross.

But as often happened throughout His ministry, none of them actually grasped the import of His words on this occasion, nor did any of them remember them while He was in the tomb. None of them would take comfort during that time, as Jesus likewise knew full well.

Within the next few hours, the disciples were going to "weep and lament" (vs. 20) as Jesus was arrested, tried, crucified, and entombed. While they had been forewarned on more than one occasion that these things were going to happen (cf. Matt. 16:21; 17:22; 20:18; Mark 8:31; Luke 9:22), they were nevertheless ill-prepared for the unfolding of these events.

While the disciples grieved and wept over their Master's death, the world would rejoice and celebrate. The religious and civil authorities had long sought to be rid of Jesus, considering Him both a dangerous heretic and a political subversive. But within three days, the disciples' sorrow would be turned into joy when they realized for themselves that Jesus had risen from the grave, proving that He was both Lord and Saviour of the world. "The subsequent narrative develops the post-resurrection period as a time in which the disciples' fears are quelled, their doubts dispelled, and their commission confirmed" (Barker and Kohlenberger, eds., *The Expositor's Bible Commentary,* Zondervan).

From anguish to elation (John 16:21-22). {To help the disciples better understand these things, Jesus compared what they would soon undergo to the anguish and eventual joy of a woman giving birth to a child.}^Q3 Just as she endures what seems an unrelenting struggle filled with fear, pain, and exhaustion, so it would be for the disciples. They would soon undergo the grief, doubts, and emotional anguish of having all their hopes and dreams apparently dashed to pieces by the death of their Lord.

But when a woman's baby is delivered at last, all her agony is eclipsed by the joy she feels at the presence of a new human life. So it would be for the disciples.

They would rejoice in the realization of their Lord's resurrection from the dead and in His vindication as the King of kings and the Saviour of the world. Their faith and hopes would be reborn!

PRAYER IN JESUS' NAME

23 And in that day ye shall ask me nothing. Verily, verily, I say unto you, Whatsoever ye shall ask the Father in my name, he will give it you.

24 Hitherto have ye asked nothing in my name: ask, and ye shall receive, that your joy may be full.

25 These things have I spoken unto you in proverbs: but the time cometh, when I shall no more speak unto you in proverbs, but I shall shew you plainly of the Father.

26 At that day ye shall ask in my name: and I say not unto you, that I will pray the Father for you:

27 For the Father himself loveth you, because ye have loved me, and have believed that I came out from God.

28 I came forth from the Father, and am come into the world: again, I leave the world, and go to the Father.

Promise of answered prayer (John 16:23-24). "That day" refers to the day of Jesus' resurrection and His reappearance among the disciples in His glorified human form. On that day, a new arrangement would commence in terms of their supplications and requests. No longer would they need Jesus to be personally present among them to bring requests to. After His resurrection, the way would be made wide open for them to boldly ask God the Father Himself for anything they needed. They would ask in Jesus' name, and the Father would graciously provide.

Jesus assured the disciples that although they had not yet asked anything in His name, they would soon be able to do so with full confidence of receiving

from the Father. Indeed, this is true for all believers. Apart from Jesus Christ, there is no admittance to the Father's presence. Neither prayer nor praise is received apart from the intercessory work of Christ. He is the one Mediator (cf. I Tim. 2:5) and our Great High Priest (cf. Heb. 4:14). Because of this, we can come boldly before the Father's throne of grace (vs. 16).

It should be noted that many interpreters of this text do not believe that prayer was the primary intent of Jesus' words here. Rather, they believe He was talking about asking Him for spiritual knowledge, something they believe followers would no longer need to do once He rose from the dead, and especially after the coming of the Holy Spirit on Pentecost (John 14:26). Yet requests for spiritual knowledge are certainly a part of a believer's overall prayer life even today.

Prior to this time, as noted, the disciples had not been encouraged to make their requests to God in Jesus' name. But that was about to change. {The purpose of such praying was to make full their joy in the Lord.}[Q4] Of course, the joy comes not so much from the things received as from the close relationship with the Father that results from answered prayer.

Direct access to the Father (John 16:25-27). Up to this time, much of Jesus' teaching had been given through parables, proverbs, allegories, or some other less direct form of speech (cf. Mark 4:34). The word translated "proverbs" here appears four times in John's Gospel (10:6; 16:25[twice], 29) and only once elsewhere (II Pet. 2:22). It is variously translated as "proverb," "parable," or "allegory." Such figurative language may have accounted for some of the lack of clear understanding among His disciples. {Jesus may have had to veil some things in figurative speech because the disciples' spiritual immaturity made plain truth hard to bear.}^{Q5}

The time was coming, however, when the Saviour would speak plainly to His apostles. This would come after His resurrection over a period of forty days prior to His ascension. The coming of the Holy Spirit would also enable them to understand teachings they had already received from Him.

They would be able to approach the Father in Jesus' name, and Jesus would also pray to the Father on their behalf. Jesus may also have had in mind His own high priestly prayer, which is the subject of next week's lesson. The words "in my name" should never be taken as "a magical formula which enable the user to get *his* will done; instead those words tied the requests to the work of the Son in doing the *Father's* will" (Walvoord and Zuck, eds., *The Bible Knowledge Commentary,* Victor).

There is no doubt that these men loved Jesus, although they were certainly confused at times regarding His teachings. If we think we would have been less confused than they were, we are probably mistaken. We have the advantage of reading and studying these things after the fact and with the help of the indwelling Holy Spirit, an advantage not yet granted to them.

{The apostles were loved by the Father because they believed that Jesus had come from God.}^{Q6} Previously, Simon Peter had confessed, "Thou art the Christ, the Son of the living God" (Matt. 16:16). This was the genuine belief of all the apostles except Judas Iscariot.

Jesus with the Father (John 16:28). Jesus expanded on His statement about the disciples' faith in His divine origin, in the process making clear what He had meant earlier (vs. 19). He had come into the world, having come forth from God the Father in heaven. And now it was almost time for Him to leave the world and return again to where He had always been, in heaven with God the Father. But with the disciples' newly granted access to the Father in heaven, in a real sense Jesus would still always be with them (cf. Matt. 28:20).

COMFORT IN TRIBULATION

29 His disciples said unto him, Lo, now speakest thou plainly, and speakest no proverb.

30 Now are we sure that thou knowest all things, and needest not that any man should ask thee: by this we believe that thou camest forth from God.

31 Jesus answered them, Do ye now believe?

32 Behold, the hour cometh, yea, is now come, that ye shall be scattered, every man to his own, and shall leave me alone: and yet I am not alone, because the Father is with me.

33 These things I have spoken unto you, that in me ye might have peace. In the world ye shall have tribulation: but be of good cheer; I have overcome the world.

A clear understanding (John 16:29-30). {Once He had stated His meaning plainly (vs. 28), Jesus' disciples realized that this was what He had been talking about all along, and they acknowledged that they now at last understood Him clearly.}^{Q7} This led them to two important conclusions: First, they acknowledged that He knew all things. Second, they acknowledged that He had come from God—He was not a mere man but the very Son of God! Although some of His disciples had indeed confessed Him as the Messiah and Son of God early in His ministry (John 1:40-41, 44-45, 49), their spiritual growth had led them to a fuller realization of what this meant.

When we first confess Christ and receive Him as Lord and Saviour, we understand the truths about Him in relatively shallow terms. Once we have matured in Christ through study, trials, and testings of our faith, our understanding of those same truths takes on a richer, more profound meaning.

A quiet warning (John 16:31-32). When the Lord said, "Do ye now believe?" He was anticipating a time that would soon challenge their faith. At this moment their faith seemed strong, but its strength would be sorely tested in just a few hours.

In the midst of a worship service we may feel so greatly blessed through the music and the message that we leave with what indeed seems a strong and vital faith. But all that can change suddenly if later we receive news of a terrible tragedy, especially about someone close to us. Sadly, the seemingly stalwart faith of many believers can quickly falter in the midst of trials and persecution.

The hour Christ had alluded to so many times previously had now arrived. During the time Jesus' disciples were with Him, they had experienced a number of trials, but nothing they had faced thus far would compare with what was about to occur. {Jesus would be arrested in Gethsemane, and all the disciples would forsake their Master in panic.}[Q8]

Since we are God's children and followers of Christ, we must remember that the Lord is always with us and will never forsake us (Heb. 13:5). Satan will use the trials of life to make us think God does not care about us. That is just a lie of the devil to weaken or destroy our faith. Remember, "we walk by faith, not by sight" (II Cor. 5:7).

A promise of peace (John 16:33). {Jesus wanted His disciples to experience peace, but peace of a different kind than the world can ever know. This peace comes only from knowing Jesus, and it can be experienced by all believers. It is produced in us by the words of Christ. The more we saturate our souls with His words and apply them to our daily lives, the greater and stronger His peace will grow within us.}[Q9]

Jesus was not looking through rose-colored glasses here. He warned His disciples of the unavoidable tribulations of this present world. This world is, to a large degree, still Satan's domain. Living for Christ in this fallen, sin-cursed world is to invite the attacks of the evil one.

{But in the face of such inescapable hardship, Jesus bids us be of good cheer. We can have peace and be of good cheer in the midst of the world because Christ, through His sacrificial redemption of sinners, has overcome the world.}[Q10]

—John Alva Owston.

QUESTIONS

1. How did the disciples feel about Jesus' earlier statement, found in John 16:16?
2. What impending events was He alluding to in this statement?
3. How did Jesus illustrate the sorrow and joy the disciples would soon experience?
4. What is the purpose of praying in Jesus' name?
5. Why did Jesus speak in parables and proverbs?
6. Why did the Father especially love Jesus' apostles?
7. What finally led the apostles to clearly understand Jesus' earlier meaning?
8. What event would cause the disciples to forsake Jesus?
9. What special peace does Jesus offer His disciples?
10. Why can believers be of good cheer in the midst of the world's troubles?

—John Alva Owston.

Preparing to Teach the Lesson

Suffering. Tragedy. Hardship. These are subjects that many of us would rather avoid. We like to focus more on topics such as success, prosperity, and blessing. It is certainly not wrong to talk about those subjects, but we must realize that we all suffer tragedy and hardship. While it is not healthy to devote an excessive amount of thought to these issues, it is also misguided to ignore them altogether.

Jesus never led His disciples to believe that life would be all roses and sunshine because they followed Him. Instead, He was honest about the suffering that He would endure and that they too would endure for their association with Him. The good news is that because of His finished work, their suffering would end in victory. We can be assured that although we suffer for a time now, Christ has overcome the world for us, and those who persevere in faith will be rewarded in the end.

TODAY'S AIM

Facts: to see how Jesus finishes His farewell discourse to His disciples by promising both suffering and joy.

Principle: to comprehend that Jesus has overcome the world that causes our suffering, so we must remain faithful to Him.

Application: to remain devoted to serving Jesus as we walk with Him and suffer with Him every day.

INTRODUCING THE LESSON

Sometimes we get confused by where God leads us and what He allows us to go through. We do not always understand His ways or His will, but we must follow Him anyway. He will never lead us astray or do anything that will destroy us. In fact, our suffering is often a blessing from Him (cf. Rom. 5:1-5; II Cor. 1:8-11; 12:7-10; Heb. 12:3-1; Jas. 1:3-4; I Pet. 1:6-7).

The Lord loves you and has endured suffering, so He knows what you are going through and cares about it. He has faced the evil of this world and has overcome it. That should cause us to rejoice in Him even in the face of adversity

DEVELOPING THE LESSON

1. Sorrow turned to joy (John 16:19-24). As they walked to the Garden of Gethsemane after leaving the upper room, Jesus told the disciples that after a little while, they would no longer see Him. Further, after another little while, they would see Him again. If you are confused by this statement, imagine how the disciples felt!

The disciples were understandably puzzled by His odd saying, and Jesus knew they wanted to ask Him about it. He explained to them that for a time they would "weep and lament" while the world would rejoice (vs. 20). This refers to His crucifixion. Their sorrow would turn to joy, however, as He would be resurrected.

To explain what He meant, Jesus said that a woman has sorrow from the pain of childbirth, but her sorrow turns to joy when her baby is born. Likewise, the disciples were sad now, but they would rejoice when they saw Him again. Once He rose from the dead, no one would ever steal their joy from them again.

Jesus then said that in that day—after His resurrection—they would not ask Him for anything; they would no longer depend on Him to convey their requests to God. They were entering a unique relationship that all believers now have in Christ. Because of Him, we can take our requests directly to God. We pray to the Father in the name of Jesus, and God answers us because He loves us and wants our joy to be full.

2. Figures of speech (John 16:25-28). Up to this point, Jesus often taught His disciples in parables and figures of speech. The hour was coming, however, when He would speak plainly to them. This would happen after His resurrection, and the Holy Spirit would also teach them plainly after the Day of Pentecost.

After Pentecost, Jesus would not have to take their requests to God for them. This does not mean that He no longer cares for us or is uninterested in our lives. He still serves as our Mediator (I Tim. 2:5) and Advocate (I John 2:1), and He still intercedes for us (Heb. 7:25). But now through the work of Christ we have direct access to the throne of the heavenly Father. We can pray directly to Him in Jesus' name.

3. Victory comes through Jesus (John 16:29-33). The disciples thought that Jesus was speaking plainly to them at this point, and they thought they understood clearly what He was saying. That is why they said that they believed He came from God. Jesus was not just a prophet sent from God. He was the Son sent from the Father.

The disciples were not as strong as they thought they were, however. Jesus said that they would soon be scattered to their own homes and would abandon Him. Jesus said that though they would leave Him, He would not be alone because the Father would be with Him.

Why was Jesus teaching them these things? To show them (and us) that we can find peace in Christ. The world is trying desperately to find peace while at the same time rejecting the Prince of Peace. Jesus is the only source of peace there is, so trying to have peace while rejecting Him is futile.

Jesus warns that this world is full of tribulation, especially to the believer.

He encourages us to be of good cheer, though, because He has overcome the world; the world that stands to oppose us has already been defeated by our Savior. We now have eternal victory in Jesus as we trust Him through our suffering, tragedy, and hardship.

ILLUSTRATING THE LESSON

The world may give us trouble, but Jesus gives us peace and ensures ultimate victory.

CONCLUDING THE LESSON

Anyone who says that being a Christian is easy is being disingenuous. Being a Christian is not easy, especially since the world is hostile to us because of what we believe and who we belong to. Following Christ through the turmoil of this life is well worth it, however, as God will extravagantly reward those who persevere in faith through the hard times of this life, both now and forever. We have victory in Jesus, and the world cannot take away what God has guaranteed.

ANTICIPATING THE NEXT LESSON

Next week, we will study a portion of what is often known as Jesus' High Priestly prayer.

—*Robert Ferguson, Jr.*

PRACTICAL POINTS

1. The Lord is not intimidated by our questions (John 16:19).
2. Regardless of how painful things may be now, pure joy is ahead (vss. 20-22).
3. Asking in the Father's name leads to joy (vss. 23-24).
4. Jesus serves as a liaison between us and God, so we never have to worry about not knowing what to pray (vss. 25-28).
5. We can be confused about many things, but the Word of God is plain regarding everything important (vss. 29-30).
6. Hardships will come, but Jesus has already overcome (vss. 31-33).

—*Charity G. Carter.*

RESEARCH AND DISCUSSION

1. Why would the world rejoice at Jesus' death (John 16:20)?
2. Have you ever allowed or nearly allowed someone to take your joy (vs. 22)?
3. Why might Jesus initially have chosen to speak to His disciples in parables (vs. 25)?
4. How do we respond if what we asked for in Jesus' name is not granted?
5. What tribulation are you currently facing? How does knowing that Christ has already overcome encourage you to keep moving forward (vs. 33)?

—*Charity G. Carter.*

ILLUSTRATED HIGH POINTS

A little while (John 16:19)

Time is relative. A little while at the dentist can seem like an eternity while a little while with your girlfriend will seem far too short.

If we could ask Jesus when He will come again, His answer would probably be "in a little while." In the meantime, we have the opportunity to remain faithful to Him and His work.

Your sorrow shall be turned into joy (John 16:20)

Jesus sought to prepare His disciples for the coming trauma of His death on the cross. It would come in a little while, but it would also last only a little while. Their suffering, though traumatic, was temporary; their joy became permanent.

Geraldine ("Mrs. Howard") Taylor (1865–1949), missionary to China, said this about our present suffering, "When sin and pain and death are no more, and all tears are wiped away, shall we ever have again the privilege that is ours now of sharing the fellowship of His sufferings 'to seek and to save that which was lost'?" (*John and Betty Stam: A Story of Triumph*, Moody).

Ye might have peace (John 16:33)

A U.S. Marine officer who served in Vietnam said he was often awakened by the enemy's nighttime artillery bombardment. He said it was terrifying. In those moments, his comfort came from Psalm 4:8: "I will both lay me down in peace, and sleep: for thou, Lord, only makest me dwell in safety."

Since he was standing in front of us telling the story, he was evidence that God had indeed kept him safe. But even if a shell had found its mark, he had peace that he would still be spiritually and eternally safe by God's grace.

—*David A. Hamburg.*

Golden Text Illuminated

"These things I have spoken unto you, that in me ye might have peace. In the world ye shall have tribulation: but be of good cheer; I have overcome the world" (John 16:33).

Human suffering raises questions for both Christians and unbelievers. Unbelievers often argue that suffering proves that a loving God cannot exist. They want absolute freedom with no negative consequences, even if they hurt themselves or others. Doubters are offended both by God's commands against sin and by the pain sin causes.

Christians, on the other hand, recognize that Adam and Eve opened the door for suffering and hurt, even for innocent people.

Job, a target of Satan's malice, paid a heavy price for being generous and righteous. Nevertheless, we never see him angry at the Chaldeans and Sabeans who committed the murders and thefts (Job 1:15, 17). As Job discovered, sorting out one type of suffering from another can be difficult. Does my stomach hurt because I ate too much, because someone poisoned me, because there is generally suffering in the world, or because of demonic attack? These are the types of questions Christians ask, and they are also the kinds of situations that harden the hearts of people without faith.

Hebrews 12 opens with the suffering of Jesus (vss. 2-3), and verse 4 compares Jesus' suffering to ours. The text speaks to Christians on earth, saying that in our "striving against sin," we "have not yet" suffered as much as Jesus suffered. Verses 5-11 encourage Christians to "endure" suffering as God's "chastening," training them to "be partakers of his holiness." By contrast, I Peter 4:15-16 says that a believer should never "suffer as . . . an evildoer. . . . Yet if any man suffer as a Christian," he should "glorify God."

Bringing this all together, we see that Christians can trust God during suffering, regardless of the reason for it. We will always have trouble while we are "in the world." Not until New Jerusalem descends shall there "be no more death, neither sorrow, nor crying, neither shall there be any more pain" (Rev. 21:4).

But after the reminder that the world will always involve suffering, Jesus states, "Be of good cheer; I have overcome the world." As certain as suffering is in this world, so too is the reality that when Jesus died and rose again, He defeated the powers of sin, hell, death, Satan, racism, legalism, and antinomianism. In short, He overcame the world. Last week we read the assurance that He is preparing a place for us in His Father's house. We have reason to rejoice in our suffering: "For our light affliction, which is but for a moment, worketh for us a far more exceeding and eternal weight of glory" (II Cor. 4:17).

Indeed, Christ's resurrection from the dead is but the beginning. He is "the firstborn from the dead" (Col. 1:18) and the "firstfruits" of our own resurrection (I Cor. 15:19-23). We now await His return, where He will make "our vile body . . . like unto his glorious body" (Phil. 3:21). In the meantime, because He has overcome the world, so too our faith in Him overcomes the world, giving us hope amid our own tribulation: "This is the victory that overcometh the world, even our faith" (I John 5:4).

—*David Samuel Gifford.*

Heart of the Lesson

After I moved eight hours from my parents' home to work at a Christian magazine, I only saw my mom and dad a few times a year. Each time I left following a visit, I sobbed all the way to the freeway.

I feared I would never see them again. Yes, I knew we would be together someday in heaven. But as a single woman in her twenties, I dreaded the thought of living here without them. In this week's lesson, Jesus tells His disciples about the grief they soon will experience as they watch Him die, but He also promises that their sorrow will turn to joy.

1. Sorrow and joy (John 16:19-22). Jesus had just told His disciples He soon would return to the Father. He knew they were hesitant to ask what He had meant when He said, "A little while, and ye shall not see me: and again, a little while, and ye shall see me" (vs. 19; cf. vs. 17), so He stated the question for them.

Jesus knew He would soon be going to the cross. The disciples would not see Him again until after His resurrection. To prepare them, He warned they soon would grieve while the world rejoiced over the same event.

He compared the disciples' sorrow to a woman's pain in labor. She writhes in anguish, but when the baby is delivered, she forgets the pain. She is instead overjoyed at holding her new child. When the disciples saw Jesus after the resurrection, they would forget their grief and experience a joy no one could ever take away.

2. Asking and receiving (John 16:23-28). Before His death, Jesus' disciples asked Him many questions; however, after His death and resurrection, they would ask God the Father directly, presenting their petitions to Him in Jesus' name. The Father would answer, filling them with joy. Jesus would not have to ask the Father for them; He already hears them. Indeed, He loves the disciples because they love Jesus and believe He came from the Father.

Jesus admitted He had spoken to the disciples in proverbs with obscure meanings. He never spoon-fed them. He asked them to ponder His words to gain understanding. But a time was coming when He would speak plainly to them about the Father, a likely reference to Pentecost and the coming of the Holy Spirit, who would direct them into all truth (cf. vs. 13). After this, He reminded them that He had come from the Father, and now He was leaving to return to the Father.

3. Belief and abandonment (John 16:29-32). Hearing these things, the disciples confidently asserted that they now understood all that He told them. Jesus questioned their confidence. Did they finally believe? Really?

In just a few hours, they were going to desert Him out of fear, scattering to the place each man felt safest. Seemingly alone, Jesus would face His captors and endure His trial, but He truly would not be alone because the Father would be with Him.

4. Peace and tribulation (John 16:33). Jesus' goal in these sayings was to bring His disciples peace. Only in Him can we find the rest and quiet our souls crave. He closes His discourse by saying that in this world, His followers will face tribulation, but through His death and resurrection, He has overcome the world. Christians, be encouraged; His victory ensures our victory. Never give up. In Jesus, we find peace and hope.

—*Ann Staatz.*

World Missions

Jesus promised to His followers eternal life, peace with God, and a heavenly home. But He also promised His people they would face persecution and distress. "These things I have spoken unto you, that in me ye might have peace. In the world ye shall have tribulation: but be of good cheer; I have overcome the world" (John 16:33).

It is estimated that over 260 million Christians experience intense persecution. Each month, about 250 Christians are killed; 66 churches are attacked; 180 Christian women face rape, sexual harassment, or forced marriage; 104 believers suffer kidnapping; and 160 are imprisoned without trial (opendoorsusa.org/Christian-persecution).

Even in countries where religious liberty is celebrated, Christians have choices to make. A business owner refuses to do something that betrays his faith and conscience. In return, the media vilifies him, and a lawsuit is filed. Sharing one's faith with a student or customer might result in being ridiculed, looked over for a promotion, or fired. Bible verses and Christian symbols are removed from as many places as possible.

People who on other days would be enemies join together in hatred of Christians. But why?

Jesus explains why believers are hated: "If ye were of the world, the world would love his own: but because ye are not of the world, but I have chosen you out of the world, therefore the world hateth you" (John 15:19).

The world hates us because we are not of the world, but have been chosen out of it. Even familial relationships can be tense or broken in light of the world's hatred of believers (Matt. 10:34-36). When I visited China, an informer was discovered in the church there. Significantly, the informer had been attending church services for years because she was the daughter of church members! Even with the betrayal by one of their own and the risk of the government knowing about them, people still flocked to the service to worship their Saviour.

These people were following the words of Isaiah: "Fear thou not; for I am with thee: be not dismayed; for I am thy God: I will strengthen thee; yea, I will help thee; yea, I will uphold thee with the right hand of my righteousness" (41:10). God gives grace and peace to His people.

The idea that one can have peace while suffering through persecution seems illogical. For most people, peace means primarily the absence of hostility. It seems impossible for God to promise peace and also persecution.

But for Christians, the peace they have is primarily a peace between themselves and God. Before Christ, "the carnal mind is enmity against God" (Rom. 8:7). But after Christ, "being justified by faith, we have peace with God through our Lord Jesus Christ" (5:1). Jesus "made peace through the blood of his cross" (Col. 1:20).

The peace we have with God can give us peace of mind as well. Jesus promises, "Peace I leave with you, my peace I give unto you: not as the world giveth, give I unto you. Let not your heart be troubled, neither let it be afraid" (John 14:27). The world cannot understand. But for the believer, "Who shall separate us from the love of Christ? shall tribulation, or distress, or persecution, or famine, or nakedness, or peril, or sword? . . . For I am persuaded that [nothing] . . . shall be able to separate us from the love of God, which is in Christ Jesus our Lord" (Rom. 8:35-39).

—Jody Stinson.

The Jewish Aspect

Jesus said, "A woman when she is in travail hath sorrow, because her hour is come: but as soon as she is delivered of the child, she remembereth no more the anguish, for joy that a man is born into the world" (John 16:21). Pain in childbirth is as old as Eve. The book of Genesis explains the reason why there is such pain in the childbirth process—the reason is the Fall. After sin entered, pain increased for Eve and all mothers after her: "I will greatly multiply thy sorrow and thy conception; in sorrow thou shalt bring forth children" (3:16). Mothers throughout history attest to the accuracy of these declarations.

Even though women experience birth pangs, the birth of a child, especially a son, is a joyous occasion. Jewish people considered children to be a blessing from God (cf. Deut. 28:4; Pss. 127:4-5; 128:3, 6). Furthermore, Jewish women considered God's words "Be fruitful, and multiply" (Gen. 1:28) the first commandment in the Bible ("Birth," *Encyclopedia Judaica*, www.jewish-virtuallibrary.org); therefore, they perceived childbirth as obedience to God.

While ancient Jewish women believed in the blessing of children, they knew the reality of birth pains, and they were not alone. The Greek playwright Euripides (around 480-406 B.C.) has his character Medea say, "Thrice would I under shield stand, rather than bear childbirth-peril once" (*Medea*). In other words, this woman would rather fight in war three times than give birth only once. Similarly, the Greek philosopher Plato (around 427-347 B.C.) used the analogy of the agony of birth pangs to describe a pupil who strives to go from ignorance to knowledge: "Yes, you are suffering the pangs of labour, Theaetetus, because you are not empty, but pregnant" (*Theaetetus*).

Mothers died in childbirth more frequently in ancient times than they do today. The United Health Foundation studied American births from 2011-2015 and "put the U. S. maternal mortality rate at 20.7 per 100,000 live births," or 0.021% (Ollove, "A Shocking Number of U.S. Women Still Die of Childbirth," *The Washington Post*). In contrast, inscriptions on ossuaries (containers into which bones of the dead were placed) from New Testament times testify that 5% of women died in childbirth (Ilan, *Jewish Women in Greco-Roman Palestine,* Hendrickson).

How greatly the pains of birth affected Jewish culture in biblical times is further identified by references in the Talmud. Rabbi Simeon ben Yohai asserted that during birth pains, a woman "swears impetuously that she will have no [future] intercourse with her husband" so that she will not endure this pain again (*Babylonian Talmud,* Niddah 31b). After the baby's birth, however, she would regret and recant her rash words.

Jewish rabbis also sought to explain why some women died in childbirth: "'For three transgressions do women die in childbirth: for heedlessness of the laws of niddah, the dough-offerings and the lighting of the [Sabbath] candle' (mShab. 2.6). These three commandments, which women and only women are obligated to carry out, are viewed not as a reward, but as punishment for the sin in the Garden of Eden" (Ilan).

In John 16, Jesus explains that the pain His disciples would feel at His death would be replaced by joy at His resurrection. Just as the same baby that caused the pain was also the cause of the joy, so Jesus' death would bring eternal joy in His accomplishment of salvation for His people.

—R. Larry Overstreet.

Guiding the Superintendent

This week's passage contains a portion of Jesus' last explicit teaching before the cross. The discouraged disciples would need these words to guide them during the days of trouble ahead. These powerful words contain deep truth for the disciple of Jesus today as well.

DEVOTIONAL OUTLINE

1. Joy comes after sorrow (16:19-24). As Jesus taught, He recognized the confusion in His disciples' minds (vs. 19), so He clarified that when He was nailed to the cross, they would be overwhelmed by sorrow while the world rejoiced. But that was not the end of the story. When He was resurrected, their sorrow would turn to joy (vs. 20). He illustrated this with the birth of a child. In childbirth, there is a time of intense, but temporary, pain that is transformed to joy when the child is born (vs. 21).

Unlike the joy of childbirth, the joy given to the disciples would last forever (vs. 22). This joy is always present, but many times it is not experienced in full because we do not request it of the Father (vss. 23-24).

2. Access to God comes through prayer (16:25-29). Jesus speaks of a day when He will teach in plain language (vs. 25). This would begin "at that day," after He left and the Holy Spirit arrived (vs. 26). In that day, the disciples will have access to God through prayer because the Father loves them (vs. 27). Though this is such a simple truth, it is one of the deepest truths we can ever know.

Jesus summarized His ministry as plainly as possible (vs. 28). He came from the Father and to the world. That is the truth of the Incarnation. He is leaving the world to return to the Father. That is the truth of the then future resurrection and ascension. After failing to understand His mission, the disciples were overjoyed when this truth seemed clear in their minds (vs. 29).

There is some question among interpreters, however, as to whether the disciples' profession in verse 29 accurately reflects their level of understanding.

3. Faith grows with knowledge (16:30-31). When they finally understood the mission of Jesus, the disciples' faith grew. They recognized that they knew this one thing, but He knew all things (vs. 30).

There is a relationship between faith and knowledge. We are unable to trust someone whom we do not know. As we come to know Christ better, we will experience a growth in our faith. If we really believe that Jesus knows all things, as the disciples did, then it should not be difficult for us to trust Him. He knows what is happening to us and knows how He will use trouble to help strengthen us.

Jesus asked them if they really believed Him. He knew that soon their claim to know and trust Him would be put to the test (vs. 31).

4. Peace is the final result (16:32-33). Jesus informed His followers that the process leading to His impending death had already begun (vs. 32). Though they would panic and flee in the moment, ultimately they would experience genuine peace (vs. 33).

CHILDREN'S CORNER

Most adults have reason to know what childbirth is like, even if just in conversation. Our children largely do not. Help your teachers to use the metaphor in a manner their parents would approve.

—*Robert Winter.*

SCRIPTURE LESSON TEXT

JOHN 17:6 I have manifested thy name unto the men which thou gavest me out of the world: thine they were, and thou gavest them me; and they have kept thy word.

7 Now they have known that all things whatsoever thou hast given me are of thee.

8 For I have given unto them the words which thou gavest me; and they have received *them,* and have known surely that I came out from thee, and they have believed that thou didst send me.

9 I pray for them: I pray not for the world, but for them which thou hast given me; for they are thine.

10 And all mine are thine, and thine are mine; and I am glorified in them.

11 And now I am no more in the world, but these are in the world, and I come to thee. Holy Father, keep through thine own name those whom thou hast given me, that they may be one, as we *are.*

12 While I was with them in the world, I kept them in thy name: those that thou gavest me I have kept, and none of them is lost, but the son of perdition; that the scripture might be fulfilled.

13 And now come I to thee; and these things I speak in the world, that they might have my joy fulfilled in themselves.

14 I have given them thy word; and the world hath hated them, because they are not of the world, even as I am not of the world.

15 I pray not that thou shouldest take them out of the world, but that thou shouldest keep them from the evil.

16 They are not of the world, even as I am not of the world.

17 Sanctify them through thy truth: thy word is truth.

18 As thou hast sent me into the world, even so have I also sent them into the world.

19 And for their sakes I sanctify myself, that they also might be sanctified through the truth.

NOTES

Jesus' Prayer for His Disciples

Lesson Text: John 17:6-19

Related Scriptures: John 6:35-40; 17:1-5, 20-26

TIME: A.D. 30   PLACE: Jerusalem

Introduction

There are many recorded prayers throughout the Bible. Some are very brief, as when the dying thief cried out to Jesus, "Lord, remember me when thou comest into thy kingdom" (Luke 23:42). Others, however, are quite lengthy. This was true of Solomon's dedicatory prayer for the temple (II Chron. 6:12-42) and Ezra's prayer of confession (Ezra 9:5-15).

Most of the prayers mentioned in the Bible are unrecorded; that is, we know a prayer was offered, but not what was actually said. For example, Jesus spent all night in prayer before selecting the Twelve (Luke 6:12), but we do not have the words He prayed. Nor do we know exactly what Paul prayed when he offered three petitions concerning his thorn in the flesh (I Cor. 12:8), though we do know he asked for its removal. This week, we look at Jesus' high priestly intercessory prayer.

LESSON OUTLINE

I. PRAYER FOR THE FAITHFUL— John 17:6-10

II. PRAYER FOR PROTECTION— John 17:11-12

III. PRAYER FOR JOY AND PRESERVATION—John 17:13-16

IV. PRAYER FOR HOLINESS— John 17:17-19

Exposition: Verse by Verse

PRAYER FOR THE FAITHFUL

JOHN 17:6 I have manifested thy name unto the men which thou gavest me out of the world: thine they were, and thou gavest them me; and they have kept thy word.

7 Now they have known that all things whatsoever thou hast given me are of thee.

8 For I have given unto them the words which thou gavest me; and they have received them, and have known surely that I came out from thee, and they have believed that thou didst send me.

9 I pray for them: I pray not for

the world, but for them which thou hast given me; for they are thine.

10 And all mine are thine, and thine are mine; and I am glorified in them.

Gift of the Father (John 17:6).

As the chapter opens, we read that Jesus "lifted up his eyes to heaven" and prayed. {This was the beginning of Christ's great intercessory prayer on behalf of His apostles and disciples. In praying this prayer, He was already undertaking the office of high priest.}[Q1] He was praying for us today as much as for them back then.

The time of Jesus' sacrifice for sins was near, and so He prayed that the Father would glorify Him so that He in turn could glorify the Father (vs. 1). He declared that He had thus far accomplished all the work that the heavenly Father had given Him to do (vs. 4).

The foundation of eternal life is to know God the Father as He is revealed fully in the Person of God the Son (vs. 3). But the whole idea of knowing God through His Son is a foreign concept to many people. Most think they will go to heaven if they are good enough, however they might define that. But "good enough" can never be good enough to merit heaven! Faith in Jesus alone is the way to the Father (cf. John 14:6; Acts 4:12; Titus 3:5).

{Christ manifested the Father's name to His disciples (John 17:6); He revealed the true character and nature of God the Father to them.}[Q2] Since a person's name represents that person, so it is with the Son representing the Father. To take God's name in vain (cf. Ex. 20:7) is to disrespect God Himself. We can only be saved through the name of Christ (cf. Acts 4:12); in other words, salvation is found in no one else.

The people Jesus prayed for here are those whom the Father had given Him. They came to Him through faith, believing in the words He spoke to them. They had belonged to the Father, and through faith they now also belonged to the Son. That they belonged to the Father became evident from the fact that they received Christ's words as the very words of God Himself. {They had also remained obedient to His words since they had begun following Him.}[Q3] To claim to know Christ without obeying His teachings is both incongruous and hypocritical (Heb. 10:26-31).

Reception of His words (John 17:7-8). Some three years with Jesus had led the disciples to the conclusion that His words and deeds were from the Father. The Lord Jesus had given the apostles the very words of God, and they had received them. Hearing the Word of God is essential to coming to faith (Rom. 10:17), but merely hearing is not enough to save anyone. We must both believe the gospel and prove our faith by putting what we hear into practice. As James reminds us, the implanted word is able to save our souls, but if we hear it without responding, we deceive ourselves (1:21-22). Rather, we are to be *doers* of the word.

The disciples believed that Jesus had been sent by the Father, but this did not mean that the apostles always understood everything Christ said. "They had embraced the essential truths. They had come to see Him as the Messiah sent from God, and they had put their faith in Him" (Sproul, *John,* Reformation Trust). The same is true for us. Although we do not yet understand all we read in the Bible, we have to be willing to act on what we do understand and seek to grow in the grace and knowledge of Christ (II Pet. 3:18).

Glory through their faith (John 17:9-10). Jesus here specifies the particular objects of His high priestly prayer. He is not praying for all people of the world without exception. His prayer is offered exclusively on behalf of those whom the Father has given to Him by faith. None of this should be taken to mean that God has no concern for the world. Indeed, God loves all the people of His creation, and His desire is that they come to a saving knowledge of Christ (I Tim. 2:4).

{The world that Jesus was not praying for was the world that is opposed to God and His redemptive plan to save sinners through faith in Jesus Christ.} Q4 In this regard, we too are not to love the world (cf. I John 2:15-17), since that would reveal a lack of love for God. Indeed, "the whole world lieth in wickedness" (cf. 5:19).

Those who belong to Jesus also belong to the Father, and vice versa. That being so, Christ is glorified in them. This is still true today. Our steadfast faith in Christ glorifies both Jesus and the Father. "For we are his workmanship, created in Christ Jesus unto good works, which God hath before ordained that we should walk in them" (Eph. 2:10).

PRAYER FOR PROTECTION

11 And now I am no more in the world, but these are in the world, and I come to thee. Holy Father, keep through thine own name those whom thou hast given me, that they may be one, as we are.

12 While I was with them in the world, I kept them in thy name: those that thou gavest me I have kept, and none of them is lost, but the son of perdition; that the scripture might be fulfilled.

Although He was physically still in the world, in a real sense Jesus could declare, "I am no more in the world." Soon He would be crucified, arrive in paradise (Luke 23:43), return bodily to the disciples after His resurrection (24:36-44), and eventually ascend bodily back into heaven (Acts 1:9-11).

Since Jesus would be taken from them, it was appropriate that He pray for the disciples' welfare in His ab-

sence. Today, Christ continues to intercede on our behalf in heaven (Heb. 2:17-18; 4:14-16). As Jude writes, Jesus "is able to keep you from falling, and to present you faultless before the presence of his glory with exceeding joy" (1:24).

{It was important that the apostles remain unified in their testimony and their mission. They all shared a single Lord and a single mission. What was true of them is still true with us. Later in His prayer, Jesus prayed specifically for those who would come to believe through the testimony of the apostles (John 17:20). He prayed that they also would be unified so that succeeding generations might likewise believe their testimony about Him.} Q5

Sadly, Christians often do not present a united testimony to the world. Many professed Christians are not true disciples, since they reject such basic doctrines as the inerrancy and inspiration of the Bible, Jesus' virgin birth, Christ's substitutionary atonement, His bodily resurrection, and many other doctrines of the faith. But even among those who hold to these teachings, there often remain petty disputes, power struggles, and unchristian attitudes. We always do great harm to the testimony of Christ in the eyes of the world when we cannot get along among ourselves.

{Mentioned almost as an aside in Jesus' prayer was "the son of perdition" (John 17:12), a reference to Judas Iscariot.} Q6 The word "perdition" includes concepts such as destruction, damnation, and hell itself. {The term conveys the truth that Judas was sent by Satan and was doomed to perdition for His betrayal of Christ, as had been prophesied (cf. Ps. 41:9; 109:8; John 13:18; Acts 1:15-20).} Q7 Jesus had earlier asked the disciples rhetorically, "Have I not chosen you twelve, and one of you is a devil?" (John 6:70).

PRAYER FOR JOY AND PRESERVATION

13 And now come I to thee; and these things I speak in the world, that they might have my joy fulfilled in themselves.

14 I have given them thy word; and the world hath hated them, because they are not of the world, even as I am not of the world.

15 I pray not that thou shouldest take them out of the world, but that thou shouldest keep them from the evil.

16 They are not of the world, even as I am not of the world.

Joy amid hatred (John 17:13-14). Knowing that His time on earth was now limited, Jesus prayed that His disciples would experience joy because of His words. Joy would become a scarce commodity for them during the next few days before His resurrection. Joy can indeed be experienced in the midst of sorrow and conflict, but the opposite emotions usually overwhelm us instead because we tend to focus on our pain and circumstances.

When Jesus taught His disciples, He was giving them God's Word. The Holy Spirit would enable them to remember these things later (John 14:26). Therefore, we can be confident in the full truth of their teachings after Christ ascended to the Father.

Because Christ had given the apostles His words, the world hated them because they were not "of the world." Faithful believers today are likewise not of the world; hence, the world hates us as it hated the apostles before us. While persecution takes various forms, "all that will live godly in Christ Jesus shall suffer persecution" (II Tim. 3:12). Jesus declared, "Woe unto you, when all men shall speak well of you! for so did their fathers to the false prophets" (Luke 6:26).

In but not of the world (John 17:15-16). While we might think that the best way to protect His disciples would be to shelter them away from the world, that is not what the Lord desires. If we were not in the world, then who would make known the gospel of Jesus Christ? Who would travel to distant lands with the message of the true God to make disciples? The apostles, followed by multitudes of Christians throughout the centuries, are to carry out the Great Commission (cf. Matt. 28:18-20).

Throughout church history there have been those who felt that the best way to deal with the world and its allurements was to remove themselves from society. To be sure, there are times when we need to step apart from the world for a brief time, but {it is detrimental to the Great Commission to isolate believers from society at large on a long-term basis. It is only as we interact and communicate with the people of the world that we can be effective witnesses for Jesus.}Q8 Common sense and reasonable cautions should be used concerning where and when we should witness, but we must go in Jesus' name to wherever the Holy Spirit calls us.

Jesus did pray that the disciples be kept "from the evil" (John 17:15). The idea here is that the disciples be protected from the evil one, that is, from Satan. All evil is inspired by the devil. Since Satan is on the prowl, seeking to devour anyone he can (I Pet. 5:8), we must be spiritually vigilant. To be victorious, we must actively resist demonic influences and temptations to sin.

{The disciples needed to be protected from the deceptive tactics of Satan. After all, their writings were to become the foundation of the church (cf. Eph. 2:20). Jesus was praying that the Holy Spirit would miraculously protect them so that they could complete their legacy of the inspired Scriptures.}Q9

The Lord can keep us from falling (cf. Jude 1:24), but that is no license to walk as close to the edge of the cliff as we can! Thinking we can do as we please and still please the Lord is presumptuous and dangerous (I Cor. 10:12)!

PRAYER FOR HOLINESS

17 Sanctify them through thy truth: thy word is truth.

18 As thou hast sent me into the world, even so have I also sent them into the world.

19 And for their sakes I sanctify myself, that they also might be sanctified through the truth.

Set apart by the Word (John 17:17). {The word "sanctify" means to be made holy—to be set apart for a holy purpose.}[Q10] The words "holy" and "saint" derive from the same root word. Sanctification is mainly a progressive process that begins after conversion and continues throughout our earthly lives. In one important sense, however, it is simultaneous with conversion: the sinner is made holy in the eyes of God by the application of the blood of Christ when he or she believes. Then, throughout our Christian lives, we grow in holiness by prayer, Bible study, worship, and the habitual practice of Christian virtues (II Pet. 1:5-8).

While we usually think of God's Word in its written form in the Bible, these men had been given God's Word directly from the mouth of the Son of God Himself. Some of them would actually be instrumental in penning the words we have in our New Testament. God's Word is God's truth. This is why we can have confidence in the Bible. The Bible not only contains God's Word; the Bible itself *is* God's Word (cf. II Tim. 3:16) and is to be proclaimed as such (cf. 4:2).

Set apart for a mission (John 17:18-19). A theme running throughout the Gospel of John affirms that Christ was sent by the Father into the world, and He willingly came to do the Father's will (cf. 6:38).

The apostles themselves were about to be sent into a hostile world to carry on the mission and ministry of Christ. Indeed, the whole church is the body of Christ to carry on His work (cf. Rom. 12:4-5). Had not Jesus' disciples done this faithfully throughout the centuries since His ascension, we today would have never even heard the name of Jesus.

For the sake of His disciples, Christ sanctified Himself to complete His divine mission. He did this so that His apostles in turn would be sanctified to carry on His mission after His ascension back to the Father. We today are the heirs of this divine mission, this Great Commission to redeem a world of lost sinners in the name of Him who sent us.

—*John Alva Owston.*

QUESTIONS

1. What office did Jesus undertake in praying the prayer recorded in John 17?

2. What does it mean that Jesus manifested the Father's name to His disciples?

3. How had the disciples responded to God's Word?

4. Which world was Christ not praying for?

5. Why is unity among Jesus' disciples important?

6. Who was the son of perdition?

7. How did this person fulfill Scripture?

8. Why is it essential that Christ's disciples remain in the world?

9. Why was it so important that the apostles be protected from Satan?

10. What does "sanctify" mean?

—*John Alva Owston.*

Preparing to Teach the Lesson

Have you ever asked someone to pray for you? Have you been heartened by the fact that Jesus is praying for you? It is also encouraging to *know* how He prays for us. John records the longest prayer of Jesus in the Bible, which He prayed the night before He was crucified. In this prayer, He thanked the Father for His disciples and asked Him to strengthen them. He loved these men and sought God's protection for them.

It is very special to see that in what was a very tense time in Jesus' life, He was thinking about His followers. He was not spending His final evening in isolation. Instead, He was focused on the needs of His disciples and glorifying His Father. Jesus never lost sight of the fact that His mission was about redeeming people and saving those who love Him.

TODAY'S AIM

Facts: to study the manner in which Christ prays before His death.

Principle: to know that we are never alone in this world because the Holy Spirit lives in us and Christ is praying for us to the Father.

Application: to live in full awareness that Christ goes with us when He sends us out.

INTRODUCING THE LESSON

One of the great and perhaps most overlooked aspects of the life of Jesus Christ is His prayer life. The Gospel writers regularly record Jesus in prayer. Many of His prayers are not recorded in the Bible, but this week's text is an exception. In His High Priestly prayer, John provides us with at least a summary of what Jesus prayed the night before His crucifixion, and not surprisingly, His disciples were among the first things on His mind.

DEVELOPING THE LESSON

1. Chosen out of the world (John 17:6-10). Jesus stated that He had made His Father's name known to the disciples. He revealed God's character and nature to the twelve men that He had chosen. The Father had separated them from the world and given them to Jesus, and in turn, He taught them about the Father that they might know and love Him.

Jesus' teaching about the Father led them to keep God's Word. This was not an attempt to earn His favor but resulted from their faith in Jesus. They certainly believed that He was sent by God. Acting in faith, they followed Him and learned to obey His commandments. They were obviously not perfect in speech or conduct, but they genuinely sought to please Christ. Although they were far from a finished product, God was still working in them, and Christ was preparing them for the work that lay ahead.

While it is true that God loves the world (John 3:16) and that Jesus prayed for unbelievers on the cross (Luke 23:34), this prayer was for those whom He called to be separate from the world. All believers belong to the Father, and the Father has given them to His Son. In turn, Jesus is glorified in every person who believes in Him. We glorify Christ by trusting Him and obeying His Word.

2. Kept by God's power (John 17:11-14). Believers in Christ are kept by the power of God. Our works do not add to our salvation, nor do they provide another dimension of God's grace to us. We are kept completely and solely by the power of the Lord. We are totally helpless without Him.

Jesus, of course, is no longer here in bodily form since He returned to the Father. Believers now represent Jesus to the world we live in (cf. II Cor. 5:20). We are not alone, however, as the Father has sent the Holy Spirit to live within us (cf. John 14:15-17).

Jesus asked His Father to keep the disciples in His name. There is power in the name of the Lord that cannot be surpassed by any of the world's forces. If God's grace is strong enough to save us, then it is strong enough to keep us.

The only one of Jesus' followers who is lost is "the son of perdition" (vs. 12), which is a reference to Judas Iscariot. Judas willingly betrayed Jesus and showed that he had never truly put his faith in Him. His betrayal fulfilled Scripture, namely, Psalm 41:9, but he chose his path; it was not forced on him.

Jesus spoke these words so that the believer's joy would be full—a joy He promised in chapter 16 (vs. 22) and which we will certainly need when we experience the hardships of the world. We should especially know this joy when we realize that Christ has forgiven us of our sins and equipped us to do His work.

Although Jesus has given us His Word to live by, the world hates us because it hates Him. Christians are not of the world but have been chosen by God for His purposes. The world has rejected God, so in turn it hates and rejects those whom God chooses.

3. Sanctified in truth (John 17:15-19). Although the world was hostile to the disciples, Jesus did not pray that God would take them out of the world. Instead, He prayed that God would keep them from Satan. They would all suffer (and most of them would die) for the gospel message they proclaimed, but Jesus' first concern was their spiritual welfare.

He prayed that they would be sanctified by truth. "Sanctify" means "to be set apart" and is closely associated with holiness. Christ sets believers apart according to His Word, and He has sent us into the world to proclaim the gospel to the lost. Our sanctification is possible because Jesus set Himself apart for the work of the cross.

ILLUSTRATING THE LESSON

Knowing that Jesus is praying for us should free us to go out and do His will in the world.

JESUS PRAYS FOR US!

JESUS

US

Praying Serving Going in His name

CONCLUDING THE LESSON

We can take comfort in the fact that Jesus is praying for us as we speak. He is our High Priest who goes to God for us. He never leaves us and is always pleading our case to the Father, seeking our protection and equipping us to go out into a world that is predisposed to hate us. We could not know God without Jesus, and in Him we can call God our Father.

ANTICIPATING THE NEXT LESSON

In next week's lesson we will study the arrest of Jesus in the garden as Judas leads a cohort of soldiers in the ultimate act of betrayal.

—*Robert Ferguson, Jr.*

PRACTICAL POINTS

1. Our relationship with the Son rests in the Father's giving us to Him (John 17:6-8).
2. Believers can draw strength from knowing that Jesus prays for them (vss. 9-10).
3. Jesus knew that His disciples would need to be strengthened upon His absence (vss. 11-12).
4. We can take great comfort in knowing that Jesus commits us to the Father for safe keeping (vss. 13-14).
5. Our goal should be to change the world for the Lord (vss. 15-16).
6. We were called to be drastically different from the world (vss. 17-19).

—Charity G. Carter.

RESEARCH AND DISCUSSION

1. Why is it important to know and firmly stand upon the truth that Jesus was sent by the Father (John 17:8)?
2. Jesus prayed for current and future believers. How does knowing this impact your thoughts today (vss. 9-10)?
3. Why did Jesus ask the Father to keep those who belong to Him?
4. Has the Father ever kept you from evil in the midst of a trying situation that He did not immediately remove you from (vs. 15)?
5. What does it mean to be sanctified through God's truth (vs. 17)?

—Charity G. Carter.

ILLUSTRATED HIGH POINTS

Not . . . out of the world (John 17:15)

Christians live in a fallen world and experience various trials and tribulations—some more than others. Many prayers are made for relief and victory. God answers every one, but not always in the way people expect or at first want.

At least three of God's prophets asked Him to take them "out of the world" (John 17:15). God, in His grace and mercy, chose not to grant the desperate prayers of Moses (Num. 11:15), Elijah (I Kgs. 19:4), and Jonah (Jonah 4:3). They learned, as did the apostle Paul, that His grace was totally sufficient for every need (cf. II Cor. 12:1-10).

Keep them from the evil (John 17:15)

During our time in New York City, we met a retired missionary couple who had spent a lifetime serving in Africa. Few would have faulted them if they had returned to the States and settled down in a quiet village to live out their remaining days in peaceful rest.

Instead, they decided to rent an apartment in busy Manhattan in order to befriend young African men and women who were in the United States to study. They trusted Christ to "keep them from the evil" as they continued to serve their Lord.

I also sent them (John 17:18)

In Sunday school over seven decades ago, a missionary was given a few minutes to speak. He held up a penny and asked, "How is this coin like a missionary?"

Since we were just kids, we did not answer. He then explained, "Just as this coin is 'one cent,' even so a missionary is 'one sent.'"

We might have groaned at the little pun, but the point is true.

—David A. Hamburg.

Golden Text Illuminated

"They are not of the world, even as I am not of the world" (John 17:16).

During Jesus' high priestly prayer, He makes a statement about His disciples that reminds me of John Denver's song "Rocky Mountain High." The man about whom Denver sings is supposedly "coming home to a place he'd never been before." This phrase is literally nonsensical, but we all understand what is meant. The man travels to the Rocky Mountains and realizes that he is more at home there than in his native environment.

We have all had similar emotions. Before I moved out of my parents' house, I started to feel not at home. Looking back, it was not anything about my parents or the house; it was just that I had grown up and was ready for the next step in life.

When the Israelites first moved to Egypt, they experienced God's blessing. Their relative Joseph was in power, they had food readily available, and they were given the land of Goshen for raising livestock. But a new pharaoh arose who had not benefited from Joseph's wisdom, and Israel began to be regarded as outsiders. Eventually they were enslaved, so God set in motion the events that resulted in their deliverance. At first they were not so sure about the move, especially when Pharaoh made their work harder. But God revealed His power over Pharaoh's stubbornness. That opened the door, and they joyfully left Egypt.

Although Abraham, Isaac, Jacob, and his sons had lived in Canaan, four hundred years had passed, and the Israel that left Egypt was a much distant generation. The people of God who entered into Canaan went home to a place they had never been before. For like reason, Hebrews 11:13 and I Peter 2:11 call the people of God "strangers and pilgrims" on earth.

Jesus asserted that His disciples were not "of" this world. In the Greek, the preposition is *ek*, which in this passage is best understood as "from." Jesus was not from this world, and He stated that His disciples are not from this world either (cf. John 1:12-13).

Accordingly, Jesus asked the Father to keep His disciples from the evil one. It is important to note that when God says something, it comes to pass. When God blessed Adam and Eve, saying, "Be fruitful and multiply" (Gen. 1:22), He also gave them power to procreate. When He said, "Let there be light" (vs. 3), light appeared. Similarly, when Jesus prayed that the Father would keep His disciples from evil, this became true as well (cf. Jude 1:24-25).

Immediately after Jesus prayed this prayer, He and His disciples went to the Garden of Gethsemane, where Jesus was betrayed. If we still wonder about our true status in this world, the events of Jesus' betrayal, arrest, and death should leave no doubt that we, along with all His disciples, are aliens and strangers here.

Now we dream of heaven as home, but more than this, our final home is New Jerusalem, where heaven and earth merge (Rev. 21:1-3). In that city, God and the Lamb sit on the throne, and the river of life is proceeding from it (22:1). This is our home, but we have never been there. If not before, I will see you at our homecoming!

—David Samuel Gifford.

Heart of the Lesson

I remember a time when I needed surgery. I was anxious about it, so I asked my sister to accompany me. Nonetheless, when it was time for the surgery, I still felt quite alone, so when a nurse asked if I wanted a chaplain to pray with me, I quickly agreed.

After the chaplain asked a few questions, he began to pray in a calm, assured voice. Somehow, this chaplain articulated my feelings and needs to the Lord even better than I had been able to. As he interceded on my behalf, I felt God's peace sweep over me. In this week's lesson, Jesus prays for His disciples while they listen. This prayer, which theologians term Jesus' High Priestly Prayer, occurred shortly before His arrest.

1. Prayer of completion (John 17:6-8). Jesus prayed, telling His Father that He had completed the work God had given Him. Through His life and teachings, Jesus had shown the Father's name to His disciples. To the Jewish people, knowing God's name meant knowing God's character and who He was.

God the Father had given the disciples to Jesus. Accordingly, these men had been receptive to His teachings, accepting His words as truth from God. They knew everything He had been given had come from God and believed God had sent Jesus.

2. Prayer for unity (John 17:9-12). The requests Jesus was about to bring were specifically for His disciples, not for all of humanity. He acknowledged (as all can) that all who are His also belong to the Father, and further that all who belong to the Father are His. The only way this latter statement can be true is if Jesus is one with the Father, who owns all things.

Jesus had protected His disciples throughout His ministry, and now He asked the Father to protect them after His departure. Indeed, He asks that His disciples share the same kind of unity that the Father and Son share—no divisiveness and power struggles! Instead, He desired that they love and serve one another—a task possible only with supernatural help.

3. Prayer for protection (John 17:13-16). One of Jesus' purposes in His prayer was that the disciples would have His joy overflowing in them. As they faced future trials, persecution, and loss, they would need His joy—the pinnacle of gladness one finds only in Him.

Jesus had taught the disciples God's Word, and as a result, their lives had changed. They had grown more and more like Jesus and less and less like the world. Just as Jesus was not of the world, so the disciples were not of the world: they now belonged to the kingdom of God rather than the kingdom of the world. Therefore, the world hated them just as it hates believers today.

The easy way to protect the disciples would have been to remove them from the world. But Jesus wants His followers to be light to the world, so He instead asked the Father to protect them from its evil influence. Today, we serve as ambassadors in this world; we live in society, but not conformed to it (cf. Rom. 12:1-2; II Cor. 5:20).

4. Prayer for sanctification (John 17:17-19). Jesus asked the Father to sanctify—to set apart and make pure—His disciples through the truth of God's Word. Jesus was sending His disciples on a mission to make disciples of all nations. To accomplish this task, disciples must meditate, know, and obey God's Word.

—Ann Staatz.

World Missions

In this week's passage, Jesus prays for His disciples and for their ministry after His resurrection. As such, there are many implications for missions. We will discuss three.

Jesus prays that we would be protected from the trouble He promised last week: "I pray not that thou shouldest take them out of the world, but that thou shouldest keep them from the evil" (John 17:15).

But why not take us out of the world? He continues, "As thou hast sent me into the world, even so have I also sent them into the world" (vs. 18). He will not ask for us to be taken out of the world because He sends us into the world! Indeed, at a later point, Jesus prays that His people be united so that "the world may believe that thou hast sent me" (vs. 21).

As Paul will later summarize: "Now then we are ambassadors for Christ, as though God did beseech you by us: we pray you in Christ's stead, be ye reconciled to God" (II Cor. 5:20).

This then is the first implication for mission work: though not all are missionaries, all Christians are called to be on mission. The second implication comes from the words repeated twice in our passage: "They are not of the world, even as I am not of the world" (John 17:14, 16). Even if a believer has never traveled, he is a spiritual foreigner amongst the lost (cf. Heb. 11:13; I Pet. 1:1). This means that for any believer, his Christianity will be distinct from his cultural upbringing.

For missionaries, they must remember the distinction between sharing the gospel and preaching conformity to their culture. One man perhaps showed this better than most.

During the dawn of modern Christian missions, a young man named Hudson Taylor headed to China. He soon made the shocking decision to shed his western clothing, don Chinese garb, and grow a pigtail. His fellow missionaries were aghast, but he held firm.

Eventually, he began a missionary society of his own, and one of his rules was that each missionary would adopt the dress of a poor Chinese teacher. The Lord led him to the realization that he needed to depend on Him. So, he faithfully prayed for 70 missionaries, and the Lord sent 76. Two years later, he begged God for 100 new missionaries, and the Lord gave him 102!

Hudson Taylor's life is an example of the goodness of our God "that is able to do exceeding abundantly above all that we ask or think" (Eph. 3:20). The mission he began remains to this day, as does Hudson Taylor's testimony to both the need to understand Christianity apart from one's own culture and the need to rely on the power of prayer ("Hudson Taylor: Faith Missionary to China," www.christianitytoday.com).

This leads us to our third implication for missions: this passage is a prayer after all, and more than that, it includes a prayer for the spread of the gospel! This demonstrates to us that we (both missionaries and non-missionaries alike) must pray for the cause of Christ to be advanced in the world.

The act of prayer should not be just asking for a list of things we want. Prayer is an admission that the one to whom we pray has the power to grant our requests, but we should pray primarily that His will be done, surrendering our own desires to His perfect will.

—Jody Stinson.

The Jewish Aspect

When Jesus prayed for His disciples' sanctification (John 17:17), they were already aware of the truth that God had called His people Israel to be sanctified. The basic meaning of the word "sanctify" (and its related terms, such as "holy" and "consecrate") is to "set apart"—specifically for God's sacred purposes. While some may think of sanctification as applying only to people, it applied to objects and broader categories as well. For example, God sanctified the tabernacle and the altar (Ex. 29:44). Further, Israel was to sanctify the sacrifices on the altar (vs. 27) and the Sabbath (20:8-11). In a similar sense, the tithe was also "holy," or "sanctified" (Lev. 27:30).

"Just as things can be set aside for sacred use, persons too can be ritually cleansed or sanctified and given or dedicated to the Lord" ("Sanctification," *International Standard Bible Encyclopedia,* Eerdmans). For example, Aaron and his sons were sanctified as priests to the Lord (Ex. 29:44). After Israel's Exodus from Egypt, God required that all the firstborn among both the people and animals be sanctified to Him; God makes clear the key element of His reason for that: the firstborn "is mine" (13:2).

The concept behind all these things or people being "sanctified" is that they were set apart for service in some way to the Lord. God is "holy," that is, set apart from all evil. He desires, therefore, that His people likewise be set apart to Him and distinct from all evil: "ye shall be holy; for I am holy" (Lev. 11:44). Peter applied these same words to believers in the church (I Pet. 1:16). Biblical scholar Craig Keener reports, "God had 'sanctified' or 'set apart' Israel for himself as holy, especially by giving them his commandments (e.g.,

Lev. 11:44-45)" (*IVP Bible Background Commentary: New Testament,* Inter-Varsity).

Jews in biblical times and afterward sought to live holy lives, sanctified to God by their works. A significant element of Judaism is *kiddush ha-Shem,* which means "sanctification of the [Divine] Name" ("Kiddush Ha-Shem and Hillul Ha-Shem," www.jewishvirtuallibrary.org).

The ancient rabbis developed this concept, drawing from the words, "Neither shall ye profane my holy name; but I will be hallowed [sanctified] among the children of Israel: I am the Lord which hallow you" (Lev. 22:32). The Jewish medieval scholar Nachmanides (c. 1194-1270) summarized God's proclamation as follows: "I desire that you be people of holiness, so that it will be fit for you to cling to Me Who is holy" ("You Shall Sanctify Yourselves and You Will be Holy," https://torah.org).

Contemporary religious Jews know that God sanctifies His own name (Ezek. 36:23). Some, however, also accept that they are "responsible for God's honor in the eyes of the world. Moses and Aaron were punished because of their failure to sanctify God's Name (Num. 20:12; Deut. 32:51). God's Name must be sanctified not only before the gentiles but in the eyes of Israel as well" ("Kiddush Ha-Shem"). Jews believe they achieve this goal when they exhibit exemplary lives of commitment to God, demonstrated in their morality and ethical behavior, which gains the respect of others in this world.

The Bible tells us that the only way to be set apart as righteous before God is by faith in His Son. God is the one who sanctifies us—in Christ!

—R. Larry Overstreet.

Guiding the Superintendent

In our study this week, we will be looking at the High Priestly Prayer of Jesus, which He prayed to the Father just before His arrest and crucifixion. It is the longest recorded prayer of Jesus in the Bible.

As the Son of God approached His own death, He spent time in prayer. Prayer is our most powerful tool to use when we face the severe trials that come to us in life.

In the first five verses of John 17, Jesus prayed for Himself. But in verses 6-19, He turned to the longest section of this final prayer, which concerned the eleven faithful disciples. He concludes by praying for all who would believe in Him throughout history (vss. 20-26).

DEVOTIONAL OUTLINE

1. Who Jesus prayed for (17:6-10). Though Jesus was the One who was going to be crucified, His heart was burdened for the men whom He had trained. So, He spent the biggest section of this prayer interceding for His disciples. Jesus told the Father that He had displayed the character of God to them during His time on earth (vs. 6). Further, they knew that all He taught was from the Father (vs. 7), though the last apparent breakthrough had not taken place until moments before (16:30). Verse 8 of this week's passage expresses Jesus' confidence that these men had truly received His words and understood that He had come from the Father.

Jesus declared that He was not praying for the whole world but for His disciples (vs. 9). Though they were rather insignificant to the rest of the world, Jesus said that they were given to Him by the Father. They were special objects of God's love and the personal possessions of both the Father and the Son. As He was about to leave the earth, Jesus knew that they would be the ones who would proclaim Him to the world.

2. What Jesus prayed for (17:11-19). After Jesus identified the objects of this part of His prayer, He began to intercede for His disciples. First, Jesus prayed that the Father would keep His disciples so that they would be one as the Father and Son were one (vs. 11). One of His concerns was that His followers would live in unity, putting aside their own selfish interests to humbly serve each other. Jesus is asking the Father to continue His work, as Jesus had also protected all those who were genuinely His (cf. 6:39). As for Judas, Jesus stated that he was never a real follower, but the son of perdition who fulfilled his role in the story of redemption unwittingly (John 17:12; cf. Ps. 41:9).

Jesus also prayed that the disciples would experience His joy fully (John 17:13). One way this joy would come was in their understanding of how much the Father cared for them.

Jesus requested that the Father would protect them from Satan, "the evil" one, while they lived here in the world (vss. 15-16). They were not to be isolated from the world, but insulated from its impact.

Finally, Jesus prayed that His disciples might be sanctified, or set apart. The means of our sanctification is the truth of God's Word (vs. 17). A prime reason for our sanctification is so that we can be sent by Jesus (vs. 18). And the grounds for our sanctification is Jesus setting Himself apart for the cross (vs. 19).

CHILDREN'S CORNER

A record of a prayer of God the Son to God the Father may well raise questions. Prepare your teachers to explain the Trinitarian nature of God: three Persons but yet one God.

—Robert Winter.

SCRIPTURE LESSON TEXT

JOHN 18:1 When Jesus had spoken these words, he went forth with his disciples over the brook Cedron, where was a garden, into the which he entered, and his disciples.

2 And Judas also, which betrayed him, knew the place: for Jesus ofttimes resorted thither with his disciples.

3 Judas then, having received a band *of men* and officers from the chief priests and Pharisees, cometh thither with lanterns and torches and weapons.

4 Jesus therefore, knowing all things that should come upon him, went forth, and said unto them, Whom seek ye?

5 They answered him, Jesus of Nazareth. Jesus saith unto them, I am *he.* And Judas also, which betrayed him, stood with them.

6 As soon then as he had said unto them, I am *he,* they went backward, and fell to the ground.

7 Then asked he them again, Whom seek ye? And they said, Jesus of Nazareth.

8 Jesus answered, I have told you that I am *he:* if therefore ye seek me, let these go their way:

9 That the saying might be fulfilled, which he spake, Of them which thou gavest me have I lost none.

10 Then Simon Peter having a sword drew it, and smote the high priest's servant, and cut off his right ear. The servant's name was Malchus.

11 Then said Jesus unto Peter, Put up thy sword into the sheath: the cup which my Father hath given me, shall I not drink it?

12 Then the band and the captain and officers of the Jews took Jesus, and bound him,

13 And led him away to Annas first; for he was father in law to Caiaphas, which was the high priest that same year.

NOTES

Jesus' Arrest

Lesson Text: John 18:1-13

Related Scriptures: John 11:45-53; Matthew 26:36-57;
Mark 14:26-50; Luke 22:39-53

TIME: A.D. 30   PLACE: Jerusalem

GOLDEN TEXT—"That the saying might be fulfilled, which he spake, Of them which thou gavest me have I lost none" (John 18:9).

Introduction

Many names have gone down in history as infamous traitors. In ancient Rome, Brutus was a conspirator in the assassination plot against his former friend, Julius Caesar. In American history, Benedict Arnold, a general serving under George Washington, is notorious for defecting to the British. In World War II, Vidkun Quisling headed the Norwegian government under the authority of Nazi occupation. After the war, he was executed for treason. The terms "benedict arnold" and "quisling" have actually become bywords for "traitor." To these we could obviously add the epithet "judas" (Iscariot).

Most people have experienced betrayal. If you have betrayed someone, you need to repent and seek forgiveness from both God and the person you betrayed. There are few things as odious.

LESSON OUTLINE

I. TREACHERY IN THE GARDEN—
   John 18:1-3

II. DEMONSTRATION OF
    POWER—John 18:4-9

III. ACCEPTANCE OF THE
     FATHER'S WILL—John 18:10-13

Exposition: Verse by Verse

TREACHERY IN THE GARDEN

JOHN 18:1 When Jesus had spoken these words, he went forth with his disciples over the brook Cedron, where was a garden, into the which he entered, and his disciples.

2 And Judas also, which betrayed him, knew the place: for Jesus ofttimes resorted thither with his disciples.

3 Judas then, having received a band of men and officers from the chief priests and Pharisees, cometh thither with lanterns and torches and weapons.

A familiar hangout (John 18:1-2). Beginning in chapter 13, John records the events that occurred in the upper room after the Last Supper. This significant body of teaching is not recorded in any of the Synoptic Gospels (Matthew, Mark, and Luke), reinforcing the view that John was intentionally supplementing the existing records of Christ's life that had been circulating for several decades before he likely wrote his Gospel (around A.D. 90).

{At length, Jesus and His apostles left the place where they had celebrated the Passover and made their way to a familiar spot. This was the Garden of Gethsemane}[Q1] and is so identified by two of the Evangelists (Matt. 26:36; Mark 14:32). Luke only identifies it as the "place" (22:40) and that it was on the "mount of Olives" (vs. 39).

To get to the garden from the city, it was necessary to cross "the brook Cedron (Kidron)" (John 18:1). The word "brook" may be misleading to Western readers. It literally means "winter flow" and refers to a gully, or wadi, where water flowed only during the rainy season. Hence, we should not envision the disciples wading through water or jumping across a flowing stream to get to Gethsemane.

Since this was a place frequented by Jesus and His disciples, Judas knew it was where Christ would be after the Passover meal. "Jesus knew that Judas was headed for the authorities to commit his act of betrayal. Therefore, we might expect that Jesus, in order to escape arrest, would have gone anywhere other than a place where He regularly met with His disciples, a place that Judas knew about. It was only natural that Judas would lead the arresting officers to the garden. But Jesus was not seeking to avoid arrest. It almost seems that He went out of His way to be apprehended" (Sproul, *John,* Reformation Trust).

The Synoptics all detail Jesus' agony in the garden as He struggled with obeying the Father's will, but John omits these details. That should not be surprising or disconcerting. Each Evangelist had certain intentions in mind for his particular narrative, and so each Gospel is written with it's own emphases. To include everything Jesus did would have been impossible (cf. John 21:25).

In numerous places, Judas is identified as the betrayer, or traitor (Matt. 10:4; 26:25; Mark 3:19; Luke 6:16). Indeed, his name itself has become a byword for betrayal. In the New Testament, the Greek *Ioudas* is also rendered "Judah" and "Jude." One of the other apostles also bore this name, as did one of the half-brothers of Jesus Himself (cf. Matt. 13:55; Mark 6:3).

A hostile intrusion (John 18:3). {Concerning Judas's motivation for betraying Christ, there are numerous theories. At the very least, greed was definitely involved (cf. 12:4-6). While thirty pieces of silver may seem a paltry sum for betraying an innocent person, thieves like Judas do not think this way. Beyond the money, he seems to have been disappointed to realize that Jesus had no plans to overthrow Rome. His false, worldly expectations for the Messiah certainly played a part in his actions.}[Q2]

Today it seems common to view Judas as a misunderstood, almost sympathetic figure who meant well but whose good intentions merely went awry. But the New Testament writers clearly share no such sympathies for Judas—only unequivocal contempt and condemnation!

{Legal systems invariably make a distinction between unplanned homicides and those that are premeditated. Judas voluntarily went to the Jewish religious leaders early in that week and contracted to betray Christ to them for money (cf. Matt. 26:14-16).}[Q3] Moreover, those with whom he made his bargain also stipulated that he single Jesus out to make sure they arrested the right person. Thus, Judas turned even the traditional kiss of friendship into a treacherous tool of betrayal (cf. Matt. 26:47-49; Luke 22:47-48).

John 18:3 says a "band" of men arrived to arrest Jesus. "The Greek word *speira* is a technical term for a detachment of infantry in the Roman army consisting of some 600 men" (Tasker, *The Gospel According to St. John,* Eerdmans). Taken at face value, this means that {a large contingent of soldiers was involved in Christ's arrest. Since it was Passover, more troops were stationed in Jerusalem, since uprisings were more likely to occur because of the influx of foreigners on the occasion.}Q4

{The "officers" would have been under the supervision of the chief priests. Since the priesthood was largely associated with the Sadducees, mention of the Pharisees indicates a collaborative effort between these otherwise adversarial factions of the Jewish Sanhedrin. They set aside their animosity for the mutual goal of ridding themselves of Jesus.}Q5

Since it was night, the torches and lanterns were needed by the soldiers. But they had no need to carry weapons, since the Saviour would offer no resistance to their intentions. Yet He was accused of being a revolutionary (cf. Luke 23:1-5), so they may have expected Him to resist. So, they came brimming with weapons to arrest an unarmed teacher. The picture is rather laughable.

Jesus' kingdom is not of this world but of the next, which will come after He returns in glory (cf. John 18:36; Matt. 25:31). Even at this stage, He could have commanded legions of angels to defend Himself (cf. Matt. 26:53), but such an action would have negated God's plan to bring about the world's redemption from sin.

DEMONSTRATION OF POWER

4 Jesus therefore, knowing all things that should come upon him, went forth, and said unto them, Whom seek ye?

5 They answered him, Jesus of Nazareth. Jesus saith unto them, I am he. And Judas also, which betrayed him, stood with them.

6 As soon then as he had said unto them, I am he, they went backward, and fell to the ground.

7 Then asked he them again, Whom seek ye? And they said, Jesus of Nazareth.

8 Jesus answered, I have told you that I am he: if therefore ye seek me, let these go their way:

9 That the saying might be fulfilled, which he spake, Of them which thou gavest me have I lost none.

A staggering answer (John 18:4-6). Being the eternal Son of God, nothing that was about to occur came as a surprise to Jesus. Undaunted by this hostile rabble, He stepped forward and asked, "Whom seek ye?" Of course, He knew they were seeking Him. Jesus had agonized in prayer concerning God's impending will for Him, and He was resolved to go to the cross as foreordained (cf. I Pet. 1:20).

Affirming that He was indeed Jesus of Nazareth, the One whom they sought, the Lord was willing to be arrested to fulfill the plan of God that would provide salvation to the world. It was because of "the joy that was set before him" (Heb. 12:2) that He was willing to suffer and die.

It is hard to imagine that one of Jesus' own disciples, after years of listening to His teaching and witnessing His miracles, could now stand with those planning His murder. Such is the power of Satan to deceive and corrupt. Judas had been blessed with the close fellowship of the Lord of glory Himself during His earthly ministry, yet he was now transformed into a son of hell! Vigilance against the deceptions of the enemy of our souls is a constant imperative.

Regarding Jesus's reply to the arresting force, note that in both verses 5 and 6, the King James Version has the word "he" in italics. This means that the word is not found in the original Greek text. Jesus' actual answer was "I am." As mentioned previously, this phrase is often used throughout John's Gospel to introduce key statements about Christ's identity and mission. Jesus used this phrase to identify Himself as Yahweh (cf. John 8:58), the one true God who appeared to Moses at the burning bush (cf. Ex. 3:14).

{In an amazing demonstration of the power of that divine name, the text tells us that when Jesus answered them with the declaration "I am," the arresting rabble staggered backward and fell to the ground, literally knocked off its feet. And this was just a small intimation of His divine identity.}[Q6] When He comes again, "He shall smite the earth with the rod of his mouth" (Isa. 11:4; cf. II Thess. 2:8).

"This scene is one of the most dramatic of the many dramatic scenes in this Gospel. On the one hand we see Judas and his 'army', representative of the world which is tainted by evil in its religion and its politics, and relies upon physical force to achieve its objects. On the other hand we are confronted with Jesus unarmed, unbefriended and apparently helpless in the face of overwhelming opposition, but having at His command invisible divine resources in virtue of His complete obedience to His heavenly Father. In consequence, His victory is assured in this last assault upon the citadel of evil" (Tasker).

An extension of protection (John 18:7-9). In some sense, Jesus was toying with His adversaries. They had approached Him with the earthly menace of armor and swords, and he had flat-

tened them with a single word! Since their sudden loss of verticality seemed to leave them speechless, Jesus again asked them, "Whom seek ye?" as they struggled to regain their feet. It was almost a wry challenge: "What's the matter with you, didn't you hear Me the first time?"

In a further demonstration of His divine authority, Jesus commanded the throng to allow His disciples to go their way. Since the officers had admitted to be seeking only Jesus, then He would be the only one they arrested. His disciples would go free. From an earthly perspective, Jesus was in no position to bargain with the armed contingent of soldiers. But as the Son of God, He was in complete control of the situation, as always. The soldiers complied without a hint of objection or remonstrance.

{The reason Jesus commanded His persecutors to let His disciples go was to fulfill the prophecy He Himself had spoken about a year earlier in John 6:39: "Of all which he hath given me I should lose nothing."}[Q7] As for Judas, he had never been one of those given to Jesus by the Father—he had never really been a true disciple, since he was of the devil.

God has absolute, sovereign foreknowledge of all events that come to pass (cf. Isa 46:10). A. W. Tozer likened God's predetermined purposes to an ocean liner. The people on the ship can do as they please, but they cannot alter the direction of the ship or its final destination. "Both freedom and sovereignty are present here and they do not contradict each other. So it is, I believe, with man's freedom and the sovereignty of God" (Tozer, *The Knowledge of the Holy,* Harper).

ACCEPTANCE OF THE FATHER'S WILL

10 Then Simon Peter having a sword drew it, and smote the high priest's servant, and cut off his

right ear. The servant's name was Malchus.

11 Then said Jesus unto Peter, Put up thy sword into the sheath: the cup which my Father hath given me, shall I not drink it?

12 Then the band and the captain and officers of the Jews took Jesus, and bound him,

13 And led him away to Annas first; for he was father in law to Caiaphas, which was the high priest that same year.

An impulsive blow (John 18:10). {John alone informs us that it was Simon Peter who attacked the servant of the high priest with a sword.}[Q8] The Synoptics simply identify the attacker as "one of them" (Matt. 26:51; cf. Mark 14:47; Luke 22:50). Perhaps they wanted to conceal Peter's identity as the attacker to protect him from incrimination. By the time John wrote, however, Peter had been martyred some twenty-five years previously, so there was no longer any reason to conceal who had done the act.

The fact that Peter took the initiative to defend Jesus without being told to do so is certainly in character with his impetuous nature. Both John and Luke note that it was the right ear of the high priest's servant that was cut off. But John alone identifies him by name as "Malchus." Perhaps John knew him personally, since he was acquainted with the high priest's household (cf. John 18:15). Luke alone records the miracle of Jesus healing the man's severed ear (cf. Luke 22:51).

Rebuke and recommitment (John 18:11). {Obviously, Jesus did not need Peter or anyone else to defend Him. For Peter to do so under these circumstances was both futile and foolish. Jesus therefore rebuked Peter, telling him to put his sword away. In Luke 22:51, Jesus adds, in essence, "No

more of this!" And in Matthew 26:52, He tells Peter, "For all they that take the sword shall perish with the sword."} [Q9] No weapon forged by human hands would be necessary to defeat this enemy.

Arrest and removal (John 18:12-13). Thus, there was no need to bind Jesus as they did; He would have gone with them without resistance.

{While Caiaphas was the currently ruling high priest, Jesus was taken first to Annas, father-in-law of Caiaphas. Although Annas was no longer the official high priest, he still wielded great authority in Jerusalem. In fact, he was very likely the driving force in the plot against Jesus.}[Q10]

—*John Alva Owston.*

QUESTIONS

1. What was the name of the garden where Jesus and His disciples went?
2. What motivations may have lain behind Judas's betrayal?
3. How do we know that Judas's act was premeditated?
4. What was the size of the force involved in Jesus' arrest?
5. What two adversarial groups collaborated to rid themselves of Jesus?
6. What caused those sent to arrest Jesus to fall backward to the ground?
7. Why did Jesus command that His disciples be allowed to go free?
8. Who tried to defend Jesus with a sword?
9. Why did Christ rebuke this disciple's action?
10. Who was Jesus first taken to after His arrest? Why?

—*John Alva Owston.*

Preparing to Teach the Lesson

Have you ever been betrayed by a close friend? Few things hurt emotionally as much as when a friend or loved one turns their back on you and uses personal information to hurt you. Unfortunately, acts of betrayal are committed by Christians and non-Christians alike. If you are still reeling from a close friend's betrayal, then this week's lesson will be of special interest to you. Jesus also was betrayed by a close companion, and He understands how you feel.

Judas Iscariot's betrayal of Jesus led to the arrest, trial, and crucifixion of the only completely innocent man to ever live. Judas had sold Jesus out to the chief priests for thirty pieces of silver (Matt. 26:15), and he waited for the opportune time to deliver Him to the authorities. This was a despicable act of treachery that exposed Judas for the scoundrel that he was.

TODAY'S AIM

Facts: to know that Jesus was never guilty of any sin or wrongdoing, yet He was arrested when Judas Iscariot betrayed Him.

Principle: to recognize that Jesus willingly bore our sin and to note that He understands the pain that betrayal brings.

Application: to always stand for Christ even if it is unpopular with those closest to us.

INTRODUCING THE LESSON

Jesus had just completed His High Priestly prayer and crossed over the Kidron Valley after exiting Jerusalem. There, He entered a garden known as Gethsemane (cf. Mark 14:32). As Jesus agonized in prayer over what He was about to endure, a band of soldiers came with torches and weapons to arrest Him. What the disciples may have found astonishing was who was leading them. Just as Jesus had predicted, it was one of their own.

DEVELOPING THE LESSON

1. Judas betrays Jesus (John 18:1-5). The Kidron Valley was located just east of Jerusalem between the city and the Mount of Olives, where the Garden of Gethsemane was. This was a familiar place for Jesus, as He often took His disciples there to pray.

Judas knew that Jesus could be found there, as he had undoubtedly spent significant time there with Him. Judas took specific, inside information that he had of Jesus and used it against Him.

Attacking a devout man while He is in prayer is repulsive, but Judas's conscience was seared at this point because Satan had entered into him (cf. Luke 22:3). Seizing a praying man was not a problem for Judas; all he cared about was getting his money.

Judas did not come alone to Gethsemane. He brought along a band of Roman soldiers and Jewish officers. They had come to arrest Jesus, and the soldiers may have also been present to prevent a potential riot.

Jesus knew in advance everything that was going to happen to Him. He asked who they were looking for, and they answered that they were looking for Jesus of Nazareth. Their intentions were now clearly on the record.

Standing with the soldiers and officers was Judas, who notably had switched sides. Once a follower of Jesus, he was now standing with (even leading!) those who would arrest and kill Him. While this visible portrayal of betrayal and switching sides would be surprising, in reality Judas never really stood with Jesus at all.

2. Jesus displays meekness (John 18:6-11). When Jesus answered, "I am he," the soldiers fell backward to the ground (vs. 6). More seems to be going on here than just simple surprise at Jesus' direct answer. Whether or not they perceived who they were actually dealing with, it seems that at His moment of greatest human weakness, His power was evident in a remarkable way.

Jesus asked them again who they were seeking, and they again said they were looking for Jesus of Nazareth. Jesus responded by saying that He had already told them that He was the one they were looking for. This time, He told the arresting officers to let the others go since they had twice said they sought Him alone. Even while facing arrest, the Shepherd protected His sheep. This fulfilled what Jesus had said earlier, that He kept all of those whom the Father had given Him (John 17:12).

Peter reacted with a violent, desperate attempt to protect Jesus and cut off the ear of the high priest's servant. This may have been how many of us would have reacted, but it was not part of God's plan. Peter's response was to cut off the man's ear. Jesus' response, however, was to heal this man immediately (cf. Luke 22:50-51).

Jesus rebuked Peter by telling him to put his sword away. Jesus had to drink the cup the Father had prepared for Him, and He had no desire to prevent it from happening. In the Old Testament, the cup is sometimes used as a metaphor for God's wrath (cf. Job 21:20; Ps. 75:8; Jer. 25:15-17). Jesus here is ready to take the cup prepared by the Father so that we will not need to.

3. Jesus appears before Annas (John 18:12-13). The soldiers arrested Jesus and tied Him up, treating Him like a common criminal. No one had ever laid hands on Jesus like this before. Many attempts were made by Satan and sinners alike to kill Jesus in the past, but all of them were unsuccessful. Now, His time to die had come (cf. 12:23).

They immediately led Jesus to Annas, the father-in-law of the high priest Caiaphas. Annas had previously served as high priest, and he still wielded considerable power.

ILLUSTRATING THE LESSON

One way to stand with Jesus is to proclaim His name even when our friends do not like Him.

CONCLUDING THE LESSON

Judas's true colors stood out clearly as he stood with Jesus' enemies in His most trying hour. If we are going to be true disciples of Christ, then we must stand with Him no matter who is against Him. This may make you unpopular and in some circumstances may put you in danger. However, those who love Jesus will never abandon Him under any circumstance.

ANTICIPATING THE NEXT LESSON

We continue following the trial of Jesus next, seeing how He was mistreated by the authorities and denied again by one of His own.

—Robert Ferguson, Jr.

PRACTICAL POINTS

1. When we follow Jesus, we can expect to face formidable opposition (John 18:1-3).
2. We can boldly meet adversity in the Lord's strength (vss. 4-5).
3. We should not be afraid to declare to others who we are—that we belong to Jesus (vss. 6-7).
4. We can take courage that Jesus has taken responsibility for our security in Him (vss. 8-9).
5. The Lord's interests are not served by rashness on our part (vss. 10-11).
6. Jesus is with us in our trials, although He stood alone in His (vss. 12-13).

—Charity G. Carter.

RESEARCH AND DISCUSSION

1. An estimated two to six hundred men and officers approached Jesus in the garden. Why were so many sent to arrest one man (John 18:3)?
2. Explain the irony of Jesus asking the men who they were looking for (vs. 4).
3. How did Jesus demonstrate love for His disciples on the night that He was betrayed (vs. 8)?
4. Jesus willingly went with the soldiers, but Peter violently cut off a servant's ear to defend Him (vss. 10-13). What do Jesus' and Peter's actions teach us about submission?

—Charity G. Carter.

ILLUSTRATED HIGH POINTS

And Judas also (John 18:2)

In my first-grade class of about thirty children, there were five Davids. It must have been a popular name in 1937.

Judas was a common name in the first century. Two of Jesus' twelve disciples were named Judas (cf. Luke 6:16; John 14:22; Acts 1:13). Additionally, one of Jesus' half brothers was called Judas (Matt. 13:55); he would later write the epistle of Jude.

Which betrayed him (John 18:5)

Betrayal and treachery are practiced throughout the world. Don Richardson, in his book *Peace Child* (Regal Books), tells of his missionary work among the Sawi tribe in New Guinea. This tribe had a culture of revenge. In this culture, the highest and most glorious form of action was to cultivate an enemy's friendship over many months, promise him safety, and then when the victim least suspected it, betray and kill him.

The people most respected in the tribe were not the most successful warriors, but the ones who were the most deceitful. So when they first heard the gospel, they admired Judas more than anyone else!

The cup (John 18:11)

In our house, we have many cups. Some are made of fine china and are seldom used. Others are ordinary cups and mugs for coffee and tea. Then there are numerous ornamental cups that are used for decoration only.

The cup Jesus mentioned refers to the cup of the wrath of God (cf. Isa. 51:17).

Jesus was well aware that His Father's cup awaited Him, and He was willing to bear the wrath of God for the sins of the world so that we may be forgiven.

—David A. Hamburg.

Golden Text Illuminated

"That the saying might be fulfilled, which he spake, Of them which thou gavest me have I lost none" (John 18:9).

In reading this text, which speaks of Jesus not losing any disciples, we might find it strange that just four verses earlier (vs. 5), John speaks of Judas betraying Him. Judas was one of the Twelve. Did Jesus lose him?

A careful look at John's Gospel reveals that Jesus did not lose Judas; He could not have, for he was never given to Him.

In the golden text Jesus uses the word "fulfilled." But He was not referring to fulfillment of Old Testament prophecy. Rather, Jesus was speaking about fulfilling His own words. Earlier that evening, He had said about His disciples, "None of them is lost, but the son of perdition; that the scripture might be fulfilled" (John 17:12). Even earlier (13:18), He implied that Judas's betrayal fulfilled Old Testament prophecy of the Messiah's betrayal by a friend (Ps. 41:9). All this was to show that Jesus did not lose him; Judas was always out for his own interests, and in the process, he fulfilled the Scripture.

Concerning Jesus' other disciples, He had said, "Of all which he [the Father] hath given me I should lose nothing" (John 6:39). That passage, together with 17:12, indicates that the golden text refers to Jesus keeping all who are His until His kingdom comes (cf. 17:11-15).

We must also find the significance of this week's text in its own context. In John 18:3 we read, "Judas then, having received a band of men and officers from the chief priests and Pharisees, cometh thither with lanterns and torches and weapons." The chief priests and Pharisees wanted Jesus arrested, and Judas knew where He would be that night. Once again, we see that Judas was not a follower of Jesus; he became the guide of those who wanted to arrest and kill Jesus.

Verse 4 tells us that Jesus already knew what was going to happen, and He was ready for it. He did not run or cower from the soldiers and thugs. When they said that they were looking for "Jesus of Nazareth," He replied, "I am he" (vs. 5). Everyone literally fell over backward at this. They may have been impressed by the power of Jesus' personal presence or shocked that He admitted his identity, but the text makes it quite clear that it was the words He used that knocked them flat. In Greek, these words are *ego eimi*, an emphatic "I am" and the equivalent of "I AM THAT I AM" in Exodus 3:14. Jesus thereby called Himself Yahweh. It is not surprising that the soldiers fell down backward—His claim was that audacious.

When they recovered, Jesus again asked their business. They again said that they were looking for Jesus of Nazareth, and He again admitted His identity. Then, despite His obvious power, He offered to go with them if they would let His disciples go. Peter first had to experience a teachable moment involving a sword; after that Jesus allowed the soldiers to arrest Him.

This arrangement between Jesus and the soldiers is what our text addresses. None of His disciples were arrested, killed, or "lost" that night. Jesus here keeps His faithful disciples from the danger of soldiers and thugs to demonstrate His ability to preserve them into His heavenly kingdom.

—*David Samuel Gifford*

Heart of the Lesson

When I first moved to Portland, Oregon, I occasionally visited a garden called The Grotto. An elevator carried me to the upper gardens, where meandering paths led past flower-lined pools. A prayer chapel with floor-to-ceiling windows provided quiet views of the Columbia River. The upper gardens were a peaceful retreat that seemed miles from Portland's traffic and noise.

Jesus loved to linger and pray in a garden near Jerusalem. In this week's lesson, He spends His last evening there with His disciples.

1. Garden retreat (John 18:1). Night had fallen. Jesus and His disciples had completed their Passover meal. They departed Jerusalem, crossed the Kidron Valley east of the city, reached the Mount of Olives, and arrived at the Garden of Gethsemane, where they often gathered.

2. Imminent betrayal (John 18:2-3). Earlier in the week, the disciple Judas had conspired with the Jewish religious leaders, offering to help them arrest Jesus. The secluded garden at night, away from the crowds that might defend Him or cause an uproar, was perfect for this treachery.

Judas had left the Passover meal early to pick up the Roman soldiers and temple guards who would arrest Jesus. They carried swords, torches, and lanterns, prepared to search for Jesus.

3. Supernatural encounter (John 18:4-9). Jesus knew exactly what was about to happen, yet He did not run or hide. Instead of waiting for the men to find Him, He courageously stepped forward to meet them and ask whom they were seeking.

"Jesus of Nazareth," they said; "I am he," Jesus replied (vs. 5). Immediately, the entire group fell backward to the ground. Something powerful in Jesus' words and presence affected them, stopping them.

Jesus asked again whom they were seeking. They again answered, "Jesus of Nazareth." They had been rattled, but their quest remained unchanged.

Jesus reminded them He already had admitted to being the person they were looking for. Because He was the one they wanted, He asked that they let His disciples go their way.

Again, Jesus was showing love for the disciples in His darkest moment. He also was partially fulfilling what He had said earlier that night in His prayer: He would lose none whom His Father had given Him (17:12). On this occasion, He kept them from loss of life; throughout all their lives, He kept them from the loss of eternal well-being and fellowship with Him.

4. Misguided defense (John 18:10-11). Impetuous, loyal Simon Peter drew his sword. He was going to defend his Master even if he was outnumbered. He only managed to slice off the ear of Malchus, the high priest's servant, before Jesus intervened.

He told Peter to put his weapon back in his sheath. The disciples were not to thwart His arrest and death; He was determined to drink of the cup His Father had given Him. He was choosing to die.

5. Callous arrest (John 18:12-13). The soldiers arrested Jesus and bound Him. Then they led Him to the home of Annas, the former high priest, to begin a series of trials.

This lesson reveals many sides of our Saviour. He was courageous in His determination to go to the cross. He remained calm as He faced a small army coming to arrest Him. Finally, He was a caring leader even in His darkest hour.
—Ann Staatz.

World Missions

People are not often given count-downs to the moments of their death. God alone knows when people will lose their mortal lives and enter eternity.

An example of such an unexpected death is that of Josh Wesson, a missionary to the Dominican Republic.

In 2015, Mr. Wesson headed to the beach with a group of Christian youth. During the day, four boys experienced some trouble in the ocean. Mr. Wesson entered the water to try to save their lives.

Although he succeeded in saving three, he and one of the boys entered eternity. He left behind a wife and four children (Theresa Schmidt, "Missionary Hero laid to Rest," August 14, 2015, kplctv.com).

His final act on earth was to exemplify the verse, "Greater love hath no man than this, that a man lay down his life for his friends" (John 15:13).

Josh Wesson did not know when he rose that day that he had begun his last day on earth. But for Christ, facing death on the cross, He knew all that lay before Him. He understood each moment of pain and agony that He would experience.

Yet even with His crucifixion looming, He took the time to pray for His disciples. In John 17, we read one of Jesus' last prayers. He prays for God's glory (vss. 1-5), then for His disciples (vss. 6-19), and finally, for His future disciples: "Neither pray I for these alone, but for them also which shall believe on me through their word" (vs. 20).

He also earnestly prayed, "Father, if thou be willing, remove this cup from me: nevertheless not my will, but thine, be done" (Luke 22:42). Mark records that He prayed this prayer three times (14:35-41).

The suffering He experienced is in-comprehensible to the human mind, and yet where were His disciples?

Sleeping. Three times He urged their wakefulness. Three times He found them sleeping. But even as they were proving faithless, "he [Jesus] abideth faithful: he cannot deny himself" (II Tim. 2:13).

On the cusp of such great suffering, many people would wallow in self-pity. In contrast, Jesus was still ministering to the very disciples who had not watched with Him (John 18:8; cf. Mark 14:43; Luke 22:47). He ensured that they were not arrested with Him.

Two times during His arrest, something miraculous occurred. First, when Jesus admitted who He was, all those sent to arrest Him "went backward, and fell to the ground" (John 18:6).

Second, when Simon Peter struck off Malchus' ear, Jesus healed it. Telling Peter to put away his sword, He added, "Thinkest thou that I cannot now pray to my Father, and he shall presently give me more than twelve legions of angels? But how then shall the scriptures be fulfilled, that thus it must be?" (Matt. 26:53-54).

As such, the miracles serve as a reminder that Jesus allowed His own death: "I lay down my life, that I might take it again. No man taketh it from me, but I lay it down of myself " (John 10:17-18).

Christ willingly died to save His people. This was the ultimate in giving one's life for another. As learned in a previous lesson, Christ calls all Christians to follow this example (12:23-26). Missionaries do this by giving of their time (and sometimes their very lives) to leave their culture behind and share the gospel with others.

—Jody Stinson.

The Jewish Aspect

How remarkable it is that the armed soldiers fell backward when they came to arrest Jesus (John 18:5-6)! John alone records this event since it precisely fit His consistent description of Jesus.

Our English version says that the armed contingent answered Jesus' question "Whom seek ye?" (vs. 4) with the words "Jesus of Nazareth" (vs. 5). To that response, Jesus replied, "I am he" (vs. 5). Verse 6 tells us that the words "I am he" sent them reeling to the ground. The Greek text in both these verses reads *ego eimi*, "I am"; the word "he" was supplied by the translators.

Jesus used the identical phrase on an earlier occasion, "Before Abraham was, I am" (John 8:58), and twice earlier in the same chapter. To a hostile audience, Jesus said, "if ye believe not that I am he, ye shall die in your sins" (vs. 24). He further stated, "When ye have lifted up the Son of man, then shall ye know that I am he" (vs. 28). The Greek text in both these verses has the emphatic *ego eimi*, "I am." To His bold declarations, the Jews reacted by seeking to kill Him through stoning (vss. 40, 59).

The background for these comments and the response of the Jews is found in the Old Testament. God's name is explained in Exodus 3 with the Hebrew word meaning "I am." When God commissioned Moses to deliver Israel from Egypt, Moses asked how he should answer the Israelites when they asked for His name. To that, God responded, "I AM THAT I AM: and he said, Thus shalt thou say unto the children of Israel, I AM hath sent me unto you" (vs. 14).

Modern Jewish writers accurately recognize that "Moses is not asking 'what should I call you;' rather, he is asking 'who are you; what are you like; what have you done.' That is clear from God's response. God replies that He is eternal, that He is the God of our ancestors, that He has seen our affliction and will redeem us from bondage" ("Jewish Concepts: The Name of God," www.jewishvirtuallibrary.org). God was concisely assuring Moses that "My nature will become evident from My actions" (*Jewish Study Bible,* Oxford).

Christian interpreters concur. "When used by God in the Bible, 'I am' never refers merely to His existence or inscrutability or changelessness or sovereignty. . . . God's 'I am' is always an expression of relationship to His people" (Youngblood, *Exodus*, Moody).

From the Hebrew word translated "I Am" comes the word *yhvh*—the proper name for God used 6828 times in the Old Testament, usually translated "Lord." "The most important of God's Names is the four-letter Name represented by the Hebrew letters Yod-Heh-Vav-Heh (YHVH)" ("Jewish Concepts: The Name of God," www.jewishvirtuallibrary.org).

In chapter 8, Jesus' words assured His listeners that in Him they could have forgiveness of sins; in the Garden of Gethsemane, however, His words demonstrated the power of His deity, as His antagonists sought to arrest Him. "The soldiers had come out secretly to arrest a fleeing peasant. In the gloom they find themselves confronted by a commanding figure, who . . . speaks to them in the very language of deity" (Morris, *Gospel According to John*, Eerdmans). Indeed, Jesus is the great "I Am," God manifest in the flesh, and the Redeemer for all Jews and Gentiles who trust in Him.

—R. Larry Overstreet.

Guiding the Superintendent

After about three years of planning and plotting, the religious leaders were led by their hatred of Jesus to arrest and crucify the promised Messiah. Their actions in the last few hours before the crucifixion were not only despicable, but also illegal. The Jews were so fixated on His death that they violated their own laws. Yet our sovereign God never lost control. All of these events were part of His sovereign plan.

DEVOTIONAL OUTLINE

1. The arrival of Jesus and the disciples (John 18:1). It was the custom of Jesus to spend time with His disciples in the Garden of Gethsemane (vs. 2). In His last prayer there, Jesus committed Himself to the plan of God (cf. Matt. 26:39; Mark 14:36; Luke 22:42). As He was finishing His prayer and speaking to the disciples, an angry mob approached to arrest Him.

2. The betrayal of Judas (John 18:2-3). Because of his greed, Judas had made a deal with the leaders to turn Jesus over to them. He led them to the Garden of Gethsemane because He knew that Jesus would take His disciples there (vs. 2). The leaders must have believed that the arrest would be difficult because they came well armed and with many soldiers (vs. 3).

3. The response of Jesus (John 18:4-9). Instead of running away as the leaders likely expected, Jesus "went forth" to meet them (vs. 4). When the leaders said they were seeking Jesus, He responded, "I am he," and they all fell down (vss. 5-6). Jesus was declaring that He was the Great I Am—Yahweh.

Jesus courageously stood there ready to do the Father's will. His concern was not for His own welfare, but for the protection of the disciples (vss. 7-8). This had been the focus of one of the requests He had made earlier in the evening (17:11-12; cf. 6:39). His calmness and His compassion for others is a great example to us.

4. The impulsiveness of Peter (John 18:10-11). Immediately, Peter pulled out his sword to defend Jesus (vs. 10). He cut off the ear of Malchus, the servant of the high priest. It is possible that Peter missed his main target. Foolish and brave, Peter was willing to fight and die if that would protect Jesus. Perhaps he was emboldened when he saw the soldiers fall down before Him. Once again, Jesus showed compassion by healing Malchus' ear (Luke 22:51). He rebuked Peter and affirmed His submission to the plan of the Father (John 18:11).

5. The finality of the arrest (John 18:12-13). The soldiers then arrested Jesus (vs. 12). From a purely earthly perspective, Jesus would not be free again. He would be taken to Annas, the former high priest, to begin a series of trials that violated the basic principles of justice (vs. 13).

CHILDREN'S CORNER

Suggest to your teachers to have their whole class reenact these events to make them stick in their minds.

The children of your church may wonder why Jesus was arrested if He was without sin. Prepare your teachers to explain that this is indeed not a proper thing and that's the point.

The betrayal of Judas provides an opportunity for your teachers to remind the children of sin. Remind them that while Judas and the officers sinned in plotting against Jesus, He would die to pardon any of them, who are also sinners, who will trust in Him.

—Robert Winter.

SCRIPTURE LESSON TEXT

JOHN 18:15 And Simon Peter followed Jesus, and *so did* another disciple: that disciple was known unto the high priest, and went in with Jesus into the palace of the high priest.

16 But Peter stood at the door without. Then went out that other disciple, which was known unto the high priest, and spake unto her that kept the door, and brought in Peter.

17 Then saith the damsel that kept the door unto Peter, Art not thou also *one* of this man's disciples? He saith, I am not.

18 And the servants and officers stood there, who had made a fire of coals; for it was cold: and they warmed themselves: and Peter stood with them, and warmed himself.

19 The high priest then asked Jesus of his disciples, and of his doctrine.

20 Jesus answered him, I spake openly to the world; I ever taught in the synagogue, and in the temple, whither the Jews al- ways resort; and in secret have I said nothing.

21 Why askest thou me? ask them which heard me, what I have said unto them: behold, they know what I said.

22 And when he had thus spoken, one of the officers which stood by struck Jesus with the palm of his hand, saying, Answerest thou the high priest so?

23 Jesus answered him, If I have spoken evil, bear witness of the evil: but if well, why smitest thou me?

24 Now Annas had sent him bound unto Caiaphas the high priest.

25 And Simon Peter stood and warmed himself. They said therefore unto him, Art not thou also *one* of his disciples? He denied *it,* and said, I am not.

26 One of the servants of the high priest, being *his* kinsman whose ear Peter cut off, saith, Did not I see thee in the garden with him?

27 Peter then denied again: and immediately the cock crew.

NOTES

Trials and Denials

Lesson Text: John 18:15-27

Related Scriptures: Matthew 26:59-75; Mark 14:55-72;
Luke 22:55-71

TIME: A.D. 30   PLACE: Jerusalem

GOLDEN TEXT—"Jesus said, I am: and ye shall see the Son of man sitting on the right
hand of power, and coming in the clouds of heaven" (Mark 14:62).

Introduction

Many people have had the experience of being in court. They may have been there as defendants, plaintiffs, jurors, witnesses, or just as observers. Few of us qualify to be in court as attorneys or judges. Unlike television courtroom dramas, the wheels of justice grind slowly in a real courtroom. Nor are most cases as exciting as portrayed in fictional courtroom scenes.

Between His arrest in the Garden of Gethsemane and His crucifixion, Christ endured six trials. Unlike under modern American justice, where a case can drag out over several months, or even years, Jesus was tried and convicted within a matter of hours. Not being a Roman citizen meant He had no right of appeal or any legal representation.

LESSON OUTLINE

I. PETER'S FIRST DENIAL—
John 18:15-18

II. JESUS' FIRST TRIAL—
John 18:19-24

III. PETER'S FURTHER DENIALS—
John 18:25-27

Exposition: Verse by Verse

PETER'S FIRST DENIAL

JOHN 18:15 And Simon Peter followed Jesus, and so did another disciple: that disciple was known unto the high priest, and went in with Jesus into the palace of the high priest.

16 But Peter stood at the door without. Then went out that other disciple, which was known unto the high priest, and spake unto her that kept the door, and brought in Peter.

17 Then saith the damsel that kept the door unto Peter, Art not thou also one of this man's disciples? He saith, I am not.

18 And the servants and officers stood there, who had made a fire of coals; for it was cold: and

they warmed themselves: and Peter stood with them, and warmed himself.

Trying to follow (John 18:15-16). {When Jesus was seized in the garden, the disciples fled into the night. But true to his bold nature, though cautiously, "Peter followed afar off" (Luke 22:54)—that is, at a distance—to see what was going to happen. While we cannot be certain, most think that the reference to "another disciple" was to none other than the author of this Gospel, the apostle John.}^Q1 But some think it was another, unnamed disciple. F. F. Bruce suggests it was an unknown Jerusalem disciple who had access to high society (*The Gospel of John,* Eerdmans).

{Whether it was an unnamed disciple or John, he was known to the high priest. We do not know what the connection was, but it did make it possible for Peter to be granted access to the courtyard of his residence.}^Q2 It is likely that the high priest, and possibly other members of his family, resided in or near the temple courts. In the time of Christ, the entire temple complex covered about thirty-six acres.

It was only after the other disciple spoke to the woman who watched the gate to the courtyard that Peter was able to gain admission to the courtyard. As is still true, access to both people and places is often contingent on whom we know. We even refer to these people as gatekeepers.

Standing in denial (John 18:17-18). {As the woman let Peter into the courtyard, she asked him if he too was not one of Jesus' disciples.}^Q3 Exactly why she suspected this about Peter is unclear. Perhaps she thought she recognized him from a previous encounter, or she may have detected his Galilean accent. A. T. Robertson notes, "She made it easy for Peter to say no" (*Word Pictures in the New Testament,* Broadman), in that "her question to

Peter is cast in the form expecting the answer 'No'" (Bruce). Worth noting too is the fact that her question is formulated to cast disparagement upon Jesus: "You're not one of *this* man's disciples, are you?" (Robertson).

At this point, Peter swiftly denied that he was one of Jesus' disciples. He would eventually deny the Lord three times, as foretold by Jesus in all four Gospels (Matt. 26:33-34; Mark 14:30; Luke 22:34; John 13:38).

The night was cool, so those gathered had built a fire to keep warm. Being "a fire of coals" (John 18:18), it was not a blazing fire that people could easily be warmed by at a distance. Such a fire would require those present to gather closely together at its edges to keep themselves warm. {Peter was likely trying to blend in with those present, and he therefore stood close to them. This decision would eventually set him up to again be challenged about knowing Jesus, leading to his further denials of Him.}^Q4

JESUS' FIRST TRIAL

19 The high priest then asked Jesus of his disciples, and of his doctrine.

20 Jesus answered him, I spake openly to the world; I ever taught in the synagogue, and in the temple, whither the Jews always resort; and in secret have I said nothing.

21 Why askest thou me? ask them which heard me, what I have said unto them: behold, they know what I said.

22 And when he had thus spoken, one of the officers which stood by struck Jesus with the palm of his hand, saying, Answerest thou the high priest so?

23 Jesus answered him, If I have spoken evil, bear witness of the evil: but if well, why smitest thou me?

24 Now Annas had sent him bound unto Caiaphas the high priest.

Interrogation and reply (John 18:19-21). {Jesus' first hearing was before Annas, the former high priest and father-in-law to Caiaphas, the current high priest.}^{Q5} The office of high priest was a lifetime position, and the Jews still considered it so despite the fact that its term was now set by the Roman authorities. Annas was still considered by many Jews as the lawful high priest, so that is undoubtedly why Jesus was brought before him first. Before things could move ahead, Annas would have to give his stamp of approval on the proceedings.

{Annas questioned Jesus about His disciples and His doctrine.}^{Q6} Since all rabbis had disciples, the high priest likely wanted to know where Jesus' followers were from and possibly why they had decided to follow Him. He may also have wanted to know how many disciples Jesus had and what revolutionary threat, if any, they might pose.

Since the high priest had connections with the Roman authorities, it is likely that he wanted to ascertain whether Jesus and His disciples were a political threat to the Jewish religious hierarchy and their always tense relationship with Rome. "This was Annas making a preliminary examination of Jesus probably to see on what terms Jesus made disciples—whether as a mere rabbi or as Messiah" (Robertson).

The high priest also questioned Jesus concerning His teaching. Since Christ had already had numerous confrontations with various religious leaders, especially the Pharisees, Annas was probably trying to decide whether His teachings were any threat to the Sadducees, the party to which he and many other priests belonged. It seems clear, however, that the religious leaders, whatever party they were associated with, were bent on ridding themselves of Jesus. While the Pharisees and Sadducees could agree on little else, they did agree that Jesus should be done away with.

{In response to the high priest's inquiry about His teachings, Jesus boldly referred him to what He had taught openly in public places of worship, both in synagogues as well as in the Jerusalem temple.}^{Q7} It was not as though Jesus had been running a covert operation. All He had taught and done had been in open, public forums.

Abusive treatment (John 18:22). Earlier in His ministry, Christ had said, "If I bear witness of myself, my witness is not true" (5:31). By this He meant that from an Old Testament legal standpoint, a person's testimony about himself does not verify any fact as true. Some objective, corroborating testimony is required to establish a fact as true. For example, if one person accuses another of a crime, but the accused person denies the charge, it is merely one person's word against another; nothing has been legally proved. Additional corroborating testimony must be presented to establish that the accused is in fact guilty of that crime.

The above being true, it was not irregular that Jesus would answer the high priest by referring him to those who had actually heard Him teach. A considerable amount of disinformation about Jesus and His teachings was circulating in Jerusalem at this time (cf. 7:12, 20, 40-43). He therefore told the high priest that he should consult those who had actually heard Him on various occasions.

{At this, one of the officers of the high priest slapped Jesus across the face with the palm of his hand. The Lord's indirect answer to the high priest was seen as insubordination and disrespect.}^{Q8} This was just the beginning of the abuse Jesus would endure at the hands of both the Jewish and the Roman authorities throughout His trial and execution.

Honest challenge (John 18:23). In response to this abuse, Jesus challenged His attacker to give a valid reason for the attack. Since Jesus had said nothing evil and had meant no such disrespect to the office of the high priest, why had the officer struck him? In a prior confrontation with the Pharisees, Jesus had challenged them by saying, "Which of you [accuses] me of sin? And if I say the truth, why do ye not believe me?" (John 8:46).

Christ was innocent of all wrongdoing, and the officer's reaction was unwarranted. This was just one of many violations of the law that occurred during the trials of Jesus. According to attorney Earle Wingo, there were fifteen obvious violations of Jewish and Roman law in the proceedings against Jesus (*The Illegal Trial of Jesus,* Charter).

Abrupt dismissal (John 18:24). {At this point, Annas had apparently heard enough. He sent Jesus to the current high priest, his son-in-law Caiaphas.}[09] As a final note concerning the term "high priest," it is used not only of the presiding high priest but of others who were leaders in the Jewish religious hierarchy. Hence, when it is used of one person, it is rendered "high priest" (John 18:10, 13, 15, 16), but when more than one priest is indicated, it is translated "chief priests" (7:32; 11:47; 18:35; 19:6). This is true in all four Gospels.

Concerning Jesus' trial before Caiaphas, the other Gospels give considerable detail (Matt. 26:57-68; Mark 14:53-65; Luke 22:54-71). These other accounts also include the fact that the Jewish supreme court, the Sanhedrin, condemned Jesus. Since not all members of the Sanhedrin had to be present to conduct business, it may have been a handpicked group that would simply rubber stamp the wishes of Annas and Caiaphas. There were, however, a few dissenters to their actions (cf. Luke 23:50-53; John 19:38-42).

PETER'S FURTHER DENIALS

25 And Simon Peter stood and warmed himself. They said therefore unto him, Art not thou also one of his disciples? He denied it, and said, I am not.

26 One of the servants of the high priest, being his kinsman whose ear Peter cut off, saith, Did not I see thee in the garden with him?

27 Peter then denied again: and immediately the cock crew.

Denial two (John 18:25). Meanwhile, Simon Peter was still warming himself at the fire along with some servants and soldiers. Someone asked him, "Art not thou also one of his disciples?" As he had done previously, Peter denied Jesus by asserting, "I am not."

This was the second time since Jesus' arrest that Peter had denied Him publicly. Peter had pledged his loyalty to Jesus, even if it meant his own death. But when he was actually faced with owning his loyalty to Christ before those who could have him arrested and punished along with his Master, his courage failed. When push came to shove, he lied to save his own skin.

This is a humbling lesson for anyone who relies on his own self-confidence in the Christian life. In I Corinthians 10:12, Paul warns us, "Let him that thinketh he standeth take heed lest he fall." It is only through the grace and power of the Holy Spirit that we can persevere in our faithfulness to Christ.

Resisting such temptation is not easy. But the Peter we see here is a stark contrast to the Peter we see in Acts 2:14-40! After the Holy Spirit had come to dwell in the church and in the hearts of every believer, Peter was emboldened to stand up and intrepidly proclaim the gospel in the very heart of Jerusalem. His preaching pierced the hearts of his listeners, compelling them to beg him to tell them what they needed to do to be saved. Even after the most dismal failure, there is yet hope of great victory if we endure in faith and reliance on God's grace.

Denial three (John 18:26-27). {One of the servants standing near the fire with Peter just happened to be related to Malchus, who had had his ear cut off by Peter. This servant had also been present in the garden when Jesus was arrested. But since it had been dark and there had been a large number of people there, he was apparently not completely certain that Peter was actually the one who had attacked Malchus. He nevertheless was suspicious. So he asked Peter pointedly, "Did not I see thee in the garden with [Jesus]?"}Q10

Upon this third denial, the rooster immediately crowed. Comparing the four accounts of Peter's denial of Christ provides additional details concerning this episode. They are all similar, but different enough to conclude that there was no collaboration between the four Evangelists.

Of note is the fact that Peter actually backed up his denials with cursing and swearing (cf. Matt. 26:72; Mark 14:71). Those present also recognized him as a Galilean because of his accent, which differed from those from Judea (cf. Matt. 26:73; Mark 14:70; Luke 22:59). Luke also mentions that Jesus looked upon Peter at this very moment (cf. 22:61), probably as He was being moved from the residence of Annas to that of Caiaphas. Upon remembering what Christ said, "Peter went out, and wept bitterly" (vs. 62).

Most believers can remember times when they have in some manner denied knowing Jesus. The world is hostile to the claims of Christ and likewise hostile to those who follow Him. This hostility is often expressed by contempt for those who publicly dare to express allegiance to Christ. It can be observed at times when a Christian sports figure gives praise and thanks to Jesus Christ for his or her success. The interviewer seldom acknowledges what has just been said, urgently endeavoring instead to change the subject. Talking about Jesus invariably makes worldly people uncomfortable. Sometimes it makes them upset or even angry and belligerent.

We must therefore be ever vigilant concerning temptations to deny Christ that are continually before us in the world (cf. I Cor. 10:12-13). Concerning Satan's tricks, Paul declares, "We are not ignorant of his devices" (II Cor. 2:11). But bold reliance on the power of the Holy Spirit who dwells in us will give us courage to represent Christ as faithful ambassadors. As John wrote to the readers of his first epistle, "Ye are of God, little children, and have overcome them: because greater is he that is in you, than he that is in the world" (4:4).
—John Alva Owston.

QUESTIONS

1. Which disciples followed Jesus after His arrest?
2. How did those disciples gain entrance to the high priest's house?
3. Who first challenged Peter about whether he was Jesus' disciple?
4. What did Peter do that set him up for his subsequent denials of Jesus?
5. Who first questioned Jesus after His arrest?
6. What two things was Jesus questioned about?
7. How did Jesus respond to the question about His teachings?
8. Why did the officer slap Jesus across the face?
9. Where was Jesus sent next?
10. Who challenged Peter about Jesus the third time?
—John Alva Owston.

Preparing to Teach the Lesson

It was the worst night of Jesus' life. How did He handle it? What did He do? To whom did He turn? On this night everyone turned their backs on Him while His enemies put in motion their plot to kill Him. Jesus had no one to turn to. One of His disciples betrayed Him, and the others abandoned Him in Gethsemane (cf. Mark 14:50). To make matters worse, one of His closest disciples would deny even knowing Him before the night was over.

We too sometimes face rejection from people, both friend and foe alike. When we are rejected by people, we can turn to Christ because He will never reject those who come to Him in faith and love. You can know that He loves you no matter what kinds of situations you may go through or mistakes you have made. He will never leave you, nor forsake you (Heb. 13:5), and He is the Friend that sticks closer than a brother (Prov. 18:24).

TODAY'S AIM

Facts: to examine how Jesus is tried by the high priest while Peter denies knowing Him.

Principle: to recognize Christ's faithfulness in a situation where men were unfaithful.

Application: to always turn to Christ when others turn away, knowing that He is always faithful.

INTRODUCING THE LESSON

After Jesus was arrested, the activity of the night began as He was put on trial before rulers who were trying to find Him guilty of a crime and execute Him. The whole focus of the religious leaders in Jerusalem was on putting Jesus to death. They were not going to rest until they masterminded a way to get the Romans to crucify their enemy; these leaders were relentless in their hatred of Jesus.

DEVELOPING THE LESSON

1. Peter's first denial of Jesus (John 18:15-18). When Jesus was taken to Annas, Peter and another disciple (probably John) followed Him. A peculiarity of John's writing style in his Gospel was not to mention himself by name but to employ other designations such as "the disciple whom Jesus loved" (cf. 13:23; 19:26; 20:2; 21:7, 20). Such a stylistic signal seems to be at play here, as there there is not really any other reason to keep only one disciple anonymous.

This other disciple knew the high priest and was able to gain access to the courtyard with Jesus while Peter stayed outside near the door. Because of his familiarity with the high priest, John was able to bring Peter in.

The girl who stood watch at the door saw Peter and immediately voiced her suspicion that he too was a follower of Jesus. When the servant girl challenged him, he denied it, thus denying Jesus. When he had been safe among his fellow disciples, he was bold to say that he would never betray or deny Jesus even at the risk of his own death. But now Peter was doing exactly what he said he would never do (cf. Mark 14:31).

Peter was trying to blend in with the others who were present that night. Because it was cold outside, the servants and officers built a fire. Peter could not resist the warmth and went and stood by the fire and warmed himself up, never confessing that he knew Christ.

2. Jesus before the high priest (John 18:19-24). The high priest mentioned here was Annas, who was actually the former high priest and the father-in-law of the current high priest. He is mentioned as the high priest because he was still very powerful and was probably still viewed as the real power behind the actual high priest.

The high priest expressed interest in Jesus' disciples and what He had been teaching them. In asking about His disciples, Annas was probably interested in knowing whether they had been training for sedition against the Roman authorities. Regarding doctrine, he was trying to get Jesus' teaching on the record for the purpose of twisting His words to condemn Him. The charge in this case would have been blasphemy (cf. Matt. 26:65; Mark 14:64).

Jesus explained that He spoke openly to everyone in synagogues throughout Galilee and Judea as well as the temple in Jerusalem and not in secret places or hidden meetings. He said to ask those who heard Him about His teaching.

At this response, one of the officers slapped Jesus in the face, accusing Him of disrespecting the high priest. Jesus, however, challenged the officer to spell out exactly what He said that was wrong. Otherwise, why did he hit Him?

After hearing this, Annas had Jesus bound again and sent to Caiaphas, the sitting high priest. It is clear that the two most powerful religious leaders in Jerusalem were conspiring to convict and kill Jesus. The guilty verdict was already determined before the trial even started.

3. Peter's second and third denials (John 18:25-27). While Jesus was being interrogated by Annas and sent to Caiaphas for further questioning, Peter was still outside by the fire. He was again asked about being a disciple of Jesus. He quickly denied any association with Jesus, making this the second time he denied Him.

A relative of the man whose ear he cut off then voiced his suspicion that he had seen Peter with Jesus in the garden, and Peter denied Jesus a third time.

Right after the third denial, the rooster crowed. Peter had denied Jesus three times, just as Jesus said he would (John 13:38). His brash talk turned out to be empty boasting.

Note the contrast between the faithfulness of Jesus in a criminal trial before powerful men and the unfaithfulness of Peter before servants.

ILLUSTRATING THE LESSON

Christians are called to stand out for Christ, not try to blend in with the world.

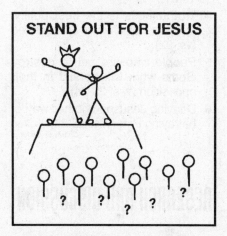

CONCLUDING THE LESSON

As we can see, Jesus' enemies used deceit and manipulation in order to execute their wicked plan to destroy Jesus. No one that night wanted to admit to knowing Jesus, including one of His closest friends—a man He had called on to pray with Him right before He was arrested. Where do you stand? Are you trying to blend in, or do you stand out?

ANTICIPATING THE NEXT LESSON

In next week's lesson, Jesus is sent before Pontus Pilate, the Roman procurator appointed by Caesar to oversee Judea, for questioning as the plan to execute Jesus continues.

—*Robert Ferguson, Jr.*

PRACTICAL POINTS

1. The Lord can use earthly connections to place us where He wants us (John 18:15-16).
2. A focus on our own comfort can keep us from testifying to others about our relationship with Jesus (vss. 17-18).
3. Integrity means doing and saying the right thing at all times (vss. 19-21).
4. Truthfulness is the best policy, but it is not always appreciated (vs. 22).
5. People who are out to destroy God's work will persist in their opposition (vss. 23-24).
6. Denying Jesus is another way of betraying Him (vss. 25-27).

—*Charity G. Carter.*

RESEARCH AND DISCUSSION

1. There were eleven disciples, not including Judas Iscariot. Discuss why only two of them followed Jesus to the palace (John 18:15).
2. The Bible is not clear on who the other disciple was, but some say it was John. Do you agree? Why or why not?
3. Why did Peter deny Jesus (vss. 17, 25)?
4. Did the officer have a legitimate reason for striking Jesus (vss. 22-23)?
5. Peter denied Jesus three times (vs. 27). List ways in which people deny Jesus today.

—*Charity G. Carter.*

ILLUSTRATED HIGH POINTS

I am not (John 18:17)

We tend to think that Peter's motivation for his denials was fear of what the authorities would do to him if he were to acknowledge an association with Jesus. After all, they had just arrested Jesus and put Him on trial.

A member of our youth group wrote a brief skit that put Peter's denials in a different light. The teen surmised that since the people who confronted Peter were not authorities, they may have wanted to know more about Jesus. In this understanding, Peter missed an opportunity to share the gospel.

Either way, his answers were failures: he denied his allegiance to his Master. We usually place enormous blame on Peter for this. But think of the many ways we have also denied our Lord at times: by being silent when we should speak, by not exercising our spiritual gifts for the building up of the church, by being stingy when we could give, by forsaking the assembling of ourselves together, by complaining instead of thanking God for His blessings, by gossiping—and the list could go on and on.

Peter then denied again (John 18:27)

This is the third time Peter was challenged. Mathew 26:74 says, "Then began he to curse and to swear." We tend to do this as well. Have you ever been asked repeatedly about the same thing? It is tempting to say something like "I swear on my life, my mother's grave," or some like thing to truly show that you mean business. That is what Peter was doing.

But James admonishes us to "swear not, neither by heaven, neither by the earth, neither by any other oath: but let your yea be yea; and your nay, nay; lest ye fall into condemnation" (5:12).

—*David A. Hamburg.*

Golden Text Illuminated

"Jesus said, I am: and ye shall see the Son of man sitting on the right hand of power, and coming in the clouds of heaven" (Mark 14:62).

Many scholars believe that Mark was the first to write a Gospel. Regardless of the order of the Gospels, it is well known that Mark contains very few accounts that are not found in one of the other three Gospels. Yet in the accounts it does have, it is more detailed than the others. This week's golden text contains a detail not found in Matthew, Luke, or John. The account of Jesus' trial in Mark is significant for two reasons.

First, this week's text represents one of Jesus' most aggressive statements. The high priest was badgering Him for a confession: "Art thou the Christ, the Son of the Blessed?" (Mark 14:61). As discussed last week, the reply, "I am," is more than a simple affirmation. The Greek is emphatic and recalls the divine name in Exodus 3:14. The high priest asked Jesus if He was the Messiah, a claimant to David's throne, and Jesus answered boldly, intimating that He was God Himself.

When Jesus stood before Pilate and Herod, He answered humbly (or not at all), but this word spoken before the high priest contained an implicit challenge. During the Davidic monarchy, king and high priest were separate offices, but during the Second Temple period, Israel's Gentile rulers usually placed a king of their own choosing over Jewish affairs. The high priesthood, therefore, became the highest office that Jews could hold, but the expected Messiah would unite the offices of priest and king (Ps. 110:4; Zech. 6:12-13), rendering the Aaronic high priest obsolete.

The second important feature in this verse is Jesus' reference to Daniel's vision of the Son of Man receiving eternal, worldwide dominion from God the Father (7:13-14). Jesus' interpretation of that passage is interesting because Daniel sees the Son of Man traveling *to* God on the clouds, which Luke seems to allude to in Acts 1:9. Psalm 110:1 continues the story: God invites the Son to sit at His right hand while He makes Messiah's enemies a footstool for His feet. Jesus, however, tells the high priest what happens next: Christ will return to earth on the clouds and take His throne.

The high priest did not have the historical perspective that we have today and likely thought that Jesus was threatening to enact this chain of events immediately. Quickly, therefore, he and the Sanhedrin sentenced Jesus to death, not knowing that they were initiating the very sequence they feared. Thus, Jesus' challenge to the high priest could be thought of in terms of the modern phrase "Go ahead, make My day!"

We often view Jesus as a passive rabbi who set children on His lap and hugged lambs, but we need to consider His response here when the high priest bullied Him.

Christians today live in an increasingly hostile environment, so we need to remember that Jesus is Lord (I Cor. 12:3). The Lamb on the cross is also the Lion on the throne (cf. Rev. 5:5; 22:3). He will soon return to earth not only with clouds, but leading an army of His saints ready to rule the earth with Him (cf. Dan. 7:27).

—*David Samuel Gifford.*

Heart of the Lesson

If I'm shopping or eating out on Fridays, the young people waiting on me often ask me about my plans for the weekend. I realize they are trying to create friendly customer relations rather than being nosy, so when I have plans, I say I'm going to a concert, for example. If I have no plans, I say I plan to relax. (Who can argue with that?)

I've also started adding I'll be going to church, a subtle witness to my faith in Jesus. Sometimes, I worry that I will never be a better witness, but I feel hope when I read this week's text about Peter.

1. Denial at the gate (John 18:15-18). After Jesus' arrest, the disciples fled. Peter worked up enough courage to follow Jesus to the high priest's residence from afar to see what would happen.

At some point in the night, he met up with another disciple, probably John. Because he somehow knew the high priest, John was able to enter the house where Sanhedrin members were trying Jesus. The Sanhedrin was the highest Jewish religious court, which the Romans allowed to oversee minor civil matters and Jewish civil law and religion.

Peter waited outside the gate. John returned and got the young woman guarding the gate to allow Peter inside. As he entered, she casually asked him if he was one of Jesus' disciples. Her question made him uneasy. Ahead was likely a hostile crowd full of temple guards and the high priest's servants. He quickly denied he was a disciple.

The evening was cold, so Peter joined a group huddled around a fire. Maybe here he could blend in.

2. Trial before Annas (John 18:19-24). Meanwhile, Annas, the high official questioned Jesus about His disciples and His doctrine. Jesus said He had spoken to the world in synagogues and in the temple. His teachings were no secret; large crowds heard Him speak. He suggested Annas ask witnesses about His doctrine. After all, Jewish law required witnesses and forbade using the suspect's words in trial as evidence against him. Jesus knew he was fishing for Him to say something self-incriminating.

At Jesus' answer, a temple guard slapped Him in the face and asked if that was any way to address the high priest. Jesus said that if He had said something wrong, the officer should specify it. But if He spoke truth about how the Sanhedrin was supposed to hold trials, Why did the guard hit Him?

3. Denial at the fire (John 18:25-27). During Jesus' trial, Peter stayed close to the fire. Those standing nearby asked if he was one of Jesus' disciples. His accent revealed he was from up north—a Galilean. Again, he denied he was a disciple.

But a servant of the high priest remembered Peter as the man who cut off his relative Malchus's ear and confronted him, "Did not I see thee in the garden with him?" They knew. Peter probably felt terrified. Again, he denied his relationship with the Lord. Then, just as Jesus had predicted, the cock crowed.

Peter's loyalty to Jesus put him in a tense situation in which he failed. All Christians stumble at times. The story of Peter's denial and restoration is a comfort to me, especially when I struggle to be a bold witness. Fortunately, when we fail, Jesus forgives, just as He forgave Peter and used him in founding the church. God's patience and mercy motivate me to never give up.

—Ann Staatz

World Missions

Jesus beckons to all, "If any man will come after me, let him deny himself, and take up his cross daily, and follow me" (Luke 9:23).

On the night Jesus was arrested, two men would face trials.

One faced the judgment of those infinitely far beneath Him in a trial with false accusers, took up the cross He was born to carry, "and became obedient unto death, even the death of the cross" (Phil. 2:8). The other would vehemently deny that he knew the Lord--not once, but three times.

We might be tempted to judge Peter's cowardice, but we must remember that we too fail often to show an appropriate boldness for Christ and a willingness to sacrifice on His behalf. We do not always deny ourselves, and we therefore find ourselves in the same sin as Peter.

Eric Liddell was an Olympic gold medalist. Although one of the fastest men in the world, Mr. Liddell shortened his athletic career and denied himself the continued renown that may have gained him. Instead, he took up his cross and followed the Lord to China, where he served as a missionary.

With World War II breaking out, Eric refused to leave the country where God had called him to serve. He would die in an internment camp.

Years before, when someone had asked him if he regretted giving up athletics to become a missionary, he said, "It's natural for a chap to think over all that sometimes, but I'm glad I'm at the work I'm engaged in now. A fellow's life counts for far more at this than the other" (Simon Burnton, "50 Stunning Olympic Moments: No. 8 Eric Liddell's 400 Metres Win, 1924," *The Guardian*, theguardian.com).

Eric Liddell remained faithful and bold, making sacrifices for the cause of Christ. Peter also remained faithful even unto martyrdom (John 21:19). This contrasts with his earlier denial of Christ.

Before Christ's arrest, He warned Peter that the flock would scatter, but Peter said, "Though all men shall be offended because of thee, yet will I never be offended" (Matt. 26:33).

Christ responded by stating that Peter would deny Him three times (vs. 34), but Peter said, "Though I should die with thee, yet will I not deny thee" (vs. 35).

The proper response to Jesus' somber promise would have been to ask Him for the strength and boldness to not deny Him. Peter's protest seems to be an indication that he thought his own strength would be enough, so he rather foolishly denies Jesus' words.

Israel also declared that they would obey God's law. Moses writes, "All the people answered with one voice, and said, All the words which the Lord hath said will we do" (Exod. 24:3). And yet how many times do we read of Israel's failure to follow God's command?

We too tend to trust in our own strength, but Jesus admonishes, "For without me ye can do nothing" (John 15:5).

After His resurrection, Jesus restored Peter (21:15-19). "And when he had spoken this, he saith unto him, Follow me" (vs. 19).

God will lead each of us on the path we need to take to glorify Him. For Eric Liddell, that meant China. What does it mean for us? "And he saith unto them, Follow me, and I will make you fishers of men" (Matt. 4:19).

We must ever follow Christ, asking Him for the boldness needed to sacrifice for Him.

—Jody Stinson.

The Jewish Aspect

After Jesus' arrest in Gethsemane, the Jews took Him to Annas, where His Jewish "trials" began (John 18:12-13). Annas was the father-in-law of Caiaphas, who was the official high priest. Annas, however, had also served as high priest from A.D. 7–15. After four men held the position during the next three years, the procurator Valerius chose Caiaphas in A.D. 18, and Caiaphas was the official high priest for the next eighteen years. Many Jews, however, continued to consider Annas the high priest (cf. Luke 3:2; Acts 4:6). Respecting his position, the Jews began the proceedings against Jesus with Annas.

The oral Jewish laws were precise in their regulations, as Rabbi Judah Ha-Nasi (ca. A.D. 135–217) demonstrated in his later codification of them in the Mishnah ("Law, Codification of," www.jewishencyclopedia.com). Many of its procedures were grossly violated during Jesus' trials. Starting with Jesus' "private" interrogation before Annas, which itself was not allowed in accepted Jewish law, the Jewish authorities did not do their job of securing witnesses at an early stage (cf. John 18:20-21). The final breach of Jewish law in this first trial was the attempt to trap Jesus into admitting something that could be used against Him later.

Annas then sent Jesus to Caiaphas for His second so-called trial (Matt. 26:57-68; Mark 14:53-65; Luke 22:54). This was held before the Sanhedrin, "the scribes and the elders" (Matt. 26:57). There were seventy members of the Sanhedrin in addition to the high priest who presided over the council. Only twenty-three, however, needed to be present for a quorum. Again, numerous Jewish legal procedures were broken in this trial.

First, it occurred at night, whereas all criminal trials were to be conducted by daylight. Second, it unlawfully sought to try a capital crime on the day preceding the Sabbath. Third, it met at Caiaphas' home when it was required to meet at the appointed location for the Sanhedrin. Fourth, it purposely sought out false witnesses, which violated not only Jewish jurisprudence but God's clear instructions as well (Deut. 19:15-19). Fifth, Caiaphas directly attempted to cause Jesus to speak against Himself. Finally, it was illegal to beat Jesus and spit on Him after pronouncing the guilty verdict. Clearly, the Jewish leaders consciously and purposefully flouted their own law to condemn Jesus.

The third Jewish trial, the sentencing phase, which was also before the Sanhedrin, sought to make the proceedings seem proper (Matt. 27:1; Mark 15:1; Luke 22:66-71). Since the Jews would take Jesus before Pilate, they had to give the appearance of legal authority. Yet they still violated their own jurisprudence. This trial was conducted on a feast day—another legal violation. In addition, Jesus' foes again tried to have Jesus incriminate Himself. Once accomplished, in their thinking, the Jewish leaders were then prepared to take Jesus before Pilate to seek a sentence of execution from the governor.

Each of the Jewish trials violated accepted Jewish legal standards. Rather than object to the illegal proceedings, however, Jesus endured it all with no objection or appeal (cf. Isa. 53:7). He did that because He fully yielded to the Father's will in all these details (Matt. 26:39, 42; John 10:17-18; 19:11). Jesus willingly "endured the cross, despising the shame" (Heb. 12:2), so that Jew and Gentile could obtain full and free salvation.

—R. Larry Overstreet.

Guiding the Superintendent

Over and over again, God reveals to us the weaknesses and sins of His choicest servants. Even Peter, the disciple who would be the most significant leader in the early church, is seen at his lowest moment after the arrest of Jesus. The one who boasted that he would be loyal to Jesus—even if everyone else failed Him—denied Him within hours of this arrogant claim.

DEVOTIONAL OUTLINE

1. Peter's first denial (John 18:15-18). John and Peter were able to enter the palace where Jesus was tried because of John's relationship with the high priest (vss. 15-16). The doorkeeper recognized Peter and asked if he was a disciple of Jesus (vs. 16). At this moment, Peter failed to take a stand and denied his relationship to Jesus (vs. 17).

When our commitment is tested, will we take a stand for Christ or will we try our best to fit into the crowd?

2. Jesus' first trial (John 18:19-24). John shifts the narrative from Peter's denials to the first religious trial of Jesus. He was led to Annas, the former high priest. The current high priest was Caiaphas, the son-in-law of Annas. Jesus was brought to Annas because the Jews still respected his authority.

Annas despised Jesus. His goal was to find a reason to have Jesus crucified that would be accepted by the Romans, so he examined Him about His disciples and His teaching (vs. 19). The questioning of Jesus was a violation of the Jewish legal procedure that the accused was not required to testify against himself.

On the surface, Jesus' response may sound disrespectful (vss. 20-21). However, Jesus was merely pointing out the hypocrisy of this religious leader. Annas was trying to make Jesus look like a revolutionary who secretly taught things that would cause a revolt. Jesus simply said that He did not teach secretly, but publicly in the temple.

One of the temple officers was upset with the answer of Jesus and struck Him with his palm (vs. 22). Jesus responded with a rebuke, exposing the failure to follow procedure. If they had witnesses, it was their responsibility to find them and bring them to the trial to testify (cf. Deut. 17:6-7; 19:15-19; John 18:23). Frustrated, Annas sent Jesus to Caiaphas for another trial (John 18:24).

3. Peter's final denials (John 18:25-27). The narrative returns to Peter. He was again recognized, and he again denied (vs. 25). A third time he was identified—this time by a relative of the one whose ear had been cut off in the garden (vs. 26). Once again Peter denied his relationship with Jesus. At that exact moment, the cock crowed (vs. 27).

Peter's life teaches us that no matter how strong we think we are, no one is strong enough to live for Christ in his own strength.

CHILDREN'S CORNER

Be sure to have your teachers explain what a trial is and what makes one fair. Perhaps you should suggest that your teachers give an analogy about the children getting in trouble at home, school, or church and procedures for fairly handling these situations.

Also, make sure your teachers explain what a denial is and why Peter's actions were so cowardly. Perhaps have them draw a parallel between how the children would feel if their sibling or parents denied knowing them out of shame.

—Robert Winter.

SCRIPTURE LESSON TEXT

JOHN 18:28 Then led they Jesus from Caiaphas unto the hall of judgment: and it was early; and they themselves went not into the judgment hall, lest they should be defiled; but that they might eat the passover.

29 Pilate then went out unto them, and said, What accusation bring ye against this man?

30 They answered and said unto him, If he were not a malefactor, we would not have delivered him up unto thee.

31 Then said Pilate unto them, Take ye him, and judge him according to your law. The Jews therefore said unto him, It is not lawful for us to put any man to death:

32 That the saying of Jesus might be fulfilled, which he spake, signifying what death he should die.

33 Then Pilate entered into the judgment hall again, and called Jesus, and said unto him, Art thou the King of the Jews?

34 Jesus answered him, Sayest thou this thing of thyself, or did others tell it thee of me?

35 Pilate answered, Am I a Jew? Thine own nation and the chief priests have delivered thee unto me: what hast thou done?

36 Jesus answered, My kingdom is not of this world: if my kingdom were of this world, then would my servants fight, that I should not be delivered to the Jews: but now is my kingdom not from hence.

37 Pilate therefore said unto him, Art thou a king then? Jesus answered, Thou sayest that I am a king. To this end was I born, and for this cause came I into the world, that I should bear witness unto the truth. Every one that is of the truth heareth my voice.

38 Pilate saith unto him, What is truth? And when he had said this, he went out again unto the Jews, and saith unto them, I find in him no fault *at all.*

39 But ye have a custom, that I should release unto you one at the passover: will ye therefore that I release unto you the King of the Jews?

40 Then cried they all again, saying, Not this man, but Barabbas. Now Barabbas was a robber.

NOTES

144

Pilate: What Is Truth?

Lesson Text: John 18:28-40

Related Scriptures: Isaiah 53:1-9; Matthew 27:11-18, 20-24;
Mark 15:1-15; Luke 18:32-33; 23:1-25

TIME: A.D. 30   PLACE: Jerusalem

GOLDEN TEXT—"Jesus answered, My kingdom is not of this world: if my kingdom were of this world, then would my servants fight, that I should not be delivered to the Jews: but now is my kingdom not from hence" (John 18:36).

Introduction

Justice is a great concern for many people and should be a concern of all. A careful observer realizes, however, that we live in a world where injustice often prevails. Criminals may get away with evil deeds for many years before being apprehended. Even then, a conviction is not necessarily assured. Sometimes an offender may even be released on a technicality. Police and judges are often bribed.

As Solomon said, "There is no new thing under the sun" (Eccl. 1:9). This certainly applies to injustice. Whatever accounts of injustice we may be aware of, either ancient or modern, none can compare to the injustice that was perpetrated throughout the trial of Jesus Christ. But even this monumental injustice was a tool in the hand of the sovereign God to bring salvation to the world.

LESSON OUTLINE

I. DELIVERED TO THE
   GENTILES—John 18:28-32

II. FACED WITH THE TRUTH—
   John 18:33-38*a*

III. TRUTH DISCARDED—
   John 18:38*b*-40

Exposition: Verse by Verse

DELIVERED TO THE GENTILES

JOHN 18:28 Then led they Jesus from Caiaphas unto the hall of judgment: and it was early; and they themselves went not into the judgment hall, lest they should be defiled; but that they might eat the passover.

29 Pilate then went out unto them, and said, What accusation bring ye against this man?

30 They answered and said unto him, If he were not a malefactor, we would not have delivered him up unto thee.

31 Then said Pilate unto them,

Take ye him, and judge him according to your law. The Jews therefore said unto him, It is not lawful for us to put any man to death:

32 That the saying of Jesus might be fulfilled, which he spake, signifying what death he should die.

Fear of defilement (John 18:28). Within a matter of hours after His arrest in Gethsemane, Jesus endured six trials. These were before Annas, Caiaphas, the Sanhedrin, Pilate, Herod Antipas, and Pilate again—a lot of legal proceedings for one day, especially when we realize that the outcome was already decided before the first trial. Jesus stood before all the authorities of His time: the Jewish authorities, the Roman authorities, and even the Galilean authorities. Providentially, this makes all the peoples of the world responsible for Jesus' condemnation and death. No one is innocent of His blood—yet His blood redeems us all!

After being formally charged with blasphemy before the Sanhedrin, over which Caiaphas presided (Mark 14:53-65), Jesus was led away to Pilate, the Roman governor. {The "hall of judgment" (John 18:28) is literally the "praetorium," the residence of the governor. Since the governor's primary residence was in Caesarea, this alternate residence was used by Pilate whenever he was in Jerusalem.}[Q1] That the Roman governor and a large contingent of soldiers were present was a precautionary measure, since Jewish nationalism ran high during the Passover. A Jewish rebellion was always anticipated at such times.

It was still early morning, not very long after Peter had denied Jesus the third time at daybreak. The trial before the Sanhedrin would not have taken long, since they had already decided that they wanted to put Christ to death. {The Jewish leaders were very scrupulous about avoiding ceremonial defilement, so they refused to enter Pilate's residence. It is ironic that they were so obsessed with avoiding defilement from contact with a Gentile yet could be oblivious to the defilement they would incur in condemning an innocent man to death by crucifixion!}[Q2]

Concerning the Passover, John's comment seems to indicate that the feast had not yet occurred. If correct, that means Jesus and the Twelve had eaten the Passover one day early. But a more likely possibility is that "Passover" is used here of the week-long Feast of Unleavened Bread that followed the actual Passover meal. Either way, the leaders' religious scruples betrayed their blatant hypocrisy. "These men were scrupulous to avoid any ritual defilement even while they were carrying out the most vile act of human history. As they delivered the Lamb of God to the slaughter, they made sure their hands were ceremonially clean" (Sproul, *John,* Reformation Trust).

Empty denunciation (John 18:29-31). Placating the Jewish leaders, Pilate came outside to hear their complaint. {As Roman governor, he alone held the legal power of life or death over those accused of crimes. Jesus' trial occurred at a time in which the Jewish authorities no longer were allowed to execute criminals themselves.}[Q3] That power had been taken from them by the Romans around 6 or 7 B.C.

This is significant because it again shows God's sovereign, providential ordering of history so that Jesus' prophecies would be fulfilled—that He would be delivered over to the Gentiles to be crucified (cf. Matt. 20:19; Mark 10:33; Luke 18:31-33). If the Jews had still retained the power of capital punishment at this time, His death would have been carried out by stoning, the prescribed Jewish method (Barnes, *Barnes' Notes on the Bible,* Baker).

Although the Jewish authorities had already condemned Jesus to death, they knew that their condemnation had to be confirmed and carried out by Roman authority. Rather than explicitly state the controversial nature of Jesus' crime to a Gentile authority, they tried to get Pilate to take their word alone as sufficient grounds for Jesus' execution. {The word "malefactor" merely means "evil doer." The word "criminal" would be a modern equivalent.}[Q4]

Fulfillment of prophecy (John 18:32). On numerous occasions (cf. Matt. 20:18-19; 26:2; Mark 8:31; 9:31; 10:33-34; Luke 9:22, 25, 51), Jesus had told His disciples that He was headed to Jerusalem, where He would be rejected and killed. That the means of His death would be by crucifixion is implied in statements about Him being "lifted up" (John 3:14; 12:32-33). {In order for all of these prophecies to be fulfilled, the Jews needed to hand Jesus over to the Romans for crucifixion.}[Q5]

The Old Testament stipulated that if a criminal was executed and then hanged on a tree, his body must be taken down and buried by nightfall (Deut. 21:22-23). This was because anyone so hanged was cursed by God, and leaving him hanging after nightfall would spread that curse upon the land itself. Quoting this verse, Paul writes, "Christ hath redeemed us from the curse of the law, being made a curse for us: for it is written, Cursed is every one that hangeth on a tree" (Gal. 3:13).

In Jesus' case, hanging on a tree had to do with crucifixion. As Peter writes, "Who his own self bare our sins in his own body on the tree" (I Pet. 2:24).

Crucifixion was an extremely painful and humiliating manner of death. In some cases, a victim would hang on the cross for days before succumbing. As a public display, it was intended to strike fear into the hearts of those witnessing it, reinforcing the seriousness of breaking Roman law.

{Realizing that the Jewish religious leaders were trying to entangle him in some religious dispute, Pilate told them to deal with Jesus on their own.}[Q6] When they made clear that they wanted Jesus' death, a sentence beyond their legal authority, Pilate likely was surprised that Jesus could have done something to merit such a serious penalty. He would have to examine Jesus personally to ascertain His guilt or innocence for himself.

FACED WITH THE TRUTH

33 Then Pilate entered into the judgment hall again, and called Jesus, and said unto him, Art thou the King of the Jews?

34 Jesus answered him, Sayest thou this thing of thyself, or did others tell it thee of me?

35 Pilate answered, Am I a Jew? Thine own nation and the chief priests have delivered thee unto me: what hast thou done?

36 Jesus answered, My kingdom is not of this world: if my kingdom were of this world, then would my servants fight, that I should not be delivered to the Jews: but now is my kingdom not from hence.

37 Pilate therefore said unto him, Art thou a king then? Jesus answered, Thou sayest that I am a king. To this end was I born, and for this cause came I into the world, that I should bear witness unto the truth. Every one that is of the truth heareth my voice.

38a Pilate saith unto him, What is truth?

Two-way interrogation (John 18:33-35). Pilate took Jesus back into the praetorium to question Him, away from the interference of the Jewish authorities. Luke tells us that the Jews had told Pilate, "We found this fellow perverting the nation, and forbidding to give tribute to Caesar, saying that he himself is Christ a king" (Luke 23:2). {Clearly, they were accusing Jesus of being a political insurrectionist, and therefore a threat to

Roman authority.}[Q7]

Having no doubt dealt with the Jews falsely accusing others, Pilate knew that he had to question Jesus himself if he was going to take responsibility for His punishment and whatever consequences it might precipitate. If the charges turned out to be false, Pilate did not wish to be a pawn of the Jewish leaders to carry out their dirty work.

When asked pointedly if He claimed to be the King of the Jews, Jesus answered as He often did by asking another question. He wanted to know if this was Pilate's own inquiry or if he was merely repeating what others had told him. "Now who was the interrogator? Suddenly, Pilate was on trial before the Judge of heaven and earth . . . Jesus understood the rules of evidence, and He knew hearsay convictions were prohibited. But Pilate responded like a seasoned, cynical politician" (Sproul).

"Pilate may also have been expressing his surprise that Jesus did not look like a pretender to the vacant throne of Judaism. He had expected to meet a sullen or belligerent rebel and met instead the calm majesty of confident superiority. He could not reconcile the character of the prisoner with the charge brought against him" (Barker and Kohlenberger, eds., *The Expositor's Bible Commentary, Abridged*, Zondervan).

To Jesus' question, Pilate answered, "Am I a Jew?" (John 18:35). Obviously, he was not, and the grammatical form of the question expects a negative answer. As the chief Roman official in the region, Pilate was not used to being questioned or challenged; he wanted answers to his questions, not counter questions from the accused. Further, he had no interest in the Jews and their obsessions with messiahs and prophecies. He needed to know only one thing: Did Jesus' alleged claim to be King of the Jews pose a threat to Roman occupation and stability? Was He planning to overthrow Roman rule?

Pilate's agitated response indicates that he was feeling frustrated with the entire affair. He wanted to establish what Jesus' legal culpability was under Roman law, if any, and get back to his morning's business. "What have you done?" he asked Christ tersely but emphatically.

A different kind of kingdom (John 18:36). Jesus' calmly profound response to Pilate's impatience changes the entire atmosphere of the interrogation. "My kingdom is not of this world" is significant on many levels. For Pilate, it was a direct clarification that Jesus was indeed no political threat to Rome. Rome's empire was of this present world only. The proof that Jesus had no such designs upon Rome's authority was that His servants did not fight to prevent His arrest. Jesus' kingdom was of another kind entirely.

{When Jesus said, "My kingdom is not of this world," He was declaring that His kingdom was from another place or realm. It is a heavenly kingdom, spiritual in nature, and incomprehensible to the fallen human mind.}[Q8] Jesus was saying, "My kingdom is not like your kingdom. My kingdom is not built on violence, on blood, on war. That's the way the kingdoms of this world function. My kingdom is not a world-like kingdom.'" (Sproul).

The challenge of truth (John 18:37-38*a*). Since Jesus had spoken of His kingdom, Pilate pressed Him to tell him more about it. Confirming that Pilate was correct in his assumption, Jesus revealed that the very reason He had been born was to bear witness to the truth and that all those who are of the truth hear and respond to His witness.

Pilate may have thought Jesus was merely making philosophical speculations, but standing right before him was the very embodiment of Divine Truth itself. {Pilate's response, "What is truth?"

has puzzled commentators. It is uncertain whether his question was sincere or scornful. Most do think he was being cynical. Being an educated man, Pilate was likely familiar with many conflicting philosophical discussions on the nature of truth.}[Q9]

TRUTH DISCARDED

38b And when he had said this, he went out again unto the Jews, and saith unto them, I find in him no fault at all.

39 But ye have a custom, that I should release unto you one at the passover: will ye therefore that I release unto you the King of the Jews?

40 Then cried they all again, saying, Not this man, but Barabbas. Now Barabbas was a robber.

An attempt at reprieve (John 18:38b-39). As the Roman authority in Jerusalem, Pilate himself was considered the arbiter of truth within his own jurisdiction. Apparently, the charges against Jesus brought by the chief priests had not passed muster with him as truth. He therefore declared to them, "I find in him no fault at all." This is one of three times in John's Gospel that Pilate fatefully declares Jesus' complete innocence (cf. 19:4, 6).

Pilate intended his words in a strictly legal sense, but as with the unintended prophetic meaning in a statement by Caiaphas (cf. 11:50-51), these three declarations of Jesus' perfect innocence carry a prophetic and theological import for John's readers. They remain a thrice-repeated and therefore supreme testimony of Christ's sinlessness.

Since there existed at this time an annual good-will gesture of releasing one prisoner at Passover, Pilate suggested that Jesus might be that one to be released at this time. But he apparently had underestimated the intense hatred the Jewish leaders had for Jesus.

Repudiation of truth (John 18:40). {Pilate had found the innocent man from Nazareth guiltless of any crimes punishable under Roman law. But instead of agreeing to His release, the chief priests and their cronies railed furiously against any such notion. They instead clamored vociferously for the release of Barabbas, a notorious criminal who was a convicted insurrectionist and murderer}[Q10] (Mark 15:7; Luke 23:18-19)! How ironic that they chose to compound their sin not only by condemning an innocent man, but also by pardoning a murderer and seditionist!

In a further ironic twist, "Barabbas" means "son of a father." The true Son of the Heavenly Father was being traded for a vile criminal with no real name.

—*John Alva Owston.*

QUESTIONS

1. What was the "hall of judgment?" (John 18:28)?
2. Why did the Jews refuse to enter the hall of judgment?
3. Why did the Jewish authorities need to take Jesus to Pilate?
4. What is a "malefactor" (vs. 30)?
5. For what other reason was it important that Jesus be turned over to the Romans?
6. What was Pilate's initial response to the Jewish leaders' demand?
7. What accusation against Jesus did the Jewish leaders bring that caught Pilate's attention?
8. What did Jesus mean by saying that His kingdom "is not of this world" (vs. 36)?
9. What did Pilate mean by his response, "What is truth" (vs. 38)?
10. Who was Barabbas?

—*John Alva Owston.*

Preparing to Teach the Lesson

In a time when much of modern-day thinking rejects the reality of objective knowledge, it is becoming more difficult for many people to recognize truth when they see it. In fact, the concept of truth has become outdated and old-fashioned to many modern critics of Christianity.

Jesus Christ stands in direct confrontation with the relativism of today's societal climate. He not only brought a timeless message of truth to the world; indeed, He is the very embodiment of truth. We cannot deal honestly with the teachings and Person of Jesus while attempting to sidestep truth. Some things are true, and other things are false. Modern theories aside, some things cannot be refuted. Truth starts with understanding who Jesus is and what His mission is all about.

TODAY'S AIM

Facts: to be clear that Jesus was tried by the Roman authorities to fulfill prophecy.

Principle: to recognize Jesus as a King of divine origin, bearing witness to the truth.

Application: to submit to the rule of Jesus over our lives and to know that objective knowledge is possible through a relationship with Christ.

INTRODUCING THE LESSON

In order to complete their plan to execute Jesus, the Jewish leaders needed to get the Romans on board. This was quite an unusual alliance since the Jews detested the Romans. However, when it served their purposes, they were willing to work with them. The man who was key to the success of Annas and Caiaphas's plot was Pontius Pilate, the Roman procurator over Judea. Our lesson this week turns to his examination of Jesus.

DEVELOPING THE LESSON

1. The Jews take their case before Pilate (John 18:28-32). Jesus had been questioned by Annas and Caiaphas, and their next step in getting Him executed was to convince the Roman leaders that He was a threat worthy of death. By this time, they had already condemned Jesus to death as a blasphemer under Jewish law (cf. Mark 14:63-64). Since they were under Roman rule, however, they did not have the authority to execute any criminal. Therefore, they needed Pilate to carry out their sentence.

The Jewish rulers and officers were religious, but not righteous. They would not enter Pilate's home because to go into a Gentile home would have made them ceremonially unclean and unable to eat the Passover. They were unwilling to defile themselves in this way, but they had no problem with killing a man on spurious charges. They celebrated Passover, but wanted to crucify the One who gave it. While they would reject Jesus' claims to be the Son of God, if they were righteously worshipping God, they would have known that His claims were true (cf. John 8:42, 46-47).

Pilate did not adhere to or understand the Jews' religious practices, but he did not flout them. Therefore, he met them outside and asked them what they charged Jesus with. The religious leaders did not answer with a particular accusation; rather, they sanctimoniously blustered that they would not have brought Jesus to Pilate if He were not a criminal.

Understandably, Pilate immediately tried to dismiss this case and told the Jews to judge Jesus according to their own law. They responded by stating that it was unlawful for them to execute anyone. Since Jesus was convicted of blasphemy (albeit with highly suspect evidence), they would have stoned Him to death if they could have (cf. Lev. 24:16; John 8:59).

John also shows that these proceedings fulfilled a prophecy of Jesus Himself about the death He would die (19:32). In John 12:32-33, John demonstrates that Jesus' references to being "lifted up" are a prediction of His crucifixion.

2. Jesus appears before Pilate (John 18:33-38a). Pilate reentered his judgment hall and called Jesus to him. He then asked Him directly if He was the King of the Jews. He needed to find out if Jesus posed any political threat to Rome. He had no reason for interest in Jewish affairs or customs—only Rome's.

Jesus asked Pilate if he was asking this question on his own or if someone else was directing him. Pilate sarcastically asked if he was a Jew, likely indicating that he did not care about Jewish disputes. Pilate further stated that Jesus' own people had delivered Him over to him, and he now wanted to know what He had done.

Jesus returned to the question about His kingship and stated that His kingdom is not of this world; in other words, it is of divine origin and substance. If it were of this world, then His followers would come and fight for Him. Undeterred, Pilate replied, So you are a king? Jesus confirmed that he was correct in saying that He was a king; He then added that He had been born to bear witness to the truth.

Pilate dismissed that thought with an abrupt "What is truth?" (vs. 38), but he did not wait around long enough to find out the answer.

3. The people reject their King (18:38b-40). Pilate then went back out to face the crowd and declared that he found Jesus not guilty. He then mentioned a custom that he and the Jews had at Passover: the release of a prisoner. He suggested that he might release Jesus their King at the Passover Feast.

The Jewish leaders and crowd, however, rejected the release of Jesus. Instead, they asked for the release of a prisoner named Barabbas. The Jews rejected the true Son of the Father in favor of a robber, rebel, and murderer.

ILLUSTRATING THE LESSON

We should bow in worship and submission to our crucified and risen King.

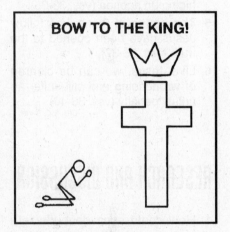

BOW TO THE KING!

CONCLUDING THE LESSON

Pilate did not want to crucify Jesus or get involved in Jewish disputes. He underestimated the leaders' desire for Jesus' blood, however, and found that they were insistent on executing Him. They had wanted to kill Jesus for a long time. Their opportunity had finally come, and Pilate was inching closer to giving in to them.

ANTICIPATING THE NEXT LESSON

In next week's lesson, Pilate gives in to the Jewish leaders and orders Jesus to be crucified in the greatest act of injustice the world has ever known.

—*Robert Ferguson, Jr.*

PRACTICAL POINTS

1. Some religious people do despicable things (John 18:28).
2. We should not expect straightforward answers from people bent on doing wrong (vss. 29-30).
3. The Lord uses the plans of evil people to bring about His own plan for our salvation (vss. 31-32).
4. We need wisdom to tell if some people's questions are sincere or hiding an agenda (vss. 33-35).
5. The hearts of those who follow Jesus have been opened to the truth (vss. 36-37).
6. Like Jesus, we can be cleared of wrongdoing and still suffer an unjust penalty (vss. 38-40).

—Charity G. Carter.

RESEARCH AND DISCUSSION

1. How could such devoutly religious people have no problem falsely accusing Jesus (John 18:28-30)?
2. Why did Pilate tell the Jewish leaders to judge Jesus (vs. 31)?
3. In order to ascertain Jesus' innocence or guilt, Pilate asked Him, "Art thou the King of the Jews?" (vs. 33). Explain why Jesus responded with His own question.
4. What did Jesus mean when He said, "My kingdom is not of this world" (vs. 36)?
5. Pilate asked, "What is truth?" (vs. 38). How would you answer that question?

—Charity G. Carter.

ILLUSTRATED HIGH POINTS

The hall of judgment (John 18:28)

Occasionally, the news media will refer to a particular trial as "the trial of the decade or century." Such trials usually cost a great deal of money and take several months with multiple witnesses and many attorneys.

In contrast, the so-called trial of Jesus involved three appearances before the Jewish leaders, two before Pilate, and one before Herod—all within the space of a few hours!

What is truth? (John 18:38)

Many in our culture assert, "There is no absolute truth. Everything is relative." Others claim there is truth, but we cannot know it; there is no objective knowledge. Pilate asked, "What is truth?" (John 18:38), then stormed off before receiving an answer.

The Bible declares that there is absolute truth, which is knowable through the revealed Word of God.

I find in him no fault (John 18:38)

Pilate three times declared Jesus innocent of the charges brought against Him (John 18:38; 19:4, 6). He tried to remain neutral and escape responsibility, but the Jewish leaders demanded that he carry out their predetermined sentence (18:30). We are reminded of a hymn by A. B. Simpson:

Jesus is standing in Pilate's hall,
Friendless, forsaken, betrayed by all,
Hearken! what meaneth the sudden call?
What will you do with Jesus?
What will you do with Jesus?
Neutral you cannot be,
Some day your heart will be asking,
"What will He do with me?"

—David A. Hamburg.

Golden Text Illuminated

"Jesus answered, My kingdom is not of this world: if my kingdom were of this world, then would my servants fight, that I should not be delivered to the Jews: but now is my kingdom not from hence" (John 18:36).

In this week's text, Jesus says that His kingdom is not of this world, meaning that it has a divine origin. John does announce a time when it will be on earth: "And the seventh angel sounded; and there were great voices in heaven, saying, The kingdoms of this world are become the kingdoms of our Lord, and of his Christ; and he shall reign for ever and ever" (Rev. 11:15). Saints, when we hear the seventh and final trumpet, everything will change: Jesus' kingdom will be on earth; the "Hallelujah Chorus" will be more than a song!

But this does not mean that Jesus' kingdom will become a worldly kingdom, with false news, false promises, and unintended consequences. His kingdom will still not be of this world. It does mean that the Lord Jesus will take over this present world system and institute a kingdom of righteousness that is based on truth and Christian love.

In explaining His kingdom to Pilate, the main idea that Jesus conveyed was the word "truth" (John 18:37), emphasizing, it seems, the spiritual nature of the kingdom. There may also have been an underlying polemic against the kingdoms of this world—they are built on falsehood. Therefore, Pilate mocked, "What is truth?" (John 18:38). To this world, truth is not absolute but subjective, dependent on who is talking or what group of people might benefit or suffer.

Theologians tell us that God's kingdom is both already here and still on the way. They use the expression "now and not yet." Our present age is a unique period in time, falling between the age of the Mosaic Law and the reign of Christ at His return Though they await the physical descent of the kingdom, Christians can now experience some of the powers of the "world to come" (Heb. 6:5).

Because He is sitting at God's right hand, Jesus is already "Lord and Christ" (Acts 2:36). "All power is given unto [Jesus] in heaven and in earth," so with the promise of this King's presence, Christians can make disciples and teach the nations to observe God's Word (Matt. 28:18-20). Prayers can be answered; miracles can happen.

One of the main points of our text today, however, concerns Christians and physical violence. For fifteen hundred years before Jesus spoke with Pilate, Israel had waged war against their enemies. The Romans, however, had defeated and ruled the Jews for about ninety years, and so for many Jews of that time their dreams of a Messiah involved His waging war against the Romans. Jesus, however, had a greater purpose in mind: to wage war against sin and man's bondage to it.

In the meantime, Christians engage in spiritual warfare. We do things like telling the truth, living righteously, preaching the gospel, trusting in God, loving our enemies, persevering through trial, and praying in the Spirit (Eph. 6:15-18). We honor our governing authorities, but if we are asked to disobey the commands of God, we know what to say: "We ought to obey God rather than men" (Acts 5:29). By God's grace, we honor Him.

—*David Samuel Gifford.*

Heart of the Lesson

When my dad was fired from his job teaching shop—working with tools and machinery—at a Christian school, he was shocked, as he had usually received high marks on evaluations. Later, the principal admitted he had promised if he ever became a principal, he would hire his brother-in-law to teach shop. Dad had to go.

Within a year, God turned the evil to good; Dad found better-paying work as a finish carpenter. This week's lesson shows the greater evil Jesus experienced during His trial. But it, too, was part of God's plan.

1. Accusation (John 18:28-32). Early Friday morning, while most Jerusalem residents were likely still asleep, the Jewish religious leaders brought Jesus from the high priest's home to the Roman judgment hall. Jesus' trial before Caiaphas was over; the next step was for Jesus to appear before Pilate, the Roman governor.

The Jewish leaders wanted to participate in the Passover meal later that day. Therefore, they refused to enter the hall because it would defile them until evening. Instead, Pilate had to go outside to ask Jesus' accusers what charges they brought against Him. They replied that if He were no criminal, they would not have brought Him.

Pilate said they should judge Jesus themselves according to their own law. The leaders protested. They wanted Jesus to die, and under Roman rule, they had no right to administer the death penalty, so they demanded that Pilate try Him.

They unknowingly were fulfilling Jesus' earlier prophetic words about how He would die: He would be "lifted up" (that is, on a cross [John 12:32-33])—an execution method only Rome could impose.

2. Interrogation (John 18:33-38a). Pilate returned to the judgment hall and asked Jesus if He was the King of the Jews. He seemed most concerned about whether Jesus presented a threat to Roman rule. Jesus often answered questions with a question. Here He asked Pilate if this was his own question or if others had suggested it.

Pilate asked Jesus what He had done to cause His own people and chief priests to turn against Him and bring Him for judgment. Jesus ignored this question and answered Pilate's prior question about His kingship. His kingdom was not earthly but spiritual. He came to establish the kingdom of God in human hearts, not overthrow governments. Jesus pointed out if His kingdom were earthly, His followers would have fought to prevent His arrest.

At this point, Pilate again asked if He is a king and Jesus said in effect, "As you say." Further, He was born to bear witness of the truth. Jesus had proclaimed the truth about God the Father, the truth that He was the Son of God, the truth about sin, and the truth about salvation. Jesus noted that lovers of truth listened to Him. Pilate said sarcastically, "What is truth?"

3. Rejection (John 18:38b-40). Pilate went outside and told the leaders he found no fault in Jesus. Every year at Passover, he released a prisoner. Surely if he offered the choice between Jesus and the murderous Barabbas, the crowd would choose to save the innocent Jesus. Then Pilate could set Him free and crucify Barabbas. But the Jewish leaders wanted Jesus crucified.

God turned the injustice Jesus suffered to good because it purchased our salvation. Have you placed your trust in Him?

—Ann Staatz.

World Missions

In Brazil, it is common to see highway police blocking the road to do random searches. They can wave you through or pull you over to examine you and your vehicle.

One day, we were driving home from the city with a gas container. While we were being examined, the policeman noticed the gas container. He informed us that carrying it inside the vehicle was against the law. We explained that we did not know and apologized for our ignorance.

Later, my father used this as an illustration to the people we taught. He asked, "Did we break the law?"

They responded, "No, you didn't break the law because you did not know the law existed." My dad then pointed out that a law broken in ignorance does not make the transgressor guiltless.

Just as the law existed even though we were ignorant of it, so truth exists whether people are ignorant, unbelieving, or rebellious. No one's beliefs, convictions, or feelings can alter the truth.

When Jesus stood before Pilate, Pilate had the opportunity to hear Truth speak. But as the following discourse will show, he did not recognize it: "Jesus answered, Thou sayest that I am a king. To this end was I born, and for this cause came I into the world, that I should bear witness unto the truth. Every one that is of the truth heareth my voice. Pilate saith unto him, What is truth?" (John 18:37-38).

Pilate did not recognize that Jesus was the Truth. As Jesus previously said to His disciples, "I am the way, the truth, and the life: no man cometh unto the Father, but by me" (14:6).

Pilate failed to understand when Jesus said, "My kingdom is not of this world: if my kingdom were of this world, then would my servants fight . . . but now is my kingdom not from hence" (18:36).

However, Pilate did seem to recognize Christ's power. When he was told of Jesus' claim to be the Son of God, Pilate "was the more afraid" (John 19:8), and he asked Jesus about His identity. When He refused to respond, Pilate made a boast of his power, to which "Jesus answered, Thou couldest have no power at all against me, except it were given thee from above . . . And from thenceforth Pilate sought to release him" (vss. 11-12).

Yet even with all the opportunities Pilate was given to accept the truth of who Christ was and humble himself in repentance, he ignored the truth and condemned Jesus to death.

Every human is given the opportunity to either accept or reject the truth of who Jesus is. The choice is to believe that Jesus is God, as He claimed to be—"I and my Father are one" (10:30)—or to believe that Christ was delusional or a liar. There is no middle ground.

The world is filled with people in need of the Truth. Christ has entrusted us to tell them about Him, for "It is given unto you to know the mysteries of the kingdom of heaven" (Matt. 13:11).

We ought to be bold in our declaration of the gospel, for "How then shall they call on him in whom they have not believed? and how shall they believe in him of whom they have not heard? and how shall they hear without a preacher?" (Rom. 10:14).

—Jody Stinson.

The Jewish Aspect

In the account of Jesus' trial before Pilate, John writes that His Jewish accusers carefully avoided entering Pilate's judgment hall themselves. They did this "lest they should be defiled" and thereby be barred from eating the Passover (18:28). So Pilate had to accommodate them by coming outside. But how could Jews be "defiled" just by being present at a trial?

Without question, the teaching on defilement was clear in the Old Testament, with five specific categories identified. One was physical defilement seen in texts such as, "I have washed my feet; how shall I defile them?" (S Sol. 5:3). A second was sexual defilement through fornication or adultery: "Thou shalt not lie carnally with thy neighbour's wife, to defile thyself with her" (Lev. 18:20).

Third was the case of ceremonial defilement, which disqualified someone or something from religious service. This would include the restrictions on what food an Israelite was allowed to eat (Lev. 11). Closely related to ceremonial defilement, the fourth type is religious defilement involving pagan worship: "He hath given of his seed unto Molech, to defile my sanctuary" (20:3). The final category was ethical defilement. This referred to disobedience to God's laws concerning proper treatment of others and could include evils such as brutality, murder, and tyranny: "Your hands are defiled with blood" (Isa 59:3).

None of those five Old Testament categories, however, explains why the Jews of Jesus' day thought entering Pilate's judgment hall would defile them. Rabbinic thinking concerning defilement of Jews by Gentiles seems to have developed greatly between the time when Jews returned to Israel after the Babylonian Captivity and the time of Jesus. Before the Captivity, a primary way the Jews turned away from God was by their worship of Gentile idols. The prophets rebuked them for this regularly. From the time the Jews returned, they were almost continually under Gentile dominion. Persia, the Ptolemies of Egypt, the Seleucids of Syria, and finally the Romans all exerted control and influence over the Jewish people. Resisting the Gentile environment of idolatry, therefore, became a priority of Jewish religious life, as seen dramatically in the time of the Maccabees.

During these years, rabbis developed ever more detailed regulations with the purpose of maintaining Jewish purity and separation. These stipulations became deeply embedded in Jewish culture. Peter himself seems to have known and lived by them before the Lord corrected his thinking. He told the Roman centurion Cornelius and the company in his house, "Ye know how that it is an unlawful thing for a man that is a Jew to keep company, or come unto one of another nation" (Acts 10:28). It was "unlawful" because of Jewish traditions, not from Old Testament teaching.

These increasing restrictions on interactions of Jews with Gentiles were recorded in the Mishnah, which is a written record of Judaism's oral law. Among the many regulations is this statement: "The dwelling places of non-Jews are unclean" ("Ohalot, Chapter 18, Mishnah 7," http://learn.conservativeyeshiva.org).

This was the teaching that the Jewish leaders sought to follow when they refused to enter Pilate's judgment hall. They sought to rigorously obey man-made laws while they were hardened to their crime of murdering an innocent man.

—R. Larry Overstreet.

Guiding the Superintendent

Jesus endured three religious trials before the high priests and the Sanhedrin. The Jewish leaders declared Him guilty of blasphemy. However, they did not have the authority to put Jesus to death.

Therefore, to have Jesus crucified, they needed to gain the approval of the Roman authorities. The key figure for that was Pilate, the governor of Judea.

DEVOTIONAL OUTLINE

1. Jewish accusations (John 18:28-32). The Jews led Jesus to Pilate early in the morning (vs. 28).

Pilate asked them to state their accusation against Jesus (vs. 29). They answered that if He were not a criminal, they would not have brought Him to Pilate (vs. 30). That was not an answer to the question, but simply a self-righteous attempt at deception. Pilate, presumably thinking this was another religious squabble, told them to handle it themselves (vs. 31). But they insisted Jesus was guilty of a crime worthy of death.

2. Pilate's examination (John 18:33-35). Seeking justice, Pilate began to ask Jesus questions and gain evidence to determine whether He was guilty of treason against Rome. He asked if He was the King of the Jews (vs. 33). Jesus answered with a question; He wondered if Pilate personally cared who He was or whether someone else had told him (vs. 34). Pilate sarcastically remarked about his ethnicity, implying that he really had no personal interest (vs. 35).

3. Jesus' explanation (John 18:36-38a). Jesus responded that His kingdom was not of this world (vs. 36). If it was of this world, then His disciples would have been in the streets fighting to prevent His arrest. Pilate again tried to understand Jesus' answer and asked again if he was a king (vs. 37). Jesus said His mission was to proclaim the truth given to Him by the Father. His kingdom was not of this world, but of truth. Before leaving the judgment hall, Pilate asked, "What is truth?" (vs. 38).

4. Pilate's verdict (John 18:38b). Pilate then turned around, went back to the Jews, and pronounced his verdict. He declared that he found no fault in Jesus. A claim to be the King of a spiritual kingdom was not a threat to Rome.

5. Pilate's concession (John 18:39-40). Justice would demand that Pilate dismiss the case and release Jesus. However, bowing to political pressure and not wanting to cause a riot, Pilate made a concession to the Jews. He offered to follow the custom of releasing a prisoner at Passover. Given Pilate's reluctance to crucify Jesus in the next chapter (19:4-7, 13-15), it appears he expected that the crowds would release Jesus (18:39). However, at the instigation of the leaders, the crowds cried for him to release Barabbas (vs. 40).

The crowds and the leaders rejected their Messiah. What will you decide to do with Jesus?

CHILDREN'S CORNER

Your teachers could use the example of Barabbas and Jesus to illustrate the substitution that they need for their own sins.

As we approach the death of Jesus, your teachers will need to revisit the idea that death means not returning, highlighting that for Jesus alone this is not the case.

Your children should know that Jesus committed no crime, not just no crime worthy of death.

—*Robert Winter.*

SCRIPTURE LESSON TEXT

JOHN 19:16 Then delivered he him therefore unto them to be crucified. And they took Jesus, and led *him* away.

17 And he bearing his cross went forth into a place called *the place* of a skull, which is called in the Hebrew Golgotha:

18 Where they crucified him, and two other with him, on either side one, and Jesus in the midst.

19 And Pilate wrote a title, and put *it* on the cross. And the writing was, JESUS OF NAZARETH THE KING OF THE JEWS.

20 This title then read many of the Jews: for the place where Jesus was crucified was nigh to the city: and it was written in Hebrew, *and* Greek, *and* Latin.

21 Then said the chief priests of the Jews to Pilate, Write not, The King of the Jews; but that he said, I am King of the Jews.

22 Pilate answered, What I have written I have written.

23 Then the soldiers, when they had crucified Jesus, took his garments, and made four parts, to every soldier a part; and also *his* coat: now the coat was without seam, woven from the top throughout.

24 They said therefore among themselves, Let us not rend it, but cast lots for it, whose it shall be: that the scripture might be fulfilled, which saith, They parted my raiment among them, and for my vesture they did cast lots. These things therefore the soldiers did.

25 Now there stood by the cross of Jesus his mother, and his mother's sister, Mary the *wife* of Cleophas, and Mary Magdalene.

26 When Jesus therefore saw his mother, and the disciple standing by, whom he loved, he saith unto his mother, Woman, behold thy son!

27 Then saith he to the disciple, Behold thy mother! And from that hour that disciple took her unto his own *home.*

28 After this, Jesus knowing that all things were now accomplished, that the scripture might be fulfilled, saith, I thirst.

29 Now there was set a vessel full of vinegar: and they filled a spunge with vinegar, and put *it* upon hyssop, and put *it* to his mouth.

30 When Jesus therefore had received the vinegar, he said, It is finished: and he bowed his head, and gave up the ghost.

NOTES

Crucifixion and Death

Lesson Text: John 19:16-30

Related Scriptures: Psalm 22:12-18; Matthew 27:27-56;
Mark 15:16-32; Luke 23:26-43

TIME: A.D. 30   PLACE: Jerusalem

GOLDEN TEXT—"When Jesus therefore had received the vinegar, he said, It is finished: and he bowed his head, and gave up the ghost" (John 19:30).

Introduction

Capital punishment has long been debated by both the church and society. Some nations have outlawed it altogether; others carry out executions capriciously, not unlike what happened in biblical times.

The execution of lawbreakers is clearly commanded under the Mosaic Law (Ex. 21:12-17). Some Christians, however, believe that we have no such mandate under the new covenant.

Capital punishment is strictly the prerogative of the civil authorities, not individuals. No one has the right to personally carry out a death sentence on his own.

The first-century Roman legal system had no prison system as we think of it. Incarceration normally was for a relatively short time prior to trial or execution. The death sentence was often imposed for crimes not considered capital offenses anywhere today.

LESSON OUTLINE

I. CHRIST CRUCIFIED—
John 19:16-22

II. PROPHECY FULFILLED—
John 19:23-24

III. PROVISION ARRANGED—
John 19:25-27

IV. MISSION ACCOMPLISHED—
John 19:28-30

Exposition: Verse by Verse

CHRIST CRUCIFIED

JOHN 19:16 Then delivered he him therefore unto them to be crucified. And they took Jesus, and led him away.

17 And he bearing his cross went forth into a place called the place of a skull, which is called in the Hebrew Golgotha:

18 Where they crucified him, and two other with him, on either side one, and Jesus in the midst.

19 And Pilate wrote a title, and put it on the cross. And the writing was, JESUS OF NAZARETH THE KING OF THE JEWS.

20 This title then read many of the Jews: for the place where Jesus was crucified was nigh to the city: and it was written in Hebrew, and Greek, and Latin.

21 Then said the chief priests of the Jews to Pilate, Write not, The King of the Jews; but that he said, I am King of the Jews.

22 Pilate answered, What I have written I have written.

Pilate found himself in a difficult situation. Neither declaring Jesus innocent (18:38) nor releasing Him as a Passover good-will gesture (vs. 39) was acceptable to the Jewish authorities and the angry mob gathered outside the praetorium. An attempt to dump the problem in Herod's lap failed as well (cf. Luke 23:6-12). When Jesus came before him again, Pilate had Him scourged (John 19:1-5). But even this failed to placate the chief priests, who relentlessly cried out, "Crucify him, crucify him" (vs. 6). At this juncture they also interjected that Jesus had "made himself the Son of God" (vs. 7).

When he heard that, Pilate became frightened. What had these Jews gotten him into? What would it mean to be an accessory to killing such a man? He demanded that Jesus tell him where He had come from, but Jesus remained strangely silent (vss. 8-9). When Pilate threatened Him with death, Jesus reminded him that any power Pilate had over Him was delegated "from above" (vs. 11) and that the greater sin was therefore upon the Jewish authorities, who were misappropriating Pilate's civil power to murder Him. At this, Pilate desperately tried to release Jesus, but the religious leaders insinuated that such an action would be tantamount to treason against Caesar (vs. 12).

{Pilate did not want to be perceived as treasonous, so he relented, giving the order for Jesus to be crucified.}[Q1] In a last, frantic appeal for mercy, he asked the chief priests, "Shall I crucify your King?" (vs. 15). But their only response was the self-condemning admission: "We have no king but Caesar."

Suffering the cross (John 19:16-18). Jesus is often depicted as bearing the entire cross to the place of His execution. But many believe He carried only the horizontal crossbar, since it would have made sense to have the vertical section of the cross permanently anchored in the ground at the site of crucifixion. Matthew's Gospel relates that Simon of Cyrene was compelled to carry Jesus' cross, presumably because in His weakened condition, Jesus was unable to do so (27:32).

{The place of execution was known as "Golgotha" or "Calvary" (cf. Luke 23:33); both words mean "skull."}[Q2] The place may have been so named because it was a place of death, and the image of a skull often symbolizes death. One purported location for the site of Jesus' execution actually does resemble a skull to this day.

Various forms of crucifixion are known to have existed in ancient times. Some prisoners were tied to crosses and allowed to die of exposure. If the goal was a quicker death, the condemned would be nailed to a cross. In contrast, modern executions tend to be carried out quickly to minimize suffering; some modern methods, such as lethal injection, even employ sedation to alleviate suffering.

{Two criminals were also crucified along with Jesus, fulfilling Isaiah 53:9 and 12: "He made his grave with the wicked" and "he was numbered with the transgressors."}[Q3] These criminals also mocked Jesus (Matt. 27:44). But one of them had a change of heart and was ultimately ushered into Christ's kingdom upon his death (Luke 23:39-43).

Inscription controversy (John 19:19-22). {Since crucifixions were carried out in public, a placard was often placed on the cross of the condemned person to identify the criminal and the crime for which he was being executed. This was usually for inspiring fear in the populace rather than for merely informational purposes.}[Q4]

Since the Jewish leaders had convinced Pilate to execute Jesus because He claimed to be the King of the Jews, Pilate had that title inscribed on His cross. Passersby would then read this proclamation, which ostensibly affirmed that Jesus indeed was the King of the Jews. This was exactly what the Magi affirmed near the time of Jesus' birth (Matt. 2:2). When Nathanael first met Jesus, he ascribed to Him the title "King of Israel" (John 1:49).

{So that anyone would be able to understand what was written, the inscription was presented in three languages: Aramaic (the language spoken by most Jews at this time, usually known as "Hebrew" to Greeks and Romans), Latin (the official language of the Roman Empire), and Greek (the universal language of the known world at this time, and used by the writers of the New Testament).}[Q5]

{The chief priests were highly indignant about this inscription. They wanted Pilate to change the message to say that Jesus only *claimed* to be the King of the Jews (19:21). But Pilate was no longer in a mood to accommodate the Jewish leaders, and so he refused to give their request any consideration. He told them brusquely, "What I have written I have written" (vs. 22).}[Q6]

PROPHECY FULFILLED

23 Then the soldiers, when they had crucified Jesus, took his garments, and made four parts, to every soldier a part; and also his coat: now the coat was without seam, woven from the top throughout.

24 They said therefore among themselves, Let us not rend it, but cast lots for it, whose it shall be: that the scripture might be fulfilled, which saith, They parted my raiment among them, and for my vesture they did cast lots. These things therefore the soldiers did.

It was a common practice at this time for those on the death detail to simply divide the clothing and other personal possessions of the condemned among themselves. The condemned were usually crucified naked, adding to their public humiliation. {There were four soldiers at the cross, so most of Jesus' clothing was parceled out among them in four ways.

But they were still left with Jesus' coat, or tunic, which was woven in one piece with no seams. Rather than tear this garment into four ruined rags, the soldiers decided on gambling to see who would get the whole garment.}[Q7] Specifically how they did this is not stated, but it probably involved something like the rolling of dice.

Like many other seemingly ordinary actions surrounding Jesus' life and death, what the soldiers did unintentionally fulfilled prophecy. The original prophecy is from Psalm 22:18. Psalm 22 is a messianic psalm. Though it was written by David about a thousand years earlier concerning events in his own life, the psalm famously contains numerous compelling parallels to Christ's sufferings on the cross.

PROVISION ARRANGED

25 Now there stood by the cross of Jesus his mother, and his mother's sister, Mary the wife of Cleophas, and Mary Magdalene.

26 When Jesus therefore saw his mother, and the disciple standing by, whom he loved, he saith unto his mother, Woman, behold thy son!

27 Then saith he to the disciple,

Behold thy mother! And from that hour that disciple took her unto his own home.

While the chosen followers largely forsook Jesus after His arrest, there were some disciples who remained faithful during that time. Among them were certain women who stood near His cross. Jesus' own mother, Mary, stood there, witnessing His pain and agony. At the time of Jesus' presentation in the temple, the elderly Simeon had solemnly prophesied that Mary's soul would one day be pierced by a sword (cf. Luke 2:35). The crucifixion was surely the fulfillment of his words.

By comparing parallel accounts in Matthew and Mark and using the process of elimination, we can be reasonably sure who "his mother's sister" was (John 19:25). Since Matthew 27:56 identifies this woman as "the mother of Zebedee's children" and Mark 15:40 names her as "Salome," we can assume that she was the mother of the apostles James and John, who were sons of Zebedee. This woman was Mary's sister; so that means James and John were actually Jesus' cousins.

As her eldest son, Jesus had a special responsibility to take care of His mother. Though He would soon rise from the dead, His time on earth was nearly over. He therefore made provision for Mary's needs in His absence.

The disciple whom Jesus loved has traditionally been understood as a reference to the author of the fourth Gospel, the apostle John himself. If in fact it refers to someone else, we have no clue who that might have been. While tradition is not inspired Scripture, long-standing traditions do have merit, especially when there is nothing to contradict them.

{When Jesus said to Mary, "Behold thy son!" (vs. 26), He was telling her she should now think of John as her son; he would be taking His place. Then, when He said to John, "Behold thy mother!" (vs. 27), He was likewise telling John he should now consider Mary his mother. It was a means whereby Jesus could be assured that Mary would be cared for after His death, since it seems evident that Joseph had been deceased for some time at this point.}Q8

The fact that Jesus addressed His mother as "woman" should not be construed as somehow disrespectful. The word was used as a common designation for a mother or a wife; it could be interpreted as something similar to the modern title "ma'am."

The statement "from that hour that disciple took her unto his own home" explains Jesus' purpose in making these declarations to them from the cross.

Taking responsibility for His mother's welfare as He hung on the cross shows us that even in untold agony and on the verge of death, Jesus kept His Father's commandments perfectly. Even at this most dire moment, when we might expect Him to be preoccupied with His own suffering, He was faithful to do His Father's will in making provision for His bereaved mother, as any dutiful son should.

MISSION ACCOMPLISHED

28 After this, Jesus knowing that all things were now accomplished, that the scripture might be fulfilled, saith, I thirst.

29 Now there was set a vessel full of vinegar: and they filled a spunge with vinegar, and put it upon hyssop, and put it to his mouth.

30 When Jesus therefore had received the vinegar, he said, It is finished: and he bowed his head, and gave up the ghost.

Hour of sacrifice (John 19:28-29). As best as can be determined, Jesus was on the cross from about nine in the morning until about three in the afternoon (cf. Mark 15:25, 33-34). These were the very hours during which sacrifices were made in the temple. As the Lamb of God (1:29), Jesus was taking away the sins of the world on the cross through the perfect, once-for-all sacrifice of Himself. All the prophecies related to His sacrificial death were being fulfilled during these hours of regular, daily sacrifice.

Indeed, "all things were now accomplished" (19:28). {And knowing that all was accomplished, Jesus fulfilled one more prophecy by declaring aloud the terrible thirst He experienced on the cross.}Q9

Psalm 69:21 says, "They gave me also gall for my meat; and in my thirst they gave me vinegar to drink." The vinegar of that era was a cheap wine vinegar commonly consumed by the soldiers. When mixed with other substances, it was used as an anesthetic.

Hyssop is also known as Syrian oregano. It is an herb used both as a seasoning and also in religious rituals (Heb. 9:19). Here it was a long branch or bunch of hyssop that had a sponge attached to it, and it was used to offer a drink to Jesus to assuage His thirst, perhaps even making it possible for Him to forcefully make His final declaration.

It is finished! (John 19:30). After receiving the wine vinegar, Jesus declared, "It is finished," a single word in the original language. The term was often used at the completion of a contract, as when a debt was paid in full. Jesus had declared the very night before, "I have finished the work which thou gavest me to do" (17:4). {Far from being an admission of defeat, "It is finished" is an affirmation of victory! Jesus' redemptive work to save lost sinners was now fully accomplished.}Q10

From the standpoint of the rest of the New Testament, what Christ did on the cross is a finished work. Nothing can be added to it, nor can anything be taken away from it. Though unworthy of his grace, we can receive salvation through faith in Christ.

Having completed His work on earth, Jesus "bowed his head, and gave up the ghost" (19:30); that is, He died.

To confirm that Jesus was indeed dead, the soldiers pierced His side with a spear (19:34), fulfilling the prophecy, "They shall look on him whom they pierced" (John 19:37; cf. Zech. 12:10). Had He not already expired, they would have broken His legs to hasten His death (John 19:32-33). This was in fulfillment of another prophecy: "A bone of him shall not be broken" (John 19:36; cf. Ex. 12:46; Ps. 34:20).

After this, Joseph of Arimathea and Nicodemus buried the body of the Lord Jesus (John 19:38-42). That, of course, was not the end of the story; Sunday was coming!

—*John Alva Owston.*

QUESTIONS

1. Why did Pilate finally give in to the demands of the chief priests?

2. What was another name for Golgotha, and what did it mean?

3. Who was crucified alongside Christ?

4. What was the purpose of the placard on the cross?

5. In what languages was the message on the placard written? Why?

6. How did Pilate respond to the request to change the words on the placard?

7. What happened to Jesus' clothing?

8. How did Jesus make provision for His mother?

9. Why did Christ utter the words "I thirst" (John 19:28)?

10. What is the significance of Jesus' declaration "It is finished" (vs. 30)?

—*John Alva Owston.*

Preparing to Teach the Lesson

Although Pilate found no guilt in Jesus, he gave in to the demands for Jesus to be crucified. He was completely bewildered by the Jewish leaders' hatred for a man who was not guilty of any crime against Rome, and he did not understand the Jews' laws and religion. All he was interested in was preserving the peace. He tried releasing Jesus, but the crowd would have none of it. The rejection of Jesus became so severe that the chief priests announced their dedication to Caesar as their only king—and they hated Caesar!

It is stunning to see that the Jewish leaders were willing to align themselves with their hated foes in order to kill Jesus. In an ironic twist, they were insisting the Romans kill the One whom others among their people had previously wanted to overthrow the Romans. Seen as the most popular man in Jerusalem just days before, Jesus was now condemned to die by His own people (cf. John 1:11).

TODAY'S AIM

Facts: to study John's account of the crucifixion of Jesus, the King of the Jews.

Principle: to become wholly assured that Jesus died on a cross to take away the sins of the world (John 1:29).

Application: to determine to live in victory over sin because Christ's death has set us free.

INTRODUCING THE LESSON

There He stood, all alone before an angry mob. He had been brutally beaten and flogged and was given a crown of thorns to wear. He was publicly ridiculed at the end of a week that had earlier seen Him praised when He rode into Jerusalem on a donkey. Public opinion had clearly swayed against Jesus as the people demanded His crucifixion. The most merciful man the world has ever seen received no mercy from anyone, and a bloodthirsty mob had their way with Him.

DEVELOPING THE LESSON

1. Jesus is crucified (John 19:16-22). After trying unsuccessfully to convince the Jews that Jesus had done nothing to deserve death, Pilate finally gave in to them and delivered Him over to them to be crucified. Since the Jews were not permitted by Roman law to execute anyone, the Romans would carry out the sentence.

Jesus was led to a place commonly known as "the place of a skull," which John gives as the translation of the Hebrew (or Aramaic) "Golgotha" (vs. 17). Some believe it was named such because the hill looked like a skull, while others believe it was a reference to the many skulls that may have been there from prior crucifixions.

John notes that Jesus was crucified in the midst of common criminals. He undoubtedly sees this as a fulfillment of the words: "He was numbered with the transgressors" (Isa. 53:12; cf. Mark 15:27-28).

It was common for Roman officials to write a criminal's offense on a placard and have it fastened to the cross above his head. This would inform everyone present or passing by what the individual's crime was. It must have been difficult to specify Jesus' offense since Pilate had not found any fault in Him. Needing to write something, he settled on "Jesus of Nazareth the King of the Jews," (vs. 19). It was inscribed in Aramaic (or Hebrew), Latin, and Greek so that anyone who could read would be able to read it in a language they understood.

After many bystanders had read the placard, the chief priests complained to Pilate about the inscription. They wanted him to add that Jesus *claimed* to be the King of the Jews, but Pilate refused, saying he had written what he had written.

2. Jesus speaks from the cross (John 19:23-27). After Jesus had been fastened to the cross, the soldiers divided His garments into four parts—one for each of them. They also took His tunic, a long, one-piece garment worn close to the skin. Instead of tearing it, the soldiers decided to cast lots, which was like rolling dice, for it. Unwittingly, they actually fulfilled prophecy by doing this (cf. Ps. 22:18).

Standing by the cross of Jesus were His mother, His aunt, Mary the wife of Cleophas, and Mary Magdalene, and along with them was John. Jesus looked down and saw them standing together and commissioned John to take care of His mother. As the eldest son, Jesus made arrangements to ensure that His mother received care even while He was suffering on the cross. This was typical of Jesus—always looking out for others no matter what degree of suffering He was enduring at the time.

3. Jesus dies (John 19:28-30). Jesus knew what He came to do. It was the plan of God since before the foundation of the world that He would suffer and die to redeem God's people and reconcile them to Himself (I Pet. 1:18-21). The crucifixion came as no surprise to Jesus. It was why He came.

After spending several hours on the cross, Jesus stated that He was thirsty. The Roman soldiers dipped a sponge in some sour wine, put it on a hyssop branch, and held it up to Jesus' mouth (cf. Ps. 69:21).

Jesus received the sour wine and then cried out "It is finished" (John 19:30). The phrase translates the Greek word *tetelestai.* This word was written on receipts in the first century to indicate that a bill had been paid in full. Jesus paid our sin debt in full; nothing else is owed. Jesus had taken the sins of the world on Himself and become the final sin sacrifice.

After saying this, Jesus hung His head and gave up His spirit. No one could take it from Him. He gave it up. Jesus Christ, the Son of God, was dead.

ILLUSTRATING THE LESSON

Jesus took our sins on the cross, so we could be forgiven.

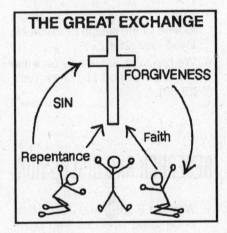

CONCLUDING THE LESSON

"It is finished!" It may not have seemed like it at the time, but this was a shout of victory. Jesus' mission was complete, and sin had been fully and finally atoned for. But how can a man shout in victory with His last words? The reason is simple: Jesus knew that He would be resurrected three days later, never to die again.

ANTICIPATING THE NEXT LESSON

Next week's lesson will study one of the appearances Jesus made to His disciples after His resurrection.

—*Robert Ferguson, Jr.*

PRACTICAL POINTS

1. Jesus bore His cross for us; we are called to bear ours for Him (John 19:16-18).
2. Those who do not know the Lord may unwittingly testify to who He is (vss. 19-20).
3. God uses even the mockery of unbelievers to shine light on the truth (vss. 21-22).
4. Everything that the Lord declares will come to pass in exact detail (vss. 23-24).
5. Even in His suffering, Jesus looked to the needs of those He loved (vss. 25-27).
6. We can trust Jesus fully because He has finished His work (vss. 28-30).

—Charity G. Carter.

RESEARCH AND DISCUSSION

1. Why did Pilate hand Jesus over to be killed when he had previously found absolutely no fault with Him (John 19:16; cf. vs. 6)?
2. The sign that Pilate hung above Jesus was offensive to the Jewish leaders. Why might Pilate have refused to change it (vs. 22)?
3. It seems that only one disciple was at the cross. Where were the other disciples (vss. 25-26)? List some possibilities.
4. Why did Jesus tell His mother and the disciple He loved that they were now mother and son (vss. 26-27)?

—Charity G. Carter.

ILLUSTRATED HIGH POINTS

They crucified him (John 19:18)

We notice the cultural difference regarding execution in Palestine in the first century and in America today. Today, when a condemned person is executed, our society seeks to make it gentle. Thus, the lethal injection needs to be quick and painless.

In Jesus' day, it was exactly the opposite. The Jews practiced stoning, which was not quick or painless. The Romans often used crucifixion, which could take many hours, even days, and was brutally painful. In fact, the brutality was precisely the point.

They crucified him (John 19:18)

When we attended a viewing of *The Passion of the Christ*, a young girl sitting nearby sobbed through the crucifixion scene, presumably crying at the physical torture of Jesus that the film emphasized. That aspect was indeed horrendous, but the worst of Jesus' suffering was being forsaken by His Father as He bore the sins of the world (cf. Matt. 27:46).

His mother (John 19:25)

One of my first tasks as a visiting professor at the Zaporozhye Bible College in Ukraine was to make a seating chart of the class. Fortunately, the students chose to sit in the same seat each day. One year, in the front row was Igor, Igor, Igor, and another fellow. I only managed to tell them apart because my interpreters knew them well.

Many women were in the crowd of people present at Jesus' crucifixion. A few are mentioned, and there seem to be three with the name of Mary. Jesus did not need an interpreter to distinguish between them. He knew each one for their faith and loyalty as well as for their love and compassion.

—David A. Hamburg.

Golden Text Illuminated

"When Jesus therefore had received the vinegar, he said, It is finished: and he bowed his head, and gave up the ghost" (John 19:30).

When I was a child, I always wondered why they gave Jesus vinegar for His thirst. Maybe it reduced pain, I thought. But that was not really the reason. Jesus knew the Hebrew Bible, and one of His last prophecies to fulfill was Psalm 69:21, which speaks of the Messiah ingesting vinegar. Roman soldiers were not known for their kindness or respect for condemned criminals. Rather than honor a dying man's last wish, they mocked His thirst with bitter drink. Maybe the next would-be Messiah would think twice before doubting the intentions of Rome.

John records that on the cross, Jesus mustered the lung power for His final proclamation: "It is finished." Similarly, when Moses died at 120, "His eye was not dim, nor his natural force abated" (Deut. 34:7). Both leaders retained their strength to the end.

The text does not say that Jesus' head drooped, but rather, "He bowed his head." Jesus' last act before His death was to bow His head as if in prayer or submission to the Father. "By the Spirit," he then "went and preached unto the spirits in prison" (I Pet. 3:18-19). When our text says Jesus "gave up the ghost," it is not envisioning paranormal activity. The phrase simply means that He surrendered His spirit to God.

In John 7:6, Jesus had said, "My time is not yet come." I remember reading this as a young man and wondering what Jesus was planning to do. When I later realized that He was speaking about His death on the cross, the mystery seemed anticlimactic. I had heard the gospel many times as a child, and

Jesus dying on the cross just seemed like a fact of life. Why did He make such a big deal of it? He was God and knew the whole plan from the beginning.

I did not understand the emotions accompanying death until I spent time with the elderly in the 1990s. Even as a pastor, I had difficulty talking with the unsaved about their spiritual need. Most people by their seventies or eighties have either made peace with God or have settled on hoping there is no hell.

The conversations that I *have* had with elderly believers have not always been what I would expect. Many of them talk hopefully about heaven and seeing God, but others have regrets about children, a spouse, or something they wish that they had or had not done. They do not fear death, but they generally take actions to avoid it.

I will never forget the time I visited a beloved sister who, physically degraded, asked for prayer for total healing. I could not refuse her, but I was daunted by all that needed to happen, medically speaking, for her to recover. She had been worsening slowly, though not yet near death.

I never saw her again. In a few days, the Lord Jesus gave her an unexpected total healing. She was "absent from the body, and . . . present with the Lord" (II Cor. 5:8).

Comparing my experiences with the dying to Jesus' death, I now recognize that His approach was fully human. He did not use His deity to make it easier.

—David Samuel Gifford.

Heart of the Lesson

Pictures I saw of Jesus' crucifixion during my childhood were sanitized images showing little blood and no evidence of pain.

Then came my college Gospels course. The professor read a medical doctor's description of what happened to Jesus' body during His trial and crucifixion. Within minutes, my stomach was churning, and my head felt light. I could hardly bear hearing of this horror; imagine actually going through it! This week's lesson examines the disciple John's record of Jesus' six hours on the cross.

1. The crucifixion (John 19:16-18). Pilate gave in to the Jewish religious leaders' demand that Jesus be crucified. Crucifixion was a Roman, not Jewish, method of execution and was usually reserved for non-citizen criminals living in the Roman provinces.

The soldiers hoisted the crossbeam onto Jesus' torn, bloody shoulders and led Him outside the city to Golgotha, the crucifixion site.

Golgotha probably was a rocky outcropping that resembled a skull. Historians currently believe that the soldiers would have nailed Jesus' hands to the crossbeam, lifted it onto a vertical post that had been set in the ground, and nailed His feet in place. Two other criminals were also crucified, one on each side of Him.

2. A protested sign (John 19:19-22). Pilate made a sign for Jesus that read, "Jesus of Nazareth, the King of the Jews." He wrote the message in the languages of the Hebrews, the Greeks, and the Romans, so anyone in Jerusalem during Passover could read who Jesus was. When the chief priests heard about Pilate's sign, they immediately asked him to change the words to "He said, 'I am the King of the Jews.'" Pilate refused.

3. The divided garments (John 19:23-24). Following accepted custom, the four soldiers divided Jesus' clothes between them: the head covering, the sandals, the girdle, and the outer garment. But the fifth garment, a coat, was woven without a seam.

Rather than ruining it by cutting it into four pieces, the soldiers gambled for it. In so doing, they unknowingly fulfilled a thousand-year-old prophecy. King David writes of the Messiah in Psalm 22:18, "They part my garments among them, and cast lots upon my vesture."

4. Concern for His mother (John 19:25-27). The disciple John and many brave women, including Jesus' mother, stood near the cross. Jesus, struggling for breath because of crucifixion's suffocating effects, told His mother, "Behold thy son," and Jesus told John, "Behold thy mother." Even while dying, Jesus lovingly provided for His mother, almost certainly a widow at that time. John writes that from that hour on, he took Mary into his own home.

5. The completed work (John 19:28-30). Jesus then said, "I thirst" (a likely reference to Psalm 22:15). In response, the soldiers soaked a sponge in vinegar, attached it to a stalk from a hyssop plant, and held it to His lips, fulfilling Psalm 69:21.

After this, Jesus lifted Himself for another gasping breath and shouted a victory cry: "It is finished!" Then He bowed His head and died.

Jesus had fulfilled His purpose: He took the curse of sin upon Himself in our place, satisfying God's just demand that sin be punished. He did it because He loves us. His death and resurrection offer us the hope of eternal life with the Father.

—Ann Staatz.

World Missions

Lizzie Atwater was a young missionary in China. She and her husband were expecting their first child when the Boxer Rebellion of 1900 struck. She wrote home, "I fear we shall not meet on earth . . . I am preparing for the end very quietly and calmly. The Lord is wonderfully near, and He will not fail me. I was very restless and excited while there seemed a chance of life, but God has taken away that feeling, and now I just pray for grace to meet the terrible end bravely. The pain will soon be over, and oh the sweetness of the welcome above! . . . Dear friends, live near to God and cling less closely to earth. There is no other way by which we can receive that peace from God which passeth understanding."

She died a very violent death twelve days later, along with her husband, their unborn child, and the other missionaries with her (James and Marti Hefley, *By Their Blood*, Mott Media).

From a human standpoint, the peace with which she faced her own martyrdom—and not only so, but also the death of her baby—seems incomprehensible. Yet as Paul said, "I can do all things through Christ which strengtheneth me" (Phil. 4:13).

The Lord is faithful to give His people the strength and grace they need to face death. "He hath said, I will never leave thee, nor forsake thee" (Heb. 13:5).

His resurrection makes death lose its fearfulness. The Christian can exclaim, "O death, where is thy sting? O grave, where is thy victory?" (I Cor. 15:55). Indeed, for Mrs. Atwater, eternity encouraged her in her trial.

So too did Jesus find motivation in "the joy that was set before Him" when He "endured the cross" (Heb. 12:2). Let us think about Jesus' horrendous death on the cross, which caused Him to cry, "My God, my God, why hast thou forsaken me?" (Mark 15:34).

Christ became sin on the cross. "For he hath made him to be sin for us, who knew no sin; that we might be made the righteousness of God in him" (II Cor. 5:21). At that point, He suffered the penalty for our sins that we deserved.

Oh, the depth of suffering Christ endured on our behalf! And yet even in these His darkest moments, He would not look only to Himself, but looked out for the interests of others. The thief beside Him repented, and Jesus promised him salvation (Luke 23:39-43). Christ endured the cross so that those who believe on his name may have life, and He promised the thief that salvation even while suffering the torment that the redemption of others cost Him.

Indeed, even knowing all He would suffer, Jesus laid down His life willingly. "Therefore doth my Father love me, because I lay down my life . . . No man taketh it from me, but I lay it down of myself" (John 10:17-18). But why? Why would He willingly suffer?

The author of Hebrews tells us that He did it for future joy and future glory. Mrs. Atwater also endured peacefully and gracefully, because her mind and thoughts were focused on her home in heaven. Perhaps we do not share the gospel well in this day because we do not treasure heaven as our home as much as we should. Perhaps we are unwilling to suffer in this world because we have not fixed our minds on our future hope.

—Jody Stinson.

The Jewish Aspect

In his account of Jesus' crucifixion (John 19:16-30), John identifies how this event fulfilled two messianic prophecies found in the Old Testament. First, when the Roman soldiers were dividing Jesus' garments, they said of His tunic, "Let us not rend it, but cast lots for it, whose it shall be." This was so "the scripture might be fulfilled, which saith, They parted my raiment among them, and for my vesture they did cast lots" (vs. 24). The fulfilled Scripture is Psalm 22:18. Second, when John writes, "Jesus knowing that all things were now accomplished, that the scripture might be fulfilled, saith, I thirst" (19:28), he notes that Psalm 69:21 has been fulfilled (cf. John 19:29-30).

John identifies the fulfillment of these two prophetic texts to verify for all his readers, among whom were many Jews, that Jesus was indeed the promised Messiah (20:30-31). Christians read this passage and readily accept the reality of Jesus' identity.

One Old Testament text that speaks of a coming personal Messiah is Daniel 9:25-26. "Most conservative [Christian] expositors have interpreted this as a reference to Jesus Christ" (Walvoord, *Daniel: The Key to Prophetic Revelation*, Moody). In contrast, Jewish interpreters understand Daniel differently: "These vv. have given rise to much Christian speculation. In the context of the other historical references, however, the anointed leader probably refers to either Zerubbabel or the high priest Joshua" (*Jewish Study Bible*, Oxford). Of course, the coming of Jesus is itself historical and therefore would fit within this reasoning as well.

In the four hundred years between the Old Testament and Jesus, Jewish teachers could not harmonize what they saw as conflicting ideas of the prophesied Messiah. They saw some prophets writing of Him as a ruling King (cf. Mic. 5:2-5). They read others as emphasizing His humility as one who suffers and dies (Isa. 52:13—53:12; Zech. 9:9), apparently overlooking elements of royalty and power in those same texts.

Some Jewish teachers, therefore, taught that the Messiah was "a preexistent, heavenly angelic being who, at the end of time, will appear at the side of God as judge of the world" ("Messiah," *Interpreter's Dictionary of the Bible*, Abingdon), while others thought he would be a simple man. In contrast, other Jewish teachers, as seen in the book of Enoch (dated between 300–100 B.C.) believed that the Messiah would be both a man born of human beings (46:1-5) and a preexistent heavenly being, coming as the anointed of the Lord (48:2-7).

The Sadducees in Jesus' day, dominant in Judea, rejected all ideas of a Messiah. Jews in Galilee, however, had strong messianic hope. As one scholar put it, "Galilee was the main seat of anti-Roman feeling and messianic ideas" (Jeremias, *Jerusalem in the Time of Jesus*, Fortress).

Psalms 22:18 and 69:21 were identified by John to demonstrate conclusively to his readers that Jesus fulfilled messianic prophecy. Like those in antiquity, some contemporary Jews ignore this reality, postulating that Psalm 22 is "a prophetic reference to Haman's plot of annihilation" (Cohen, *The Psalms*, Soncino). Others recognize that Jesus applied Psalm 22 to Himself on the cross, but still do not identify Him as the Jewish Messiah (*Jewish Study Bible*). However, Jesus is the promised Messiah, and one day He will return.

—R. Larry Overstreet.

Guiding the Superintendent

There is nothing pretty about executions. Though today we make beautiful jewelry of the cross, in the first century the cross was the Roman means to execute a criminal.

DEVOTIONAL OUTLINE

1. The preparation (John 19:16-17). After Pilate succumbed to the pressure of the Jewish leaders, he delivered Jesus to them to be crucified. Accompanied by Roman soldiers, they led Jesus out of the city of Jerusalem (vs. 16), forcing Him to carry His own cross (vs. 17). When He could no longer bear the weight, Simon of Cyrene was conscripted to help carry the cross (Matt. 27:32). The procession through the city was a reminder to its residents of the penalty for rebellion against Rome. They arrived at the place of the skull, called Golgotha.

2. The process (John 19:18). John records that Jesus was crucified in between two thieves. He was truly "numbered with the transgressors" (Isa. 53:12).

3. The controversy (John 19:19-22). History teaches that a sign was displayed above the crucifixion victim, listing his crime as a warning to the city. Since Jesus committed no crime, Pilate had the sign read, "Jesus of Nazareth the King of the Jews" (vs. 19) in three languages (vs. 20). This infuriated the religious leaders, and they demanded that it be amended to say that this was merely His claim (vs. 21). Pilate stood firm, however, and this sign was not changed (vs. 22). Its claim of Jesus' kingship was in fact true.

4. The clothing (John 19:23-24). The Roman soldiers gambled away the clothing of Jesus, as was their custom (vs. 23). In God's sovereign control of the crucifixion, the soldiers inadvertently fulfilled the prophecy of Psalm 22:18.

5. The witnesses (John 19:25-27). Though all the disciples, other than John, had deserted Jesus, a few women demonstrated their courage and remained close to Jesus while He died (vs. 25). The agony Mary must have felt as she watched her Son be murdered is immeasurable (cf. Luke 2:35). Concerned about others more than Himself, Jesus spoke to His mother and John. He committed the care of Mary to John, possibly because His half-brothers were not believers at that time.

6. The death (John 19:28-29). Thirst was one of the elements of torture endured during crucifixion. Jesus' cry, "I thirst" proves He did not escape the agony of crucifixion (vs. 28). The soldiers filled a sponge with vinegar that would help alleviate some of His thirst (John 19:29). This was probably not an act of kindness, but a way to prolong the agony of crucifixion. This was also a fulfillment of prophecy (Ps. 69:21).

7. The victory (John 19:30). In triumph, Jesus proclaimed, "It is finished." The plan of God for our salvation was fulfilled.

CHILDREN'S CORNER

It is tempting in teaching the crucifixion to focus on historical details of the torture of this method of execution, but you should prepare your teachers to fight this temptation. You want your children to come away with a biblical understanding of the event and its significance, not a fixation on blood and gore. If your teachers go into detail about the torture of the cross, it is possible that your children would be traumatized.

—*Robert Winter.*

SCRIPTURE LESSON TEXT

JOHN 21:1 After these things Jesus shewed himself again to the disciples at the sea of Tiberias; and on this wise shewed he *himself.*

2 There were together Simon Peter, and Thomas called Didymus, and Nathanael of Cana in Galilee, and the *sons* of Zebedee, and two other of his disciples.

3 Simon Peter saith unto them, I go a fishing. They say unto him, We also go with thee. They went forth, and entered into a ship immediately; and that night they caught nothing.

4 But when the morning was now come, Jesus stood on the shore: but the disciples knew not that it was Jesus.

5 Then Jesus saith unto them, Children, have ye any meat? They answered him, No.

6 And he said unto them, Cast the net on the right side of the ship, and ye shall find. They cast therefore, and now they were not able to draw it for the multitude of fishes.

7 Therefore that disciple whom Jesus loved saith unto Peter, It is the Lord. Now when Simon Peter heard that it was the Lord, he girt *his* fisher's coat *unto him,* (for he was naked,) and did cast himself into the sea.

8 And the other disciples came in a little ship; (for they were not far from land, but as it were two hundred cubits,) dragging the net with fishes.

9 As soon then as they were come to land, they saw a fire of coals there, and fish laid thereon, and bread.

10 Jesus saith unto them, Bring of the fish which ye have now caught.

11 Simon Peter went up, and drew the net to land full of great fishes, an hundred and fifty and three: and for all there were so many, yet was not the net broken.

12 Jesus saith unto them, Come *and* dine. And none of the disciples durst ask him, Who art thou? knowing that it was the Lord.

13 Jesus then cometh, and taketh bread, and giveth them, and fish likewise.

14 This is now the third time that Jesus shewed himself to his disciples, after that he was risen from the dead.

NOTES

Jesus by the Sea of Tiberias

Lesson Text: John 21:1-14

Related Scriptures: Luke 5:1-11; John 20:19-29; 21:15-25

TIME: A.D. 30   PLACE: Sea of Tiberias

GOLDEN TEXT—"This is now the third time that Jesus shewed himself to his disciples, after that he was risen from the dead" (John 21:14).

Introduction

The resurrection of Christ is at the very heart of our Christian faith. It is essential to the gospel (I Cor. 15:4). Christ died for our sins, but without His resurrection, we would still be trapped in them (vs. 17).

Depending on how they are counted, there are about a dozen recorded appearances of Jesus after His resurrection. In some cases, the details are not clear. For example, Paul says that Christ appeared to "all the apostles" (I Cor. 15:7), but we are not sure whether this refers to an event recorded in the Gospels or to another appearance. Paul records an appearance of Jesus to him on the Damascus road, although that occurred after Jesus' ascension (vs. 8). And there may have been other unrecorded appearances.

LESSON OUTLINE

I. UNSUCCESSFUL FISHING TRIP—John 21:1-3

II. SUDDEN ABUNDANCE— John 21:4-8

III. FELLOWSHIP WITH JESUS— John 21:9-14

Exposition: Verse by Verse

UNSUCCESSFUL FISHING TRIP

JOHN 21:1 After these things Jesus shewed himself again to the disciples at the sea of Tiberias; and on this wise shewed he himself.

2 There were together Simon Peter, and Thomas called Didymus, and Nathanael of Cana in Galilee, and the sons of Zebedee, and two other of his disciples.

3 Simon Peter saith unto them, I go a fishing. They say unto him, We also go with thee. They went forth, and entered into a ship immediately; and that night they caught nothing.

Introductory statement (John 21:1). "After these things" refers to the events of chapter 20. These include Peter and John's initial visit to the empty tomb (vss. 1-10), Jesus' appearance to Mary Magdalene (vss. 11-18), Jesus' appearance to the ten disciples (vss. 19-23), and then His appearance a week later, when Thomas was present (vss. 24-29).

At this point, the Gospel of John comes to what seems like its ending. The writer affirms that many other signs were performed by Jesus that are not recorded. John then states his purpose in writing, namely, to bring people to faith, that is, that they "believe that Jesus is the Christ, the Son of God" (vs. 31).

If the Gospel had concluded at this point, it would have seemed quite natural, but then we have chapter 21. Often referred to as John's epilogue, it contains information about an otherwise unknown appearance of the risen Lord that occurred at the {Sea of Galilee, identified here by its alternate name, the Sea of Tiberias.}Q1

The lake got this alternate name from a city on its western shore, founded by Herod Antipas to honor Tiberius Caesar. This same body of water is called the Sea of Chinnereth in the Old Testament (cf. Josh. 13:27) and also the Lake of Gennesaret (cf. Luke 5:1) in the New. Not understanding this detail might lead some readers to conclude that these were all different places, when, in fact, they are different names for the same body of water.

Since most of Jesus' first disciples were Galileans, it would be natural for Him to appear there. Except for Judas, all the apostles were from Galilee (Acts 2:7). They had also been told that He would appear to them in Galilee (Matt. 26:32; 28:7, 10, 16). Many think Christ's appearance to more than five hundred disciples (cf. I Cor. 15:6) likely took place in Galilee.

Return to fishing (John 21:2-3). {On this particular occasion, seven disciples were together.}Q2 In John's Gospel, Peter is nearly always referred to as "Simon Peter." Simon was his given name, but he was nicknamed Peter by Jesus

(cf. 1:40-42). While not stated specifically, Peter was clearly the leader of the disciples and their spokesman.

Regrettably, Thomas is usually remembered for his doubt (20:24-29). But he was only asking to see the same evidence the others had already seen. Once that evidence was given, he was quickly and completely convinced. The name Didymus simply means "twin" (cf. 11:16; 20:24). The name Thomas also means "twin" and may not have been his given name. As to who his twin was, it is assumed that it was either Matthew or James the son of Alphaeus, since all three seem to have been siblings (Easton, *Easton's Bible Dictionary,* CreateSpace).

Nathanael is mentioned early in John (cf. 1:44-51) as having a negative opinion of the town of Nazareth. He nevertheless was quickly convinced that Jesus was the Son of God. Only now is the reader informed that Nathanael was from Cana, the town where Jesus performed His first miracle (cf. 2:1). Nathanael is most likely the same person as the apostle Bartholomew, mentioned elsewhere (Matt. 10:3; Mark 3:18; Luke 6:14; Acts 1:13).

"Bartholomew" is a family designation, meaning "son of Tolmai." "Nathanael" is a common Hebrew name that means "gift of God." It may have been that John always used this disciple's actual first name, while the Synoptics knew him primarily by his family name. He is always listed right along with Philip in all the Gospels, whether as Bartholomew or Nathanael.

The sons of Zebedee were James and John (Matt. 4:21). As to who the two other disciples were, we can only guess, though they were most likely part of the Twelve.

We are given scant information about how long after Jesus' resurrection this event occurred. The apostles seem to have stayed in Jerusalem for at least a week or so afterward (John 20:26). They were also in Jerusalem just prior to Christ's ascension (Luke 24:50-53; Acts 1:4).

{That Peter decided to go fishing should not be seen as unusual. He was, after all, a professional fisherman, along with his brother Andrew.}[Q3] They were in the same fishing business with James and John (Luke 5:10).

While some have seen Peter's decision to go fishing as a retreat from his commitment to serve Christ, this is unlikely. But it may have been a retreat for the purpose of regrouping and waiting for further instructions from the Lord. Since we know little of what Jesus said between His resurrection and ascension, speculation about such things can be fodder for overactive imaginations. The early centuries of Christian history are replete with spurious writings that purport to fill in the blanks concerning many things left unmentioned in the Bible.

Peter's decision to go fishing may have been a response to economic necessity. These men had not amassed great wealth in following Christ. To be sure, those called to gospel ministry should be adequately compensated (cf. Luke 10:7; I Cor. 9:14; Gal. 6:6; I Tim. 5:17). But making money should never be the motivation for Christian workers (I Pet. 5:2).

The other disciples mentioned above decided to go with Peter. If they were hoping to catch a lot of fish to take to market, these seven men were going to be disappointed. {They fished all night and caught nothing at all!}[Q4]

SUDDEN ABUNDANCE

4 But when the morning was now come, Jesus stood on the shore: but the disciples knew not that it was Jesus.

5 Then Jesus saith unto them, Children, have ye any meat? They answered him, No.

6 And he said unto them, Cast the net on the right side of the ship, and ye shall find. They cast therefore, and now they were not able to draw it for the multitude of fishes.

7 Therefore that disciple whom Jesus loved saith unto Peter, It is the Lord. Now when Simon Peter heard that it was the Lord, he girt his fisher's coat unto him, (for he was naked,) and did cast himself into the sea.

8 And the other disciples came in a little ship; (for they were not far from land, but as it were two hundred cubits,) dragging the net with fishes.

A concerned question (John 21:4-5). Returning from a night of futile fishing, the disciples must have been discouraged. As you may recall, when Christ called the fishermen to be His disciples, He promised them, "I will make you fishers of men" (Matt. 4:19). The time for them to begin carrying out the Great Commission (Matt. 28:19-20) was at hand.

Like us, the original disciples needed to learn lessons about patience in ministry as fishers of men. While there are many conversions recorded in Acts, there are also noteworthy refusals to obey the gospel. As Jesus pointed out in the Parable of the Sower, there will be varied responses to the gospel (Matt. 13:3-8, 18-23).

As the disciples were making their way back to shore, Jesus was waiting for them. But they did not recognize Him at first. {The light was probably still dim in the early morning, and there may have been a fog or mist hovering over the shoreline. We can therefore understand why it would be difficult to discern who was standing on the shore.}[Q5]

Calling out to His disciples, the Lord asked them if they had any food. The word translated "meat" in verse 5 simply means something to eat—in this case, fish. Since they had caught nothing, they answered no.

Profitable advice (John 21:6). Taking a tip from a stranger is not something most professional fishermen would care to do. But if what they have already tried has not been working, they might conclude they have nothing to lose. {That being so, the disciples were willing to follow the stranger's advice—namely, to cast their nets to the right of their boat in order to catch some fish.}Q6

Some have surmised that Jesus merely had a better vantage point than the disciples to see where the fish were. That might be possible, but it really does not do justice to the underlying purpose of Jesus' advice at this time. What was taking place here was an unmistakable demonstration of Jesus' divine wisdom and sovereign power over Creation. Clearly, the reason He told the disciples to cast their nets to the right was to remind them of the miracle they had witnessed near the beginning of their discipleship, recorded in Luke 5:1-6.

On that occasion, Peter and the other fishermen had likewise been fishing all night with no success. Jesus told Peter to try casting his nets for fish once again. Peter protested, since he was undoubtedly exhausted from fishing all night and had had his fill of it. But he obeyed the Lord's words anyway. Of course, their nets were immediately filled to the breaking point with fish.

Since Peter, James, and John had all been there on that previous occasion, what happened next was an unmistakable sign that immediately revealed to them the true identity of this stranger.

Sudden comprehension (John 21:7-8). At this point, the "disciple whom Jesus loved," presumably John, identified the figure on the shore. Since it was none other than the Lord Jesus Himself, John declared, "It is the Lord!" {Peter immediately put on his outer tunic ("naked" likely indicates he was clothed only in the undergarments suitable to his trade), jumped into the sea,

and swam to shore.}Q7 The other disciples followed in the boat, still dragging the net teeming with a heavy load of fish. Since they were two hundred cubits (about one hundred yards) from shore when Peter jumped out, we can again understand why they had been unable to recognize Jesus by sight. But the miracle of the fish left no doubt about His identity.

FELLOWSHIP WITH JESUS

9 As soon then as they were come to land, they saw a fire of coals there, and fish laid thereon, and bread.

10 Jesus saith unto them, Bring of the fish which ye have now caught.

11 Simon Peter went up, and drew the net to land full of great fishes, an hundred and fifty and three: and for all there were so many, yet was not the net broken.

12 Jesus saith unto them, Come and dine. And none of the disciples durst ask him, Who art thou? knowing that it was the Lord.

13 Jesus then cometh, and taketh bread, and giveth them, and fish likewise.

14 This is now the third time that Jesus shewed himself to his disciples, after that he was risen from the dead.

A hearty breakfast (John 21:9-10). {Arriving on shore, the disciples found that a breakfast of fire-grilled fish, with bread, had been prepared for them by the Lord Jesus.}Q8 Exactly how He came to have the prepared bread and fish is unknown. But on at least two occasions Jesus fed people miraculously (Matt. 16:9-10).

Those who had been at the Last Supper, where the Lord had been the host, now enjoyed His presence, sharing a meal with Him once again. This might perhaps be called "the last breakfast." Jesus also invited His disciples to contribute some of the fish they had just caught with His miraculous help.

A great number of fish (John 21:11). Obeying the Lord's request, Peter took it upon himself to single-handedly pull the net full of fish ashore. John tells us that although {the net was heavy with 153 large fish,}Q9 it suffered no fraying or tearing at all. This surely was another providential work of the Lord.

Whether there is any particular significance to the number of fish caught is mere speculation. True, some biblical numbers are notable, but others are included merely to serve in relating concrete facts about an actual, historical event.

An invitation to dine (John 21:12-14). Although these seven disciples now realized that they were indeed in the presence of the risen Lord Jesus, they were reluctant to ask Him anything about Himself. Perhaps in His glorified body, there was something about His appearance that made them hesitant to speak. Christ was not immediately recognizable more than once after His resurrection. This is made clear in the episode on the Emmaus road (Luke 24:13-35).

Jesus took from the bread and fish and shared it with His disciples. It had to be somewhat reminiscent of the scene in the upper room when He hosted the Passover and instituted the Lord's Supper.

It is significant that Jesus devoted His post-resurrection appearances to simply spending time with His disciples doing ordinary daily things such as eating a meal or walking down a road. We might be reminded of John 13:1: "When Jesus knew that his hour was come that he should depart out of this world unto the Father, having loved his own which were in the world, he loved them unto the end." Jesus loves to spend time with His disciples, so it should likewise be our hearts' desire to spend frequent quality time with Him as well.

John tells us that this was the third time that Christ appeared to His disciples after His resurrection. John only records three post-resurrection appearances of Jesus to the disciples as a group. The two prior appearances are seen in chapter 20. On the day of His resurrection, Jesus appeared to ten disciples, Thomas being absent (vss. 19-25). About a week later, He appeared to them again with Thomas present (vss. 26-29).

{John may simply be saying that this appearance at the Sea of Tiberias was merely the third one he was recording in his Gospel or that this was the third time the risen Jesus appeared to a group of disciples of which he personally was a part.}Q10 There were many other things Jesus did that John does not record in his Gospel, as he freely affirms in its final verse.

—John Alva Owston.

QUESTIONS

1. What is another name for the Sea of Tiberias?
2. How many disciples are mentioned in this post-resurrection appearance?
3. Why did Peter decide to go fishing?
4. How did the disciples' fishing expedition turn out?
5. Why might Jesus not have been immediately recognized by the disciples?
6. What did the Lord tell His disciples to do?
7. What did Peter do once he realized that it was Jesus on the shore?
8. What had the Lord prepared for His disciples?
9. How many fish did the disciples catch?
10. What might John have meant in saying that this was the third time Jesus appeared after His resurrection?

—John Alva Owston.

Preparing to Teach the Lesson

Jesus died, but death did not have the final say—He rose from the dead on the third day after He was crucified (I Cor. 15:3-4), in fulfillment of His own prophecy. The disciples were in stunned disbelief when Jesus died, and they were in fear for their own lives, as evidenced by Peter's denials of even knowing Him.

After His resurrection, Jesus made several appearances to His followers, in which He handled material things and ate food. He did not undergo a merely spiritual resurrection, which was what many Greek Gnostics taught; He secured a physical, bodily resurrection. The body that died was now alive again; only it was glorified and immune from experiencing future death. Jesus is alive today and is actively interceding for you as your High Priest and Advocate before God. Death could not finish Jesus off, and the grave could not hold Him.

TODAY'S AIM

Facts: to confirm that Jesus Christ rose from the dead on the third day and appeared to His disciples.

Principle: to recognize that Jesus' resurrection was physical and guarantees life to all who believe in Him.

Application: to know the power of Jesus' resurrection by firmly trusting that He is the Giver of life to those who believe in Him (cf. John 6:25-36; 14:19).

INTRODUCING THE LESSON

The resurrection of Jesus was not something the disciples came up with by putting their heads together on the subject. The resurrection is more than just a doctrinal belief; it has its basis in fact. It is a historical reality that can be verified through historical research, including multiple eyewitness accounts.

Jesus rose from the dead and made appearances to His disciples, some of whom were skeptical at first. If you are skeptical of the resurrection of Jesus, you are not alone. But know that untold numbers of skeptics, upon examining the scriptural record and considering the historical evidence, have become convinced followers of the resurrected Lord of life.

DEVELOPING THE LESSON

1. Gone fishing (John 21:1-3). As stated above, Jesus appeared to His disciples several times after His resurrection. They saw, heard, and even touched Him on numerous occasions. The focus of our lesson this week is on the third and final appearance to His disciples recorded in John's Gospel.

At some point after the Feast of Unleavened Bread, the disciples left Jerusalem and returned home to Galilee. They were at the Sea of Tiberias, which was also called the Sea of Galilee.

John records that seven disciples gathered together on this occasion: Peter, Thomas, Nathanael, the sons of Zebedee (James and John), and two other unnamed disciples.

When a group of fishermen get together at a lake, it is not surprising to hear one of them say that he is going fishing, which is exactly what Peter said he was going to do. The others decided to go with him, so they got into a boat and went out to fish. They fished all night, but they did not catch anything.

2. Famine to feast (John 21:4-8). After daybreak, Jesus stood on the shore, waiting for the men to come back in. They did not recognize Him yet. Perhaps it was because they were too far out to distinguish facial features, or maybe it was too foggy to see clearly, or maybe the Lord had clouded their eyes supernaturally (cf. Luke 24:16).

No fisherman who has spent a whole night fishing without catching anything wants to be asked if he caught any fish, but that is exactly what happened here. Knowing the answer to His own question, Jesus asked them if they had caught anything.

When the disciples answered this unidentified figure with a no, He told them to cast their net out on the right side of the boat. With nothing to lose, they cast their nets and caught so many fish that they could not draw the net in.

At this moment, the light went on in John's head as he exclaimed, "It is the Lord" (vs. 7). He had seen this happen before (Luke 5:4-7), and no one else could bring such a large catch as Jesus. As far as John was concerned, this could not be anyone else.

When Peter heard this, he threw on his tunic and jumped in the water right away. He wanted to get to Jesus as soon as possible. The others came along in the boat, dragging a net full of fish from around two hundred cubits (one hundred yards) away from the shoreline.

3. Breakfast on the beach (John 21:9-14). When the disciples reached land, there was a charcoal fire already going with fresh fish being cooked over the flame, along with bread. Since the fire was already made and the fish cleaned and cooking before the disciples arrived with their catch, Jesus had apparently already procured these fish on His own.

Jesus then told them to bring some of the fish they caught, so Peter went and brought in the net from the boat; it held 153 large fish. In spite of the great number of fish, the net was not torn.

Jesus then invited them to come eat. None of the disciples dared to ask who this was, nor did they need to. They knew it was Jesus, and Jesus fed them the fish and bread He had prepared for them. We will always be satisfied if we will let God feed us. This can have literal application, as here, but more often it will involve spiritual nourishment. Jesus is the Bread of Life, and we partake of Him by faith (6:26-35). Our lesson closes with the statement that this was a third appearance of Jesus to the disciples after He had been raised from the dead.

ILLUSTRATING THE LESSON

The resurrected Jesus gives life to all those who trust in Him.

JESUS GIVES US LIFE

LIFE

CONCLUDING THE LESSON

We will never run out of strength if we will rely on God's strength. We will never fail if we obey what God says. Doing God's will is a guarantee of success in God's eyes. As we close this quarter, please take a moment and thank the Lord for dying for your sins and rising from the dead.

ANTICIPATING THE NEXT LESSON

Next quarter, we will study Paul's instructions to the Corinthian church to prepare us to live as churches built on the firm foundation of Christ.

—*Robert Ferguson, Jr.*

PRACTICAL POINTS

1. The Lord shows Himself today in a myriad of different ways (John 21:1-2).
2. Sometimes we are so preoccupied that we do not notice the Lord standing right in front of us (vss. 3-4).
3. We can confidently do what Jesus says because of who He is (vss. 5-6).
4. We ought to leap at any opportunity to spend time with Jesus (vss. 7-9).
5. The Lord's abundant provision points us to His bountiful grace (vss. 10-13).
6. There is no mistaking the sure testimony that Jesus rose from the dead (vs. 14).

—*Charity G. Carter.*

RESEARCH AND DISCUSSION

1. Describe a time when you spent a great deal of effort on a task that proved futile (John 21:3). How did you feel?
2. Immediately after they caught the fish, one disciple recognized Jesus (vs. 7). What might have spurred this insight?
3. The disciples were only three hundred feet from the shore. Why did Peter jump into the water rather than stay in the boat a few moments?
4. What is the significance of Jesus showing Himself to His disciples three times (vs. 14)?

—*Charity G. Carter.*

ILLUSTRATED HIGH POINTS

I go a fishing (John 21:2)

The six basic questions of journalism and life are Who? What? When? Where? How? and Why? The first five are fairly easy. The sixth is more difficult to figure out.

Some Bible scholars suggest that Peter's decision to go fishing indicates that he was abandoning his call to ministry. Others say he simply wanted to do something while he waited for more guidance from Jesus (cf. Matt. 28:10).

Have ye any meat? (John 21:5)

Suppose you are walking along a stream, and you come upon a fellow fishing. You might say something like, "Hi, how are you doing; how's the fishing?" What you really want to know is "Have you caught anything?" But you don't want to embarrass him if he hasn't. No fisherman likes to go home "skunked," so you delicately step around your question.

Jesus asked the direct question even though He knew the answer. He had arranged this entire scenario for the apparent purpose of reminding Peter and the others what He had taught in John 15:5: "Without me ye can do nothing."

Fish . . . and bread (John 21:9)

The teacher of a class on world religions asked her young students to bring in a symbol of their religion. A Muslim child brought in a prayer rug. A Jewish child brought in a menorah. A Roman Catholic child brought in his mother's rosary. A Greek Orthodox child brought in an icon of his patron saint. The last child said, "I'm a Baptist, and this is my casserole."

Jesus knew what His disciples needed: a hearty breakfast and uninterrupted time together.

—*David A. Hamburg.*

Golden Text Illuminated

"This is now the third time that Jesus shewed himself to his disciples, after that he was risen from the dead" (John 21:14).

During Jesus' trial, Peter had denied knowing Him three times. The third time that Jesus appeared to His disciples after His resurrection, He asked Peter the same basic question three times: "Simon, son of Jonas, lovest thou me more than these?" (John 21:15; cf. vss. 16-17).

This third time that Jesus appears, some of His disciples, including Peter, had been fishing all night and had caught nothing. Appearing as an unknown figure on the shore, Jesus hollered to the men in the boat and asked their results. After hearing their answer, Jesus told them to fish on the right-hand side of the boat (John 21:6).

After they took His advice and made a colossal catch, John declared that the unknown man was the Lord, whereupon Peter immediately swam to shore. There Jesus had built a fire and was cooking fish. Jesus invited them all to breakfast. At the end of this narrative, John records that it was the third time that Jesus had shown Himself to His disciples after He was risen from the dead.

The appearances of Jesus prior to this had been quite alike. In the first one, the disciples are hiding from the Jews with the doors shut. Jesus appears in their midst and perhaps to put them at ease, tells them, "Peace be unto you" (John 20:19). However, Thomas was not present at this appearance and still doubted the Saviour's resurrection (vss. 24-25). So, at a later gathering of all eleven disciples, again "came Jesus, the doors being shut, and stood in the midst, and

said, Peace be unto you" (vs. 26).

The third appearance stands in stark contrast as it is not in a closed house, but on an open shore. The apostles appear to have gained a little courage from their Master's previous appearances. In our verse, John may be intentionally featuring the number three to transition to the next narrative: after Jesus was resurrected on the third day, He for the third time appears to His disciples to ask the same question three times of His disciple Peter, who had denied Him three times.

When Jesus used the pronoun "these" in His question, we might suppose He was asking if Peter loved Him more than the other disciples loved Him, but Jesus was not the kind of rabbi that encouraged competition among His students (cf. Mark 10:40). He may have been asking if Peter loved Him more than he loved the other disciples. But perhaps we should look to the morning's previous conversation to find Jesus' actual intent.

The subject of discussion that morning was fish, and Jesus wanted to know if Peter loved Him more than fish. It is a question we all need to answer. Whatever our professions, whatever our hobbies, whatever our successes in life, will we leave our entanglements to follow the Lord and fish for men? Peter had said the wrong thing three times in a hostile environment on a dark night, but now, in the light of day and among friends, Jesus made Peter confess the right answer three times. "Yea, Lord; thou knowest that I love thee" (John 21:15).

—*David Samuel Gifford.*

Heart of the Lesson

One afternoon, I walked home from work a few yards behind a young man. I could see a young woman approaching on the same side of the street. When the two were half a block apart, they began running toward each other. Within seconds, they were in a joyful embrace.

I like to imagine they were newlyweds, thrilled to see each other after a workday apart. In this week's lesson, Peter shows a similar exuberant enthusiasm when, from a distance, he realizes Jesus, the risen Lord, is there.

1. Time of uncertainty (John 21:1-3). The disciples had seen the resurrected Jesus twice since His crucifixion. He had told them that after He was raised, He would meet them in Galilee. Now they had returned home to Galilee as Jesus instructed.

The inactivity and uncertainty of waiting must have been getting to Peter and the six disciples with him. What was coming next? Peter announced he was going fishing.

They climbed aboard a boat—perhaps Peter's or John's—and fished all night. Though night was the best time to catch fish, they caught nothing.

2. Catch of fish (John 21:4-6). Morning came. On shore stood a lone figure. It was Jesus, but they could not recognize Him. Like a loving father, He called them "children" and asked if they had caught any fish. Dejectedly, they answered no.

He told them to cast their net over the right side of the boat and they would catch fish. They did and caught so many fish they were unable to raise the net into the boat. Do we see once again His concern for the men's everyday activities?

3. Glimpse of Jesus (John 21:7-8). John, the disciple whom Jesus loved, was first to recognize the man on shore as Jesus. He told Peter, who immediately donned his tunic, climbed over the side of the boat, and swam to shore. He could not wait to see Jesus. Peter did not allow his sin and recent failure to keep him from the Lord, and neither should we (Richards, *The Bible Readers' Companion*). The other disciples were only about a hundred yards from shore. They quickly landed the boat, dragging their catch behind them.

4. Breakfast with the Lord (John 21:9-14). On the beach, they saw bread and a charcoal fire with fish frying over it. Jesus knew they would be hungry after a night of fishing. A hot breakfast was just what a group of hungry, tired men needed.

Jesus did not scold them for fishing or even ask why they were fishing. He simply told them to bring some of their fish, apparently to add to what He had ready. Peter boarded the boat, grabbed the net, and dragged it to shore.

Then Jesus invited them to eat with Him. John notes that no one asked anymore who He was; they knew. He was the risen Lord, making His third appearance to them. He was no vision; one man might have a vision and think he saw the Lord. But seven men would never have the same vision simultaneously, nor would they eat fish and bread during a vision.

This was real: Jesus was alive, cooking for them and eating with them. As at the Last Supper, He waited on them, serving them fish and bread—a reminder that we are to love and serve one another. Perhaps we are also to see in this abundance of fish the abundance of the kingdom that awaits us.

—Ann Staatz.

World Missions

This occasion at the Sea of Tiberias is the third appearance of Jesus to His disciples after His resurrection and ultimate triumph over death (John 21:14). In these appearances, He has given them instructions about their ministry.

Every believer is called to follow Christ. The paths we take will be different, but the call is the same.

Two such believers were Heather Mercer and Dayna Curry, who serve God in the Muslim world.

They became famous during their imprisonment in Afghanistan shortly before the attacks on the World Trade Center. God chose to deliver them from their captivity, and they returned to the United States to share their testimony.

But their story doesn't end there. After donating the money that they had earned sharing their story, both women returned to the Muslim world where they still serve today.

Heather spoke about entering a Muslim country again just two years after her release. "For a brief moment, I had one of those thoughts of 'Do I really want to do this again?' I think that was the point where it solidified for me that, yes, this is what I'm made for. Even if something goes wrong, my hope is in Jesus" (J.B. Smith, "Once Held Captive by Taliban, Waco Missionaries still Serve in Muslim World," *Waco Tribune-Herald*).

She certainly follows the call God has given, just as every Christian should do.

Some will go to foreign nations. Others will minister to their own. Yet each of us is sent. Jesus told His followers, "Peace be unto you: as my Father hath sent me, even so send I you" (John 20:21). And again, "Go ye therefore, and teach all nations, baptizing them in the name of the Father, and of the Son, and of the Holy Ghost" (Matt. 28:19).

After the miracle described in this week's passage, near the end of this account, we find three words spoken to Peter: "Follow thou me" (John 21:22). Interestingly, this was not the first time that Jesus had performed a miracle of a magnificent catch, and in the earlier account, the disciples were commanded to "catch men" (Luke 5:10).

Though the response of His disciples was slightly different on each occasion, Jesus followed up both miracles with a call to a ministry.

At the occasion near the beginning of Jesus' ministry, Peter fell at His feet and said, "Depart from me; for I am a sinful man, O Lord" (vs. 8).

At the second great-catch miracle, Peter swam quickly to shore (John 21:7) and later declared his love for Jesus three times (vss. 15-19).

As the disciples were called on these two occasions to be fishers of men and follow Christ, so too are we called to repent, follow Him, and spread the gospel. Carrying the gospel to the world is not easy. There is no guarantee that people will listen to the message. There is no certainty that one's life will not end in a prison cell or martyrdom.

When discouragement strikes, we must remember that the Lord is faithful. In Jesus' call for people to deny themselves, take up their cross, and follow Him, He also promised, "For whosoever will save his life shall lose it; but whosoever shall lose his life for my sake and the gospel's, the same shall save it" (Mark 8:34-35). Though we may lose our life here, we gain it unto eternal life.

In this promise, we find hope.

—Jody Stinson.

The Jewish Aspect

On the shores of the Sea of Galilee, we see a remarkable scene after Jesus' resurrection. John tells us that after a night of unsuccessful fishing, the disciples spotted Jesus on the beach. Initially, they did not recognize Him, and when they did, He invited them to breakfast. "Jesus then cometh, and taketh bread, and giveth them, and fish likewise" (21:13).

At first, a reader might wonder why John included such a mundane detail. The reality is, however, that in the action of giving out bread and fish for a meal, Jesus assumed the role of "the head of the household," demonstrating hospitality to His disciples (Keener, *IVP Bible Background Commentary: New Testament*, InterVarsity). Throughout their history, Jews practiced hospitality as one of their vital responsibilities.

Jews were well aware of God's commands concerning hospitality (cf. Deut. 24:17-22). Also, the need for hospitality was great in ancient times. Living conditions were often harsh, travel was difficult, and for the vast majority of people, vacations were unknown. When ancient people did travel, motels and hotels were non-existent. Therefore, hospitality was crucial. Throughout their history, Jews developed their ideas on hospitality from the examples of biblical figures.

Abraham is considered a classic example of hospitality (Gen. 18). When three strangers approached "in the heat of the day" (vs. 1), "he ran to meet them" (vs. 2). He insisted that they stay with him, be refreshed, and eat "a morsel of bread" (vss. 3-5), which was a drastic understatement in view of the sumptuous meal he provided (vss. 6-8). Although he had many servants, Abraham personally served his guests (vs. 8).

In addition to Abraham, the Jewish people extolled the hospitality virtues of other biblical characters, including Reuel (Jethro) toward Moses (Ex. 2:20), Manoah toward the angel (Judg. 13:15), the Shunammite woman toward Elisha (II Kgs. 4:8-10),and Job toward traveling strangers (Job 31:32). The rabbis expanded on the example seen in this last verse to teach that Job "had forty tables spread at all times for strangers and twelve tables for widows" ("Hospitality," www.jewishencyclopedia.com).

In stark contrast to these positive examples, Nabal's refusal to show hospitality almost resulted in his death at David's hands (I Sam. 25:13, 22); only Abigail's quick intervention saved him (vs. 33). Nabal would nonetheless die ten days later (vs. 38). Many Jews take his early death as his just punishment for his stinginess.

Hospitality was still expected in Jesus' day. He often received hospitality (cf. Mark 1:29-31; Luke 10:38), and hospitality is the setting for some of His parables (cf. Luke 11:5). When He sends His disciples out two-by-two, He tells them to accept hospitality for all their needs (Mark 6:8-11; Luke 10:1-12).

"Even in later times, when the Jews were settled in cities, this virtue was held in highest esteem" ("Hospitality"). Although modern times have changed some emphases, Jews continue to regard hospitality as a sacred responsibility.

As Christians, we are also called to be hospitable. As exemplars to the church, pastors are supposed to be "given to hospitality" (I Tim. 3:2; cf. Titus 1:8), but God commands all Christians to show hospitality (Luke 14:12-14; Rom. 12:13; I Pet. 4:7-10).

—*R. Larry Overstreet.*

Guiding the Superintendent

John records three post-resurrection appearances of Jesus to His disciples. In the third one, Jesus appears to seven of His disciples while they are fishing and enjoys a morning meal with them.

DEVOTIONAL OUTLINE

1. Going fishing (John 21:1-3). "After these things"—Jesus' death and first two appearances after His resurrection—Jesus appeared to His disciples in Galilee (vs. 1; cf. 6:1). They were likely awaiting His instructions about their future (cf. Matt. 28:10, 18-20). A large group of the disciples were together when Peter suggested they go fishing (vs. 3). They spent all night fishing and caught nothing.

2. From drought to draught (John 21:4-8). While they were out fishing in the Sea of Galilee about a hundred yards from shore (vs. 8), Jesus called to them (vs. 4), but they did not recognize Him. Jesus used the word "children" as He asked them if they had caught anything; they answered with one word, "No" (vs. 5). Jesus told them to cast their nets on the other side of the boat.

Perhaps they heard authority in His voice or they were just desperate to try anything, but they obeyed. Immediately, they caught a large number of fish (vs. 6). It is hard not to wonder if this abundance of fish is a glimpse into the abundance expected in the messianic kingdom.

At this miracle, John identifies the person on shore as Jesus, and Peter immediately jumps into the water and swims back to shore (vs. 7). Is this not a very concrete example of the appropriate response to the signs of Jesus (cf. 20:30-31)? The other disciples came back to the shore in the boat, dragging the fish behind (21:8).

3. Breakfast with the Lord (John 21:9-14). As they returned to shore, they saw that Jesus had prepared a breakfast for them (vs. 9). He asked them to bring to Him the fish they had caught (vs. 10). As they dragged the catch to shore and counted the fish, they found that they had caught 153 fish (vs. 11). What a provision this was! Jesus invited them to sit down and eat with Him.

What a great time of fellowship this must have been for the weary disciples! As great as this meal with Jesus must have tasted, the words from His lips must have been even better. None of them had the need to ask who He was, since they were positive that this was the Lord Himself (vs. 12). Their calling to be fishers of men was affirmed by this time with Christ.

John summarized by stating this was the third time that Jesus had appeared to the disciples after the resurrection (vs. 14). Their faith was bolstered for the days of ministry that lay ahead.

This story reminds the believer today that Jesus' resurrection was real; seven men will not simultaneously have the same vision. It also reminds us that His resurrected body is physical.

God is gracious to us to supply our needs as He supplied the needs of His disciples. He will supply our need for both physical bread and the Bread of Life (cf. John 6).

CHILDREN'S CORNER

The most significant part of this lesson for the children to understand is that Jesus rose again and is alive today. Have your teachers remind the children what death is, and how Jesus was dead but is now alive. Have them also emphasize the physicality of Jesus' body.

—Robert Winter.

your life (Ps. 23:1-6; 90:12; Rom. 12:1-2).

Your birthday may not be celebrated worldwide, but you, like the Lord Jesus, can walk by faith and finish in triumph, as Paul declared in II Corinthians 2:14: "Now thanks be unto God, which always causeth us to triumph in Christ." Notice that Paul said God Himself causes us to triumph, and to triumph in Christ. Victory does not come by our own power or necessarily in the way we expect, but it is guaranteed as we abide in Christ.

The world contains many trials and temptations, but according to the apostle John, we can persevere through them all: "For whatsoever is born of God overcometh the world: and this is the victory that overcometh the world, even our faith" (I John 5:4).

Even through His suffering, Jesus Christ lived a life of total triumph. His life's walk with the Father was a triumph because he always did the Father's will and could say, "He that sent me is with me: the Father hath not left me alone;

for I do always those things that please him" (John 8:29).

You were born for a purpose. As a skillful artisan, God formed you in your mother's womb (cf. Ps. 139:13-15) and constantly watches over you (vss. 1-12). You can take comfort in God's guidance and protection as you pray, worship, and live in the light of the Scriptures.

But you will need the help of the Holy Spirit to obey God in your weakness, especially when presented with trials and opposition. Jesus encouraged his disciples with His final marching orders: "Go ye therefore, and teach all nations, baptizing them in the name of the Father, and of the Son, and of the Holy Ghost: teaching them to observe all things whatsoever I have commanded you: and, lo, I am with you alway, even unto the end of the world" (Matt. 28:19-20).

May we be encouraged that Christ is always with us so that, in the end, we can claim the words of the apostle Paul: "I have fought a good fight, I have finished my course, I have kept the faith!" (II Tim. 4:7).

Only the Truth

ALAN ALLEGRA

When a witness takes the stand in a courtroom, he or she is admonished to "tell the truth, the whole truth, and nothing but the truth, so help you God." But one wag replied, "If I knew the truth, the whole truth, and nothing but the truth, I would be God!"

The purpose of this oath is so the judge and jury can ascertain the facts of a case and draw a fair conclusion. Only by knowing and evaluating the facts can justice be truly served.

Jesus made many startling statements about Himself. One of the most notable is, "I am the way, the truth, and the life" (John 14:6). He followed this self-designation with, "No man cometh unto the Father, but by me." In other words, Jesus made clear that the only way to God is through Him. He alone reveals the truth about God and bestows eternal life.

Jesus Christ is the embodiment of truth. Every word He spoke corresponded to reality, which is what truth is. As God incarnate, He could not lie.

Titus's words regarding salvation can be applied to Jesus' life (cf. Titus 1:2). Jesus spoke the truth, the whole truth, and nothing but the truth, and He expects His disciples to exhibit the same honest behavior. This is made plain by the apostle Paul in Colossians 3:9: "Lie not one to another, seeing that ye have put off the old man with his deeds." In salvation, we put off the old way of life and thereafter live a life of truth.

On the other hand, Satan is the master of deceit, as Jesus told the Pharisees in John 8:44: "Ye are of your father the devil, and the lusts of your father ye will do. He was a murderer from the beginning, and abode not in the truth, because there is no truth in him. When he speaketh a lie, he speaketh of his own: for he is a liar, and the father of it." Those who lie fall into the devil's trap at their own peril.

When Christ stood before Pontius Pilate, "Pilate saith unto him, What is truth? And when he had said this, he went out again unto the Jews, and saith unto them, I find in him no fault at all" (John 18:38). Ironically, Pilate was questioning the existence of truth while standing face-to-face with the embodiment of all truth!

Movements such as Postmodernism teach that all truth is relative and subjective; in other words, what is true for one person is not true for another; it is all up to each individual person to decide what is true in any given circumstance. There is no objective standard.

This is an era of deception, where facts go unchecked and lies can be repeated long and loud until people are convinced they are true. As we saw earlier, after Jesus proclaimed Himself the Truth, Pilate sarcastically answered, "What is truth?" (John 18:38). Pilate was a pre-modern Postmodernist!

When it comes to a matter as serious as the salvation of a soul and reconciliation with God, it is vital to know and accept the truth. There are many theories about how to reclaim, restore, or even recycle the human soul, but there can be only one truth, and Jesus is that Truth. That did not sit well with the false leaders and teachers of Christ's day; however, Jesus maintained the truth of the gospel all the way to the cross.

As a fascinating yet intimidating side note, the Greek word often translated "witness" is the same word that is generally translated as "martyr," someone willing to die for what they believe—who will not give up or compromise truth, even if it means suffering and death. A quick survey of the book of Acts fleshes out the concept of martyrdom, as Stephen and others were persecuted and murdered for their faith in Christ (Acts 22:20; Rev. 2:13). This is a commitment Jesus' disciples are expected to make until His return, when He will bring justice (Rev. 6:9).

Christ expects nothing less from his followers than for them to walk in the truth, no matter the cost. He made this clear in Matthew 16:24: "If any man will come after me, let him deny himself, and take up his cross, and follow me." The Apostle John, the closest disciple to Jesus, said: "I have no greater joy than to hear that my children walk in truth" (III John 1:4). John, the Apostle of Love, rejoiced that the children of God were walking, not only in love, but in truth.

Children will imitate their parents. God is as good as His word, and His children should strive to imitate His character (Eph. 5:1). One characteristic of God's nature that brings comfort to us is this: "God is not a man, that he should lie; neither the son of man, that he should repent: hath he said, and shall he not do it? or hath he spoken, and shall he not make it good?" (Num. 23:19). For our witness and our sanctification, we should strive to speak only the truth—especially the truth of salvation in Christ. False teaching, above all, is to be shunned; there is no compromise to be had with lies. Our deeds should back up our words as we show the love of Christ to others and lead them to saving faith.

The assumption in Numbers 23:19 is that all humans lie. It takes a supernatural work of the Holy Spirit to change human nature and impart God's nature that lives in the truth (II Pet. 1:4). Consequently, God commands, "Wherefore putting away lying, speak every man truth with his neighbour: for we are members one of another" (Eph. 4:25; cf. Prov. 8:7; Zech. 8:16). Only through the work of the Holy Spirit can we say, "Through thy precepts I get understanding: therefore I hate every false way" (Ps. 119:104).

Jesus triumphed through truth, and truth always triumphs over lies. So we must also "put on the new man, which after God is created in righteousness and true holiness" (Eph. 4:24).

TOPICS FOR NEXT QUARTER

March 6

Divisions in Corinth

I Corinthians 1:1-16

March 13

True Wisdom

I Corinthians 1:17-31

March 20

Christ—Our Only Foundation

I Corinthians 3:10-23

March 27

Members of Christ

I Corinthians 6:12-20

April 3

Concern for a Weaker Brother

I Corinthians 8:1-13

April 10

Thoughts on the Lord's Supper

I Corinthians 11:20-34

April 17

Witnesses to Christ's Resurrection (Easter)

I Corinthians 15:1-11

April 24

God's Comfort in Trouble

II Corinthians 1:1-11

May 1

Glory of the New Covenant

II Corinthians 3:7-18

May 8

Our Heavenly Dwelling

II Corinthians 5:1-10

May 15

Ambassadors for Christ

II Corinthians 5:11-21

May 22

Spiritual Weapons

II Corinthians 10:1-12, 17-18

May 29

Paul's Thorn in the Flesh

II Corinthians 12:1-10

PARAGRAPHS ON PLACES AND PEOPLE

KIDRON VALLEY

Separating the eastern slope of Jerusalem from the Mount of Olives is the Kidron Valley. This deep ravine stretches north beyond the temple mount and extends south into the Judean wilderness. In biblical times it was even deeper than it is today. David made his way from Jerusalem to the Mount of Olives through the Kidron Valley while fleeing from his son Absalom (II Sam. 15:23, 30).

A thousand years later, the long-anticipated Messiah of the Davidic covenant retraced the steps of His ancestor David through the Kidron Valley. Jesus often passed this way in going from the temple courts to the Mount of Olives (Luke 21:37).

Situated a short distance up the western slopes of the Mount of Olives was the olive grove known as the Garden of Gethsemane. Upon the conclusion of the Last Supper and His high priestly prayer, Jesus came to Gethsemane via the Kidron Valley to pray (John 18:1).

BETHANY

The village once known as Bethany is located in what is now considered Palestinian territory on the West Bank. This was the hometown of the two sisters Mary and Martha as well as the place where Jesus raised their brother, Lazarus, from the dead.

Positioned near the base of the eastern slope of the Mount of Olives, Bethany served as Jesus' headquarters in the days leading up to His triumphal entry. Approximately two miles east of Jerusalem, this is the site where Mary anointed Jesus' feet with expensive oil (John 12:3).

CAIAPHAS

During New Testament times, Roman officials appointed Israel's high priests. They routinely did so from among the wealthy sect of Jews known as the Sadducees. Caiaphas held the appointment of high priest during Jesus' earthly ministry; his father-in-law, Annas, was linked to the office as well (Luke 3:2).

As Jesus' honor grew among the people, Caiaphas was among the Jewish religious leaders plotting against Him. In fact, a meeting to devise a plan that would lead to Jesus' arrest and death was held at his palace (Matt. 26:3-4).

JUDAS ISCARIOT

Some artists have depicted Judas as looking devious, but he apparently did not come across that way to his fellow disciples. He was trusted enough to be left in charge of the group's money—even though he secretly stole from it (John 12:6). They trusted him right up through the night of the betrayal (cf. 13:27-30).

Nevertheless, Judas's infamous act of treachery did not take the Lord by surprise. Jesus proclaimed to His apostles, well before He was betrayed, "Have not I chosen you twelve, and one of you is a devil?" (6:70).

It should not be surprising that Judas suffered from a guilty conscience later. He was complicit with the workings of the devil (13:2) and willingly completed the dastardly task of betraying Jesus for thirty pieces of silver, which were eventually used to purchase a field for burying foreigners who died in Jerusalem (Matt. 27:7).

—*Reginald Coats.*

Daily Bible Readings for Home Study and Worship

(Readings are for the week previous to the lesson topics.)

1. December 5.   Sorrow Before Triumph
M — Anointed at Bethany. Matt. 26:6-13.
T — Perfume Poured Out. Mark 14:3-9.
W — A Sinful Woman. Luke 7:37-39.
T — The Most Desirable Thing. Ps. 27:1-6.
F — A Soul's Thirst for God. Ps. 63:1-8.
S — Serve with Gladness. Ps. 100:1-5.
S — Sent to Save by His Death. Matt. 1:18-21; John 12:1-8.

2. December 12.   A King Comes Forth
M — Give Thanks to God. Ps. 118:22-29.
T — The Triumph of God. Ps. 47:1-9.
W — The Triumph of the Gospel. II Cor. 2:14-17.
T — Welcoming the King. Luke 19:35-38.
F — A Joyful Procession. Mark 11:7-10.
S — Hosanna to the Son of David. Matt. 21:4-9.
S — Your King Is Here. Isa. 9:6-7; John 12:12-16.

3. December 19.   A Mission from Birth (Christmas)
M — Early Steps in Christ's Journey. Luke 2:21-24.
T — Anna Gives Thanks for Jesus. Luke 2:26-38.
W — Jesus as a Boy. Luke 2:40-52.
T — The Father's Pleasure in His Son. Matt. 3:13-17.
F — Jesus' Greatest Motivation. John 4:31-34.
S — The Lord's Supper. Matt. 26:26-30.
S — Loving and Following Christ. Luke 2:25-35; John 12:23-26.

4. December 26.   A Humble Lord Is Born
M — Jesus Came to Serve. Matt. 20:20-28.
T — Who Is Greater? Luke 22:24-30.
W — The World Hated Christ First. John 15:18-25.
T — Follow Christ's Steps. I Pet. 2:21-24.
F — Humble Service. I Pet. 5:1-5.
S — Christ the Chosen Saviour. Matt. 12:15-21.
S — The Matchless Heart of Christ. Phil. 2:5-11; John 13:12-17.

5. January 2.   The Way, the Truth, and the Life
M — Peter's Denial Foretold. John 13:31-38.
T — Greater Deeds Than These. John 14:12-21.
W — Christ Is Supreme. Col. 1:15-20.
T — Sent from the Father. John 12:44-50.
F — Hear and Live. John 5:19-30.
S — Full of Grace and Truth. John 1:14-17.
S — The Way to the Father. John 14:1-11.

6. January 9.   Abide in the True Vine
M — Live in Righteousness. Matt. 5:21-48.
T — Spiritual Fruit. Gal. 5:22-26.
W — Thirst for God. Ps. 42:1-11.
T — Grafted Branches. Rom. 11:11-21.
F — A Tree and Its Fruit. Matt. 7:15-23.
S — Love One Another. John 15:9-17.
S — The Vine and the Gardener. John 15:1-8.

7. January 16.   Peace and Trouble
M — Treasures in Jars of Clay. II Cor. 4:7-12.
T — One in Christ. Eph. 2:11-18.
W — Believers Are from God. I John 4:4-6.
T — Faith That Overcomes the World. I John 5:1-5.
F — Do Not Love the World. I John 2:15-17.
S — A Touch of Power. Luke 8:40-48.
S — In Him We Have Peace. John 16:19-33.

8. January 23.   Jesus' Prayer for His Disciples
M — Paul's Prayer for the Ephesians. Eph. 3:14-21.
T — Approaching the Throne of Grace. Heb. 4:14-16.
W — The Peace of God. Phil. 4:4-7.
T — The Bread of Life. John 6:35-40.
F — Jesus Prays for Himself. John 17:1-5.
S — A Prayer for Unity. John 17:20-26.
S — Sanctified by the Truth. John 17:6-19.

9. January 30.   Jesus' Arrest
M — Hidden Plots of Men. Isa. 29:11-16.
T — Powerful Prayer. Jas. 5:13-16.
W — A Prayer for Mercy. Ps. 51:1-12.
T — Mount of Olives Prayer. Luke 22:39-46.
F — The Plot to Kill Jesus. John 11:45-53.
S — Preparing for Betrayal. Luke 22:1-6.
S — Judas Betrays Jesus. John 18:1-13.

10. February 6.   Trials and Denials
M — The Messiah Oppressed. Isa. 53:7-9.
T — Peter Weeps. Luke 22:55-62.
W — The Soldiers Mock. Luke 22:63-71.
T — The Son of Man. Mark 14:55-72.
F — Jesus Before the Sanhedrin. Matt. 26:57-68.
S — Peter's Denial. Matt. 26:69-75.
S — The Rooster Crows. John 18:15-27.

11. February 13.   Pilate: What Is Truth?
M — Jesus Predicts His Death. Luke 18:31-33.
T — Jesus the King. Luke 23:1-12.
W — Barabbas Released. Luke 23:13-25.
T — Pilate Amazed. Mark 15:1-15.
F — No Reply. Matt. 27:11-18.
S — The Cry of the Crowd. Matt. 27:20-26.
S — Jesus Before Pilate. John 18:28-40.

12. February 20.   Crucifixion and Death
M — His Bones Out of Joint. Ps. 22:12-18.
T — Jesus Led Away. Luke 23:26-43.
W — Jesus Breathes His Last. Luke 23:44-49.
T — The King of the Jews. Mark 15:16-32.
F — Simon Carries the Cross. Matt. 27:27-44.
S — Darkness over the Land. Matt. 27:45-56.
S — It Is Finished. John 19:16-30.

13. February 27.   Jesus by the Sea of Tiberias
M — Jesus Calls His First Disciples. Luke 5:1-11.
T — Fishers of Men. Mark 1:16-20.
W — Shepherds and Sheep. Ezek. 34:11-16.
T — The Good Shepherd. John 10:11-18.
F — Jesus Appears to His Disciples. John 20:19-29.
S — Jesus Reinstates Peter. John 21:15-25.
S — A Great Catch of Fish. John 21:1-14.

REVIEW

What have you learned this quarter?

Can you answer these questions?

Triumph

UNIT I: Jesus' Triumphant Arrival

December 5

Sorrow Before Triumph

1. How did Mary come to be with child?
2. Who were Mary, Martha, and Lazarus?
3. What reason did Judas offer for objecting to Mary's extravagant offering?
4. What significance did Jesus ascribe to Mary's act of devotion?
5. How should we understand Jesus' statement concerning the poor?

December 12

A King Comes Forth

1. Which of the titles in Isaiah 9:6 is the most commonly remembered at Christmas?
2. What are two qualities mentioned in Isaiah 9:7 that will characterize Messiah's reign?
3. On what day of the week did Christ triumphantly enter Jerusalem?
4. Why were there so many people in Jerusalem at this time?
5. What does "Hosanna" mean?

December 19

A Mission from Birth (Christmas)

1. What event brought Joseph, Mary, Jesus, and Simeon together in the temple at the same time?
2. How did Simeon see God's salvation?
3. What promise had God made concerning salvation and the Gentiles?
4. How would a sword pierce Mary's soul?
5. What hour had come for Christ? How would He be glorified?

December 26

A Humble Lord Is Born

1. To what group of epistles does Paul's letter to the Philippians belong?
2. What is clear from the word "robbery" in Philippians 2:6?
3. What was the ultimate demonstration of Christ's obedience?
4. What is the ultimate goal of confessing Christ?
5. Why did Jesus wash His disciples' feet?

UNIT II: Teaching on Truth and Trials

January 2

The Way, the Truth, and the Life

1. Why were the disciples troubled?
2. What is the "Father's house" (John 14:2)?
3. What did Jesus mean when He said He would come again?
4. What primary implication follows from the fact that no one can come to the Father except through Jesus?
5. How can we see God the Father?

January 9

Abide in the True Vine

1. What was Jesus' point in the various "I am" statements found in John?
2. What must be done to a branch on the vine that does not bear fruit?
3. What did Jesus mean when He said, "Without me ye can do nothing?"
4. What is the significance of the burning of dead branches?
5. What promise did Jesus make

about prayer?

January 16
Peace and Trouble
1. How did the disciples feel about Jesus' earlier statement, found in John 16:16?
2. How did Jesus illustrate the sorrow and joy the disciples would soon experience?
3. Why did Jesus speak in parables and proverbs?
4. Why did the Father especially love Jesus' apostles?
5. What event would cause the disciples to forsake Jesus?

January 23
Jesus' Prayer for His Disciples
1. What office did Jesus undertake in praying the prayer recorded in John 17?
2. Which world was Christ *not* praying for?
3. Who was the son of perdition?
4. How did this person fulfill Scripture?
5. Why is it essential that Christ's disciples remain in the world?

UNIT III: Triumph over Trials
January 30
Jesus' Arrest
1. What was the name of the garden where Jesus and His disciples went?
2. What motivations may have lain behind Judas's betrayal?
3. What two adversarial groups collaborated to rid themselves of Jesus?
4. What caused those sent to arrest Jesus to fall backward to the ground?
5. Who tried to defend Jesus with a sword?

February 6

Trials and Denials
1. Which disciples followed Jesus after His arrest?
2. How did those disciples gain entrance to the high priest's house?
3. Who first challenged Peter about whether he was Jesus' disciple?
4. What two things was Jesus questioned about?
5. Who challenged Peter about Jesus the third time?

February 13
Pilate: What Is Truth?
1. Why did the Jews refuse to enter the hall of judgment?
2. Why did the Jewish authorities need to take Jesus to Pilate?
3. For what other reason was it important that Jesus be turned over to the Romans?
4. What did Jesus mean by saying that His kingdom "is not of this world" (John 18:36)?
5. Who was Barabbas?

February 20
Crucifixion and Death
1. Why did Pilate finally give in to the demands of the chief priests?
2. What was another name for Golgotha, and what did it mean?
3. What was the purpose of the placard on the cross?
4. In what languages was the message on the placard written? Why?

February 27
Jesus by the Sea of Tiberias
1. What is another name for the Sea of Tiberias?
2. Why did Peter decide to go fishing?
3. How did the disciples' fishing expedition turn out?
4. What did the Lord tell His disciples to do?